AF471276

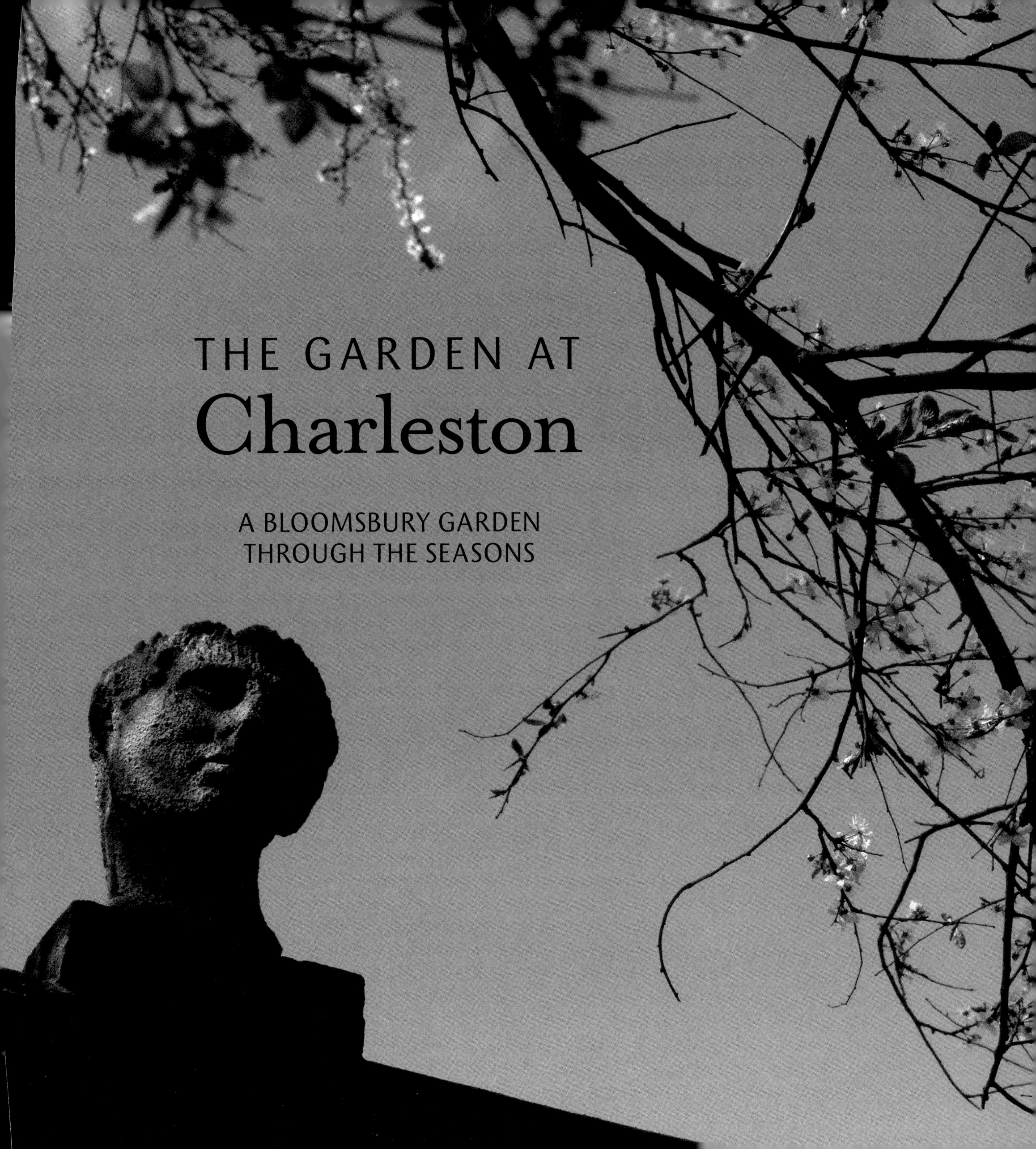

THE GARDEN AT Charleston

A BLOOMSBURY GARDEN THROUGH THE SEASONS

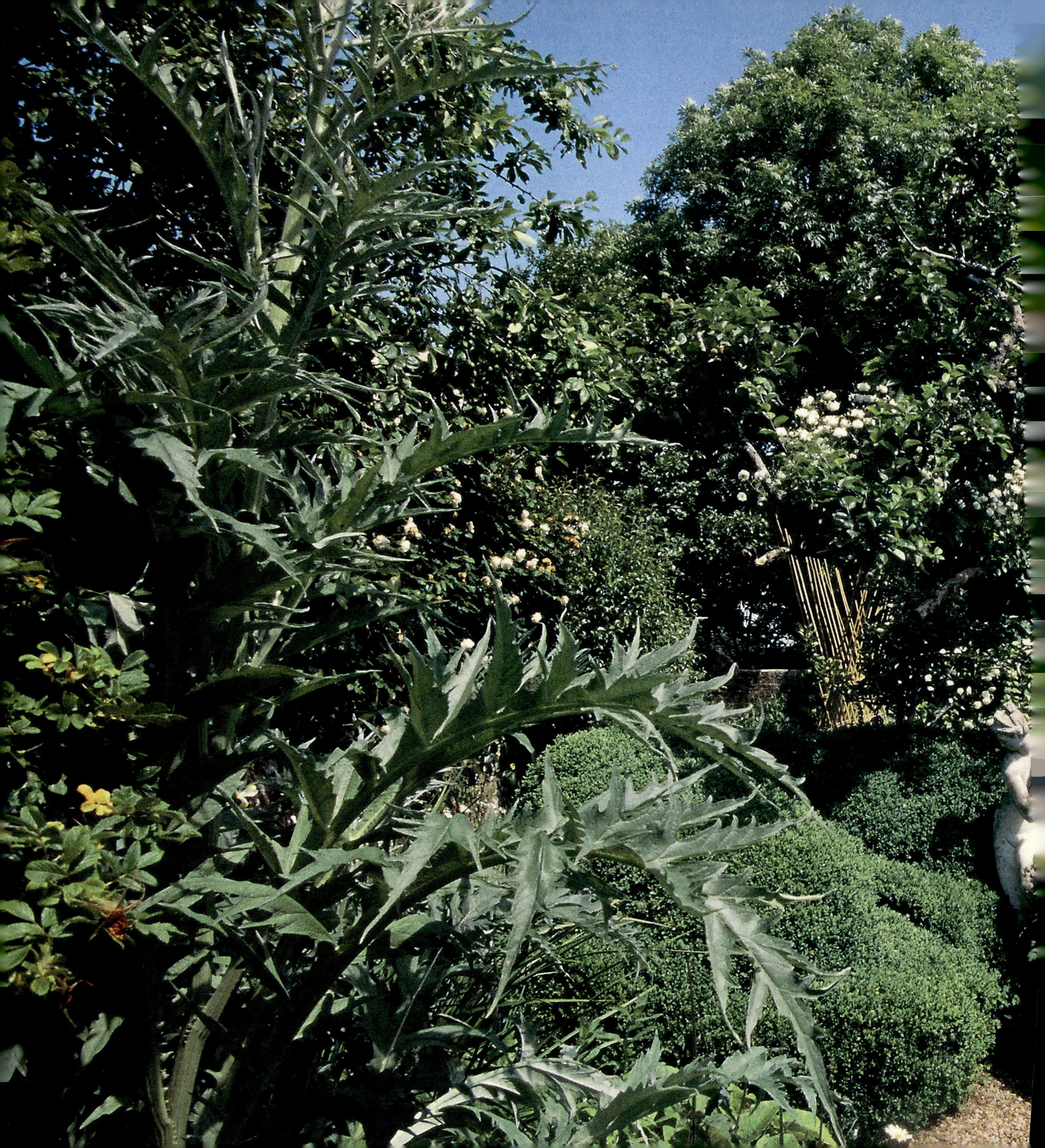

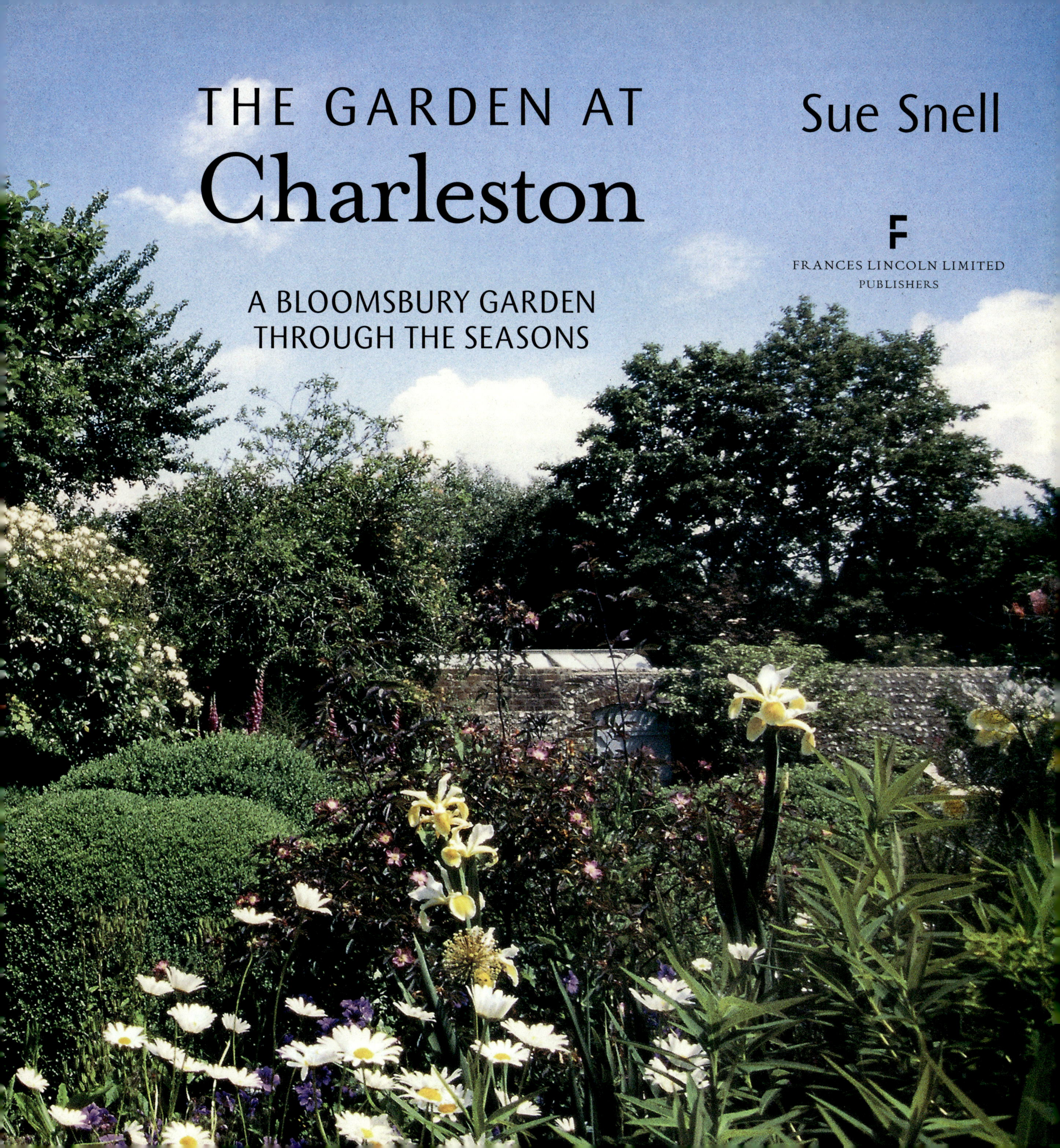

THE GARDEN AT Charleston

A BLOOMSBURY GARDEN THROUGH THE SEASONS

Sue Snell

F
FRANCES LINCOLN LIMITED
PUBLISHERS

To my parents Ella and John, and Peter

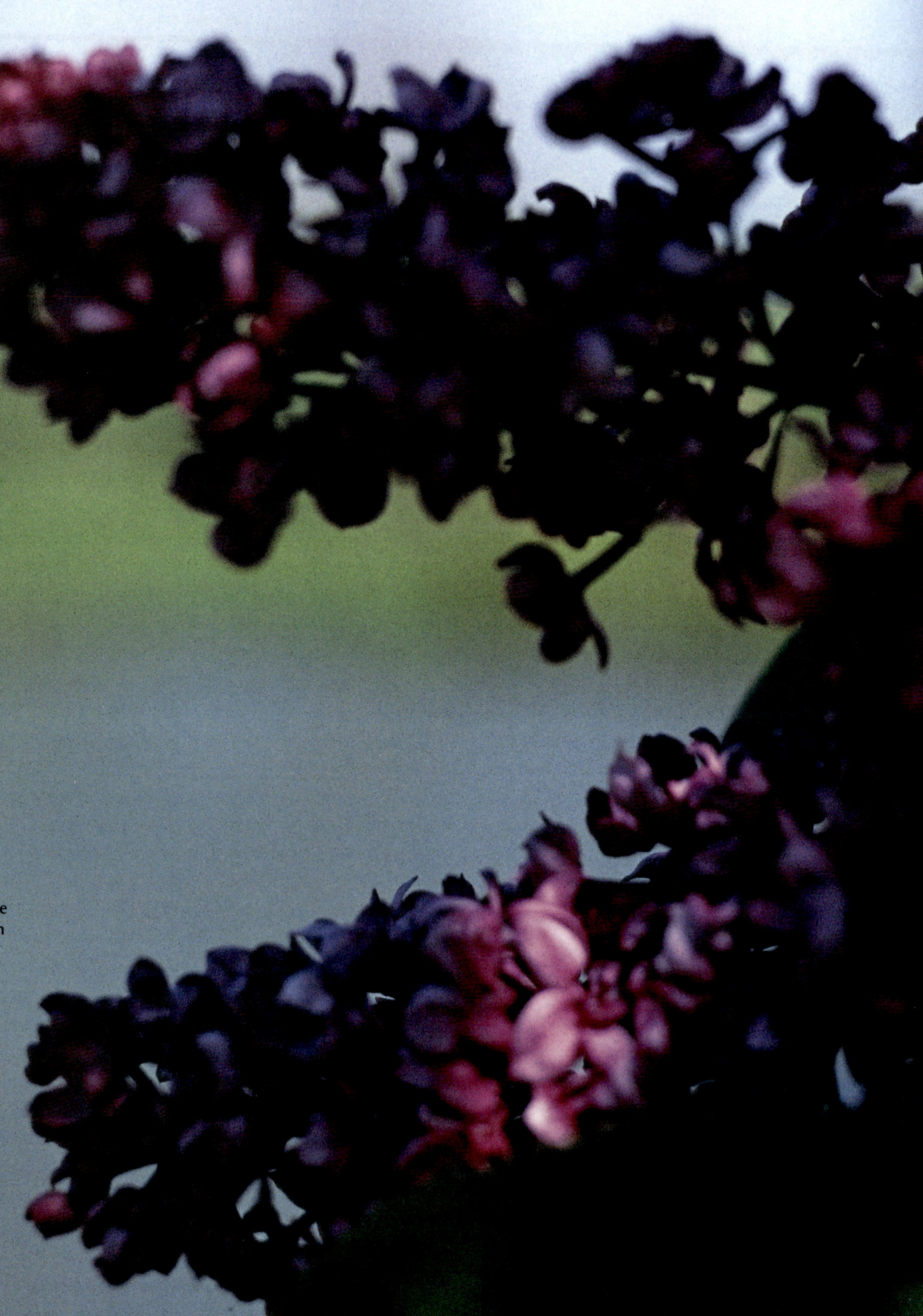

Frances Lincoln Limited
4 Torriano Mews
Torriano Avenue
London NW5 2RZ
www.franceslincoln.com

The Garden at Charleston

First Frances Lincoln edition 2010

British Library cataloguing-in-publication data
A catalogue record for this book is available from the British Library

ISBN 978-0-7112-3112-2
Printed and bound in China by C&C Offset Printing Co Ltd

HALF-TITLE PAGE Plum blossom and cast head
TITLE PAGE The walled garden in summer
THIS PAGE Lilac by the pond

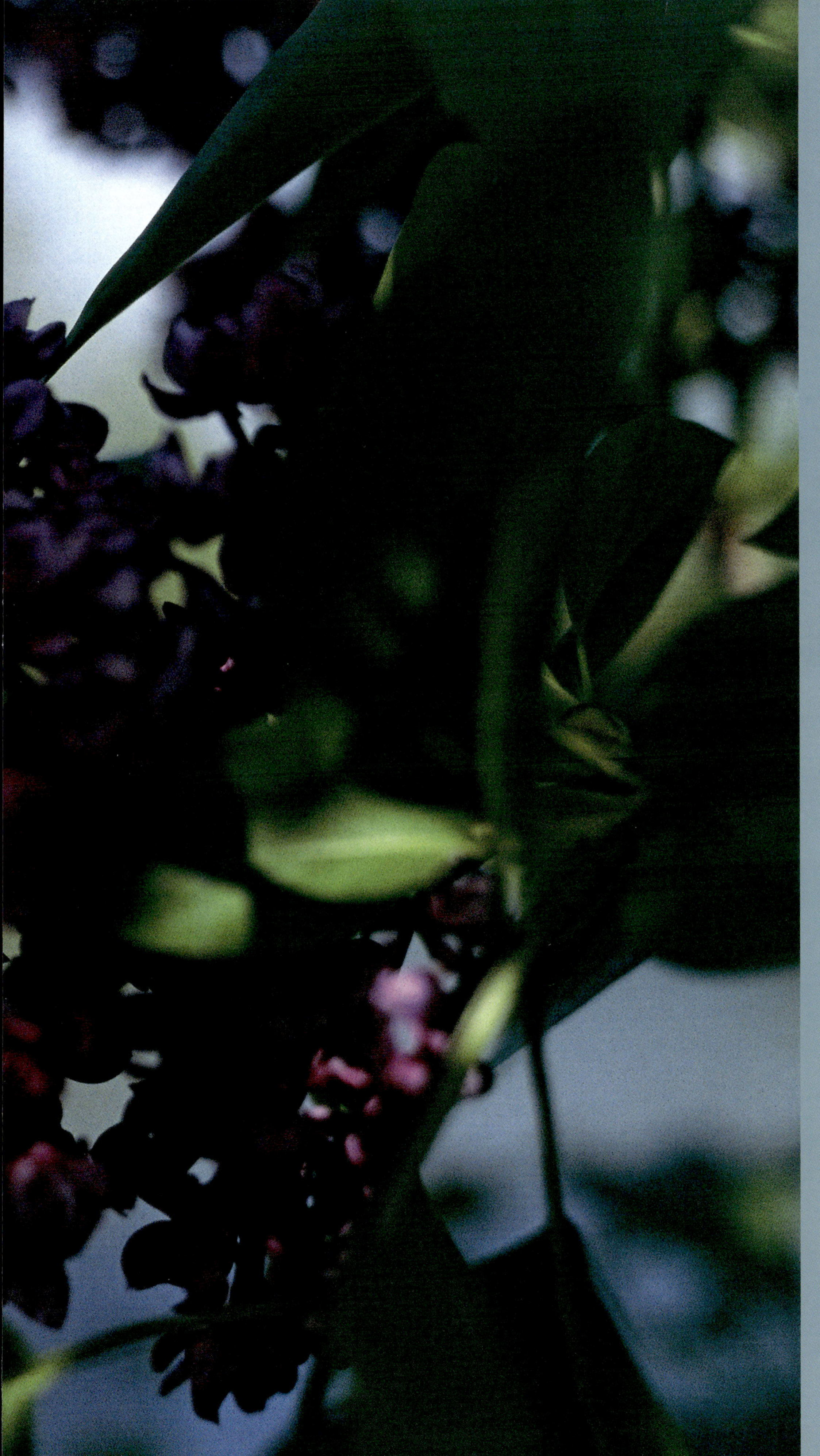

Contents

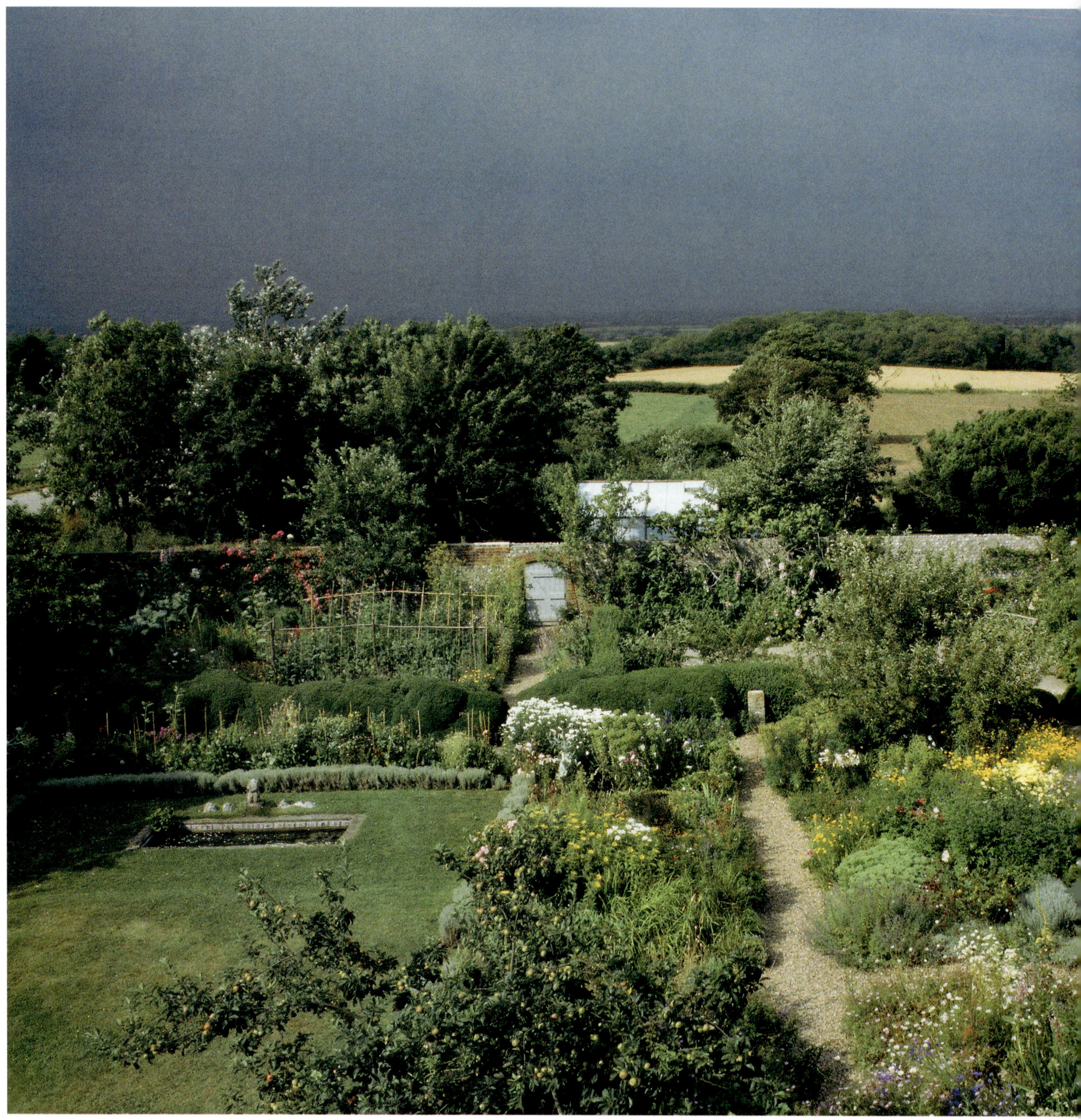

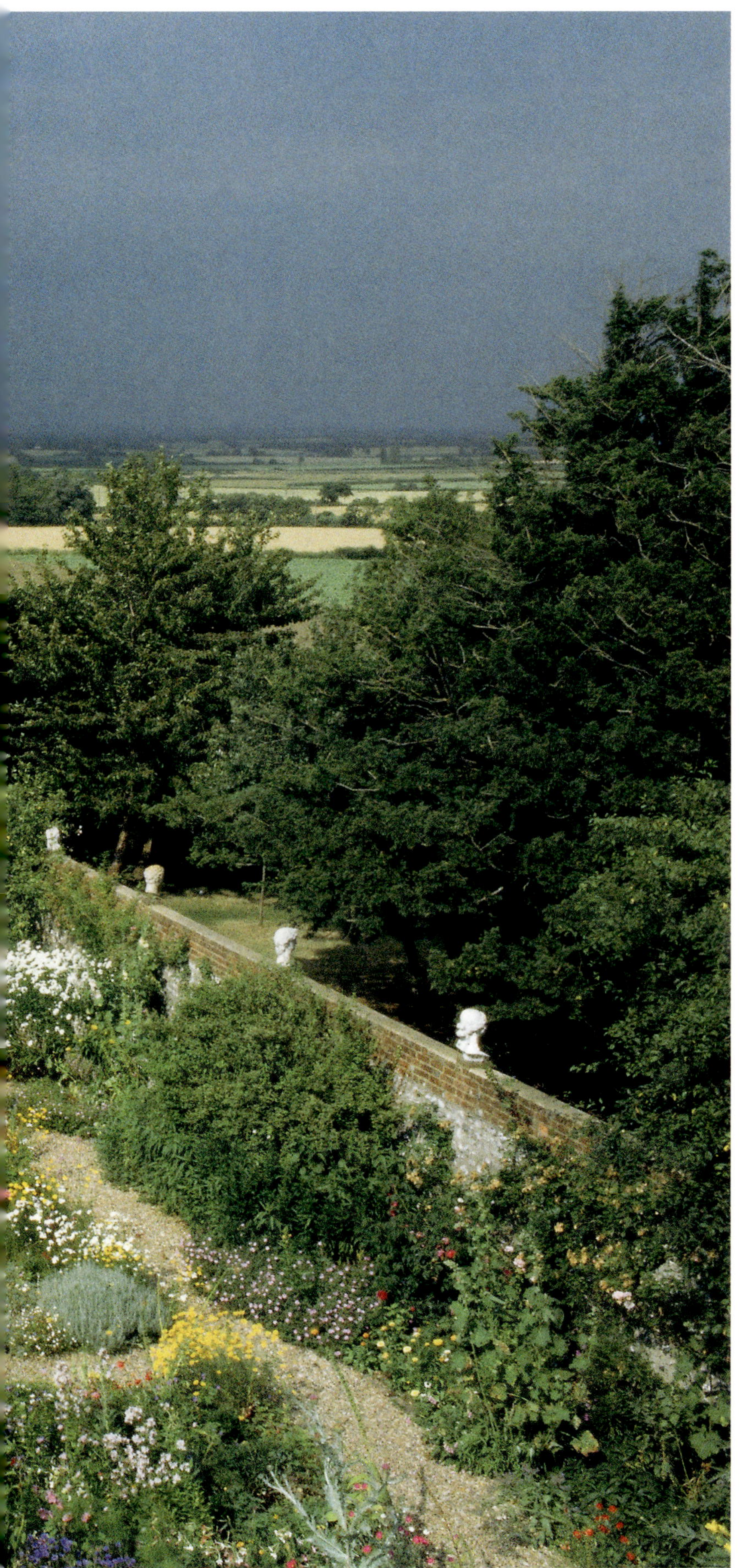

Foreword

It is now almost quarter of a century since Charleston opened for the first time to the general public. What had been a very private place that provided a means of escape and sanctuary to the group known as Bloomsbury has since been discovered, visited and enjoyed by hundreds of thousands of people.

Its Bloomsbury residents would undoubtedly have been horrified at this annual invasion of their space, though they themselves had anticipated it in a theatrical performance given in the studio at Charleston in the 1930s. But at the same time they would have recognized what it was about visiting Charleston that made it so alluring, and would have understood why so many visitors feel compelled to return again and again. Through her long association with Charleston Sue Snell has captured perfectly in her photographs of the garden and grounds so many of the elements that combine to make this such a magical place.

Charleston's location in the East Sussex Downs – it lies just below and across the fields from Firle Beacon – would always have been remote and isolated. It was this isolation that first brought Bloomsbury to the house in October 1916, when the artist Vanessa Bell, her two children Julian and Quentin, the artist Duncan Grant, his then partner David Garnett and a dog called Henry arrived at Charleston for the first time. Its rural location provided the opportunity for Grant and Garnett to find work on the land rather than go to prison as conscientious objectors. It was not just the convenience and the isolation of Charleston's setting that appealed; it was beautiful and there was the potential to make it yet more beautiful. Vanessa Bell's sister, the author Virginia Woolf, wrote to her in May 1916, 'It has a charming garden, with a pond, and fruit trees, and vegetables, all now rather run wild, but you could make it lovely.'

Grant and Bell had an inherent appreciation of the natural beauty of the different elements that make up Charleston, and from the moment they first occupied the house they started to add their own creative

The walled garden from Vanessa Bell's studio

interventions. Their interior decoration and the display of their own paintings and those of the artists they admired have turned the house itself into a work of art. Both artists were also interested in gardening and began to transform the garden, working within a structure devised by their friend, the critic and artist Roger Fry. By the mid-1920s the garden as we know it was well established, providing a riot of spring and summer colour (reflecting the fact that in the 1920s and 1930s Charleston was used mainly during the late spring and summer months). From 1939 the house became the permanent wartime home of Vanessa Bell, her son Quentin (Julian, Vanessa Bell's oldest son, had been killed in 1937 while serving as an ambulance driver in the Spanish Civil War), her husband Clive Bell and Duncan Grant. This occupation brought some changes, not least the creation of the piazza by Quentin Bell in 1946 and the increasing number of statues and sculptures that started to appear in the garden.

Vanessa Bell died at Charleston in 1961, and by the time of Grant's death in 1978 the beautiful gardens (and the house itself) had fallen into neglect. When the Charleston Trust was created in 1981 to restore Charleston for the public benefit, the task of returning the garden and grounds to their former glory was every bit as challenging as that of restoring the fabric and decoration of the house. Fortunately the Trust secured the services of the great English landscape gardener Sir Peter Shepheard (and very generous funding from the American philanthropist Lila Acheson Wallace) to oversee the project to return the garden to what he described as 'an apotheosis of the traditional English cottage garden'. The restoration work took two years; many of the original shrubs, trees and perennials were retained and the beds were planted with varieties that would have been in the garden in the 1930s, 1940s and 1950s (many identified from close study of family photographs).

Charleston's garden and the beautiful surrounding countryside were profoundly important to the Bloomsbury inhabitants, providing a magical environment for Vanessa Bell's children to grow up in, a haven for the family and their many friends and, in the riotous colours of the borders, a source of constant inspiration for Grant and Bell as artists. It was the garden, as much as the house, that formed the backdrop against which the story of Bloomsbury unfolded – a constant to which its main characters returned over a period of fifty years. The studio, garden room and Vanessa Bell's bedroom on the ground floor of the house became an extension of the garden.

For most of us words on a page are an inadequate means of evoking the qualities that make a garden like Charleston's so memorable. There is no substitute for walking by the pond on a spring morning to witness life, in the form of snowdrops, crocuses and narcissi, return after the long Sussex winter. And it is difficult to conjure in writing the heady combination of colour and scent in the walled garden on a July afternoon. The photographs in this volume not only succeed in transporting us there, but also provide the closest thing to a complete experience of this beautiful landscape as is possible.

This selection of images spans fifteen years, season to season, revealing the beauty of Charleston's surroundings not just in the spring and summer months but in the period from November to April when the house is closed to visitors. Not just in the middle of the day but from the early morning to the late evening. Not only in fine weather, but when the sky is dominated by cloudy menace or the mist is spilling from the Downs towards the house. Sue's photographs bring out the crucial relationship between the garden and the surrounding countryside – an agricultural landscape – that Charleston (as a farmhouse) was always firmly within and of which it was always a part.

Even if you know Charleston well, you will find in this book aspects and moods of Charleston that are new. The garden at Charleston is one to explore and to discover, and this collection of photographs enables the reader to return to it at will, at any time of the day or season of the year, and to be inspired and uplifted by it. And it is a book that will, of course, make one long to return to re-explore the garden itself.

Colin McKenzie
Director of the Charleston Trust

Introduction

Charleston's garden is a sensory treat from the moment you arrive. Your journey takes you from the busy A27 Brighton–Eastbourne road and you venture along a narrow farm track leading towards the folds of the glorious East Sussex South Downs. Recently preserved as a National Heritage Park, the downs are an area of outstanding natural beauty, where shaped, windswept trees seemingly hug the landscape with the promise of nearby sea. The sixteenth-century farmhouse and adjoining farm, with its extensive barns and the daily round of cows being milked, sits simply, surrounded by fields in the sight of Firle Beacon; a footpath connects walkers to Firle village and beyond. It is an almost timeless scene, similar to that when Vanessa Bell and her family and friends initially arrived at Charleston in 1916, when a new episode in the character of the house and garden began, separate from the working farm.

It is a place that evokes many memories. Of sharp spring beginnings, after the first snowdrops have arrived in late winter, with new lambs gambolling in the surrounding fields. In the magical walled garden the blousy box cloud hedges display new growth; primroses, narcissi, brash tulips and forget-me-nots burst into flower; the air is full of the perfume of wallflowers; and delicate fritillaries flourish. Later come aquilegia and sweet William, while pale pink apple blossom floats like snow on the breeze and salad seedlings sprout in the kitchen garden.

Summer follows on slowly from spring, and the garden becomes ablaze with a rainbow of abundant jewel-like colours and textures. There is a profusion of various-coloured and perfumed roses, with numerous butterflies and bees collecting pollen. Red and pink peonies and oriental poppies tangle with pink foxgloves. Phlox, orange-flecked tiger lilies, purple iris, blue delphiniums and white daisies continue the season, with palest pink and deep red, almost-black hollyhocks and dahlias, shocking-pink gladioli, soft-coloured and delicate sweet peas, red hot pokers, yellow and burnt-umber sunflowers, and brash nasturtiums that climb or curl in their own individual ways – just a few of the hundred or so flower species planted in the garden. It is a time to pick and eat apples, plums, pears, raspberries, red currants and, from the kitchen garden, globe artichokes, runner beans, broad beans, radish, lettuce and tomatoes.

All too soon summer seems to fade into the haze of autumn, and with the possibility of frost the leaves challenge the earlier flowers with their deep and vibrant yellows, reds and oranges. Medlars and quince, pumpkin and squash are picked, cooked and preserved. Leeks and potatoes are carefully lifted and stored. Then, far too hastily, comes winter, when the sky seems to rule with its grey, black and brown tones, the dankness occasionally lifted by a dusting of white snow or the sun peeping over the backdrop of the high downs.

The garden, of less than an acre, is naturally enclosed by fields and tall trees, with flint and brick walls that both form boundaries and add extra protection for the beautiful walled garden with its intricate paths, box hedging and cotton lavender edgings. There is a small lawn with a tiny pond, a glorious piazza with a second pond, a kitchen garden for vegetables and flowers to cut for the house and numerous fruit trees. There is also, to the front of the house, a large pond that reflects the house, once used as a cattle pond and now teeming with fish; an orchard with a black mulberry and yellow quinces; an internal folly garden with its own tame robin; a greenhouse; a potting shed; discreetly placed garden seats; and fun statuary by Quentin Bell, Vanessa Bell's youngest son. These pieces are made from brick, ciment and ceramic, all with unusual names – *The Spink*, *Leaning Female Figure*, *Pomona*. There are also copies of various cast heads, which Vanessa Bell and Duncan Grant collected on their travels, some small torsos, and other pieces, all with a special twist or use – like the ceramic fountain head for a small pond and the piazza in the walled garden made entirely of pieces of broken household china set in cement. A tour of the house affords various glimpses and views of the garden and ends with visitors spilling directly out into it, via Duncan Grant's studio; or you can simply visit the garden on its own, entering by the latched and painted gates flanked by flower-filled ciment fondu urns to be found at the front of the house.

This is a garden that feels secret and personal, even though many people see it each year. Each visitor feels they have discovered an extremely private and vibrant place. Frances Partridge (1900–2004), writer and naturalist, who kindly supported my work during the last few years of her life, said of it: 'I see it as an enchanted place . . . a place of potent individuality . . .

so many rich and various visual sensations. I tend to picture it at noon on a summer's day . . . with the tall flowers motionless in the hot still air' (Charleston Symposium, Victoria and Albert Museum, 1985).

It was Vanessa Bell's painterly imagination and her love of sumptuous colours and evocative planting that allowed me to feel so immediately at home in the garden. She had a wonderful eye for colour, shape and form, and a passion for gardening which she had acquired from her mother, Julia Stephens, and shared with her sister, Virginia Woolf. When Vanessa Bell was bringing up her family here, the garden was not only a space in which to garden and to escape to from the war but a sanctuary which all who visited could enjoy. Initially, because of the war, growing food was imperative, so there were mostly cabbages, potatoes and carrots, fruit trees and chickens. The family used the large cattle pond for boating. Only after 1918 was the walled garden transformed gradually into a sea of colours with overflowing herbaceous flowerbeds that became an inspiration for drawings, paintings, writings and design.

I initially came to the garden in 1986, after Sir Peter Shepheard had completed his careful and painstaking restoration for the then newly formed Charleston Trust. The restoration was complemented by the work of Mark Divall and Clifton Nurseries. Mark worked alongside Sir Peter Shepheard and stayed on to become the Trust's first gardener. Now, twenty or so years later, after an absence spent living and gardening in Provence, Mark again nurtures this garden with knowledge, passion and enthusiasm, while taking it forward in his own creative, artistic and instinctive way and capturing, as Angelica Garnett tells him, 'the spirit of the place'. He says, 'I can see the garden as a theatre. Throughout the year the plants contrive to put on many performances; by July, the glow of the peonies and oriental poppies will have been extinguished, but there is the promise of red hot pokers, dahlias and cosmos as they prepare for the garden's final act.' Mark's love of this garden ensures Charleston's continuing enchantment and ever-changing and crowded seasonal planting, as well as its place in and affinity with the stunningly beautiful surrounding countryside. Thanks to all these efforts, the garden today has evolved and developed, and, in the words of Sir Peter Shepheard, continues as '. . . a garden filled to overflowing. The plants jostling and blending with one another as in a meadow, not too precise but with a sweet disorder.'

I was extremely privileged to begin my photography of the garden in 1995 by the kind invitation of the then curator, Peter Miall, an exceptionally knowledgeable and caring man. Andrew Caverly was the gardener at the time, and for several years he very positively continued Mark's work with an equal passion for Charleston's past and future. During that time the large pond was restored and some of the surrounding trees sensitively pruned and felled, as part of the nurture, maintenance and ongoing life of Charleston. It is thanks to these three men that I have been able to work so continuously in such a beautiful garden.

Initially I began a one-year project, which culminated in an exhibition at Charleston, entitled 'A Garden's Year 1995–1996'. Shaun Romain, the arts coordinator, introduced the exhibition as follows:

> Sue has during the last twelve months recorded through her photography a unique insight into the changing seasons at Charleston. The garden has been described as a painter's garden, which has evolved through an awareness of colour, pattern, texture and tone. She has managed to capture with a considerable degree of sympathy an impression of the garden which supports the notion of it being derived from the ideas and conventions of painting. More importantly she has given us all a vision of this space which is seldom witnessed by those who visit Charleston . . . it is hoped that all who come to visit will take away with them a slightly different view of what is certainly an unusual and very idiosyncratic place.

Now, a decade or so later, I am still photographing, mostly before the visitors arrive or when they have just gone home. I had no idea on my first visit that Charleston would come to mean so much to me. It is a vibrant and colourful place, at the same time peaceful and thought provoking, and each time I visit I encounter new, very personal surprises. Some days the weather is unfavourable and the sky tells its own stories, with stormy clouds or even snow. But there is always some very beautiful light to photograph. This work began as a simple essay, a narrative on film in both colour and black and

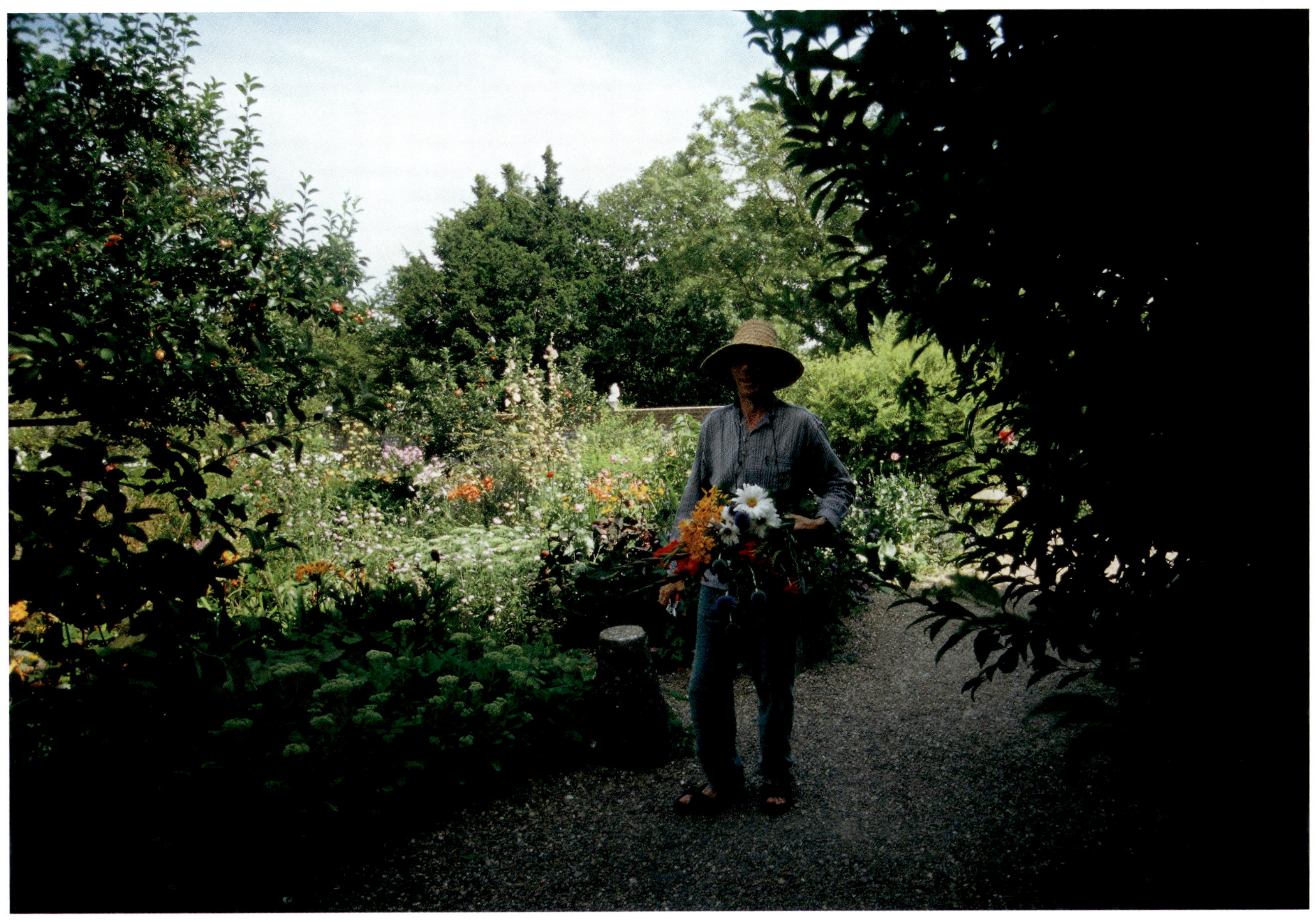

white, and has continued into an extensive, considered ongoing archive that has enabled me to put together this book of meticulous memories we can all share. Charleston continues being for me a place of enchantment, continually going forward in a positive way.

I use SLR or single lens reflex cameras with simple lenses and fast film, which suits the instinctive, unstructured, spontaneous images I like to make. My creative eye as a photographer is influenced by journalism, film, television and advertising, as I have also worked as a fashion editor and a costume designer with wonderful clothes and talented people. My images have a rhythm of their own and are always simply constructed, intended to have a soft, painterly feel. It is always very important for me to visually interpret my own individual story, so as to ensure that my work combines a vision of a place and its connection to people – people not necessarily seen but who always play a very important part, especially in a garden.

My life has been spent in London and abroad, but my grandparents and their family, including my father during his childhood, farmed near Charleston at Sedlescombe, East Sussex, when both Virginia Woolf and Vanessa Bell first came to live in this part of the country. So Charleston is, for me, also a reminder of my family, especially my father and mother, who both gardened passionately, influenced by their formative years, which for my mother was in very colourful India.

Today, Charleston's house and garden are still loved and cared for by the families of Vanessa Bell and Duncan Grant and by the very independent Charleston Trust. Under the excellent directorship of Colin McKenzie the Trust not only enables visitors to take a step back in time but also preserves Charleston for the future. Both the house and garden are open each year from April to October. Details of opening times, tours, special events and other information can be found by contacting the Charleston Trust by telephone (01323 811265) or via its website (www.charleston.org.uk).

Sue Snell
www.suesnell.co.uk

spring

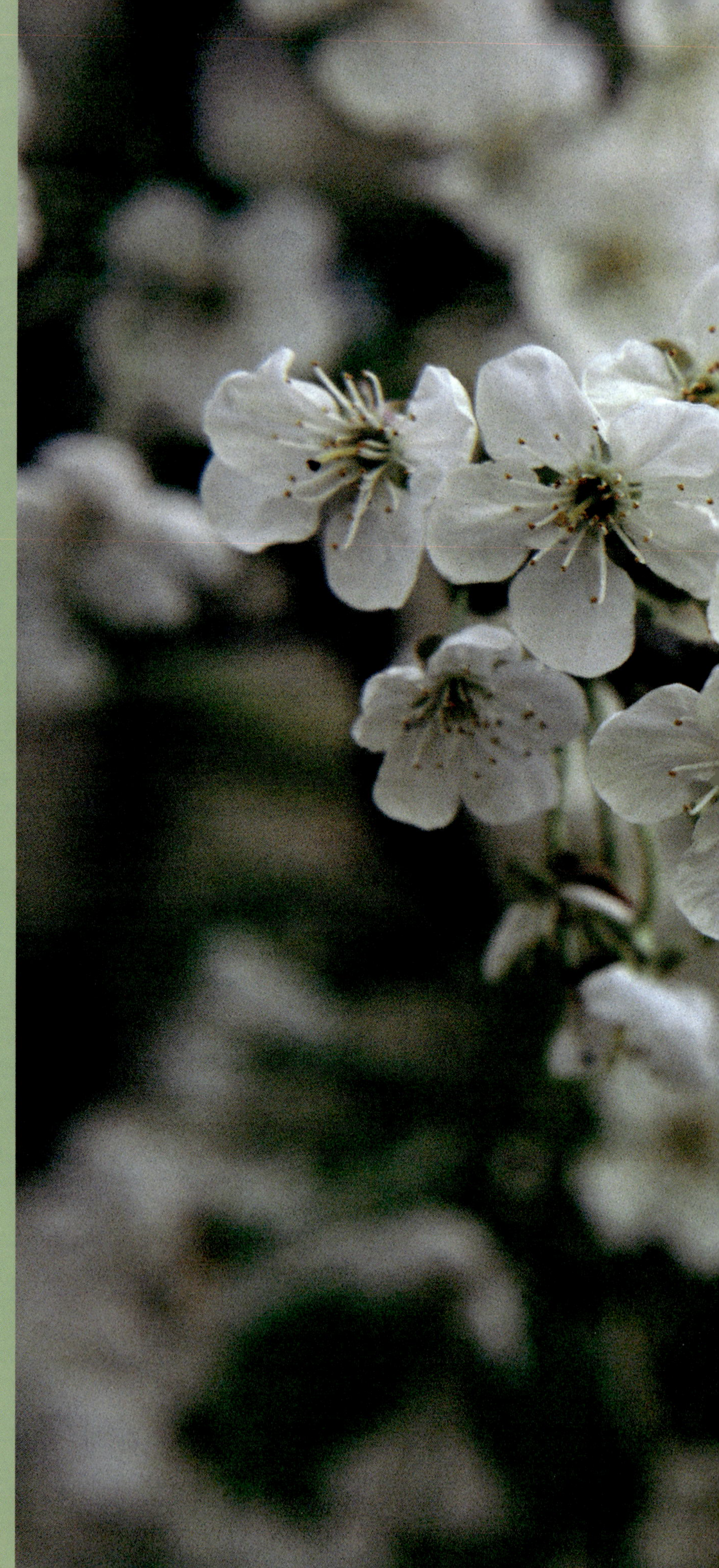

Cherry blossom

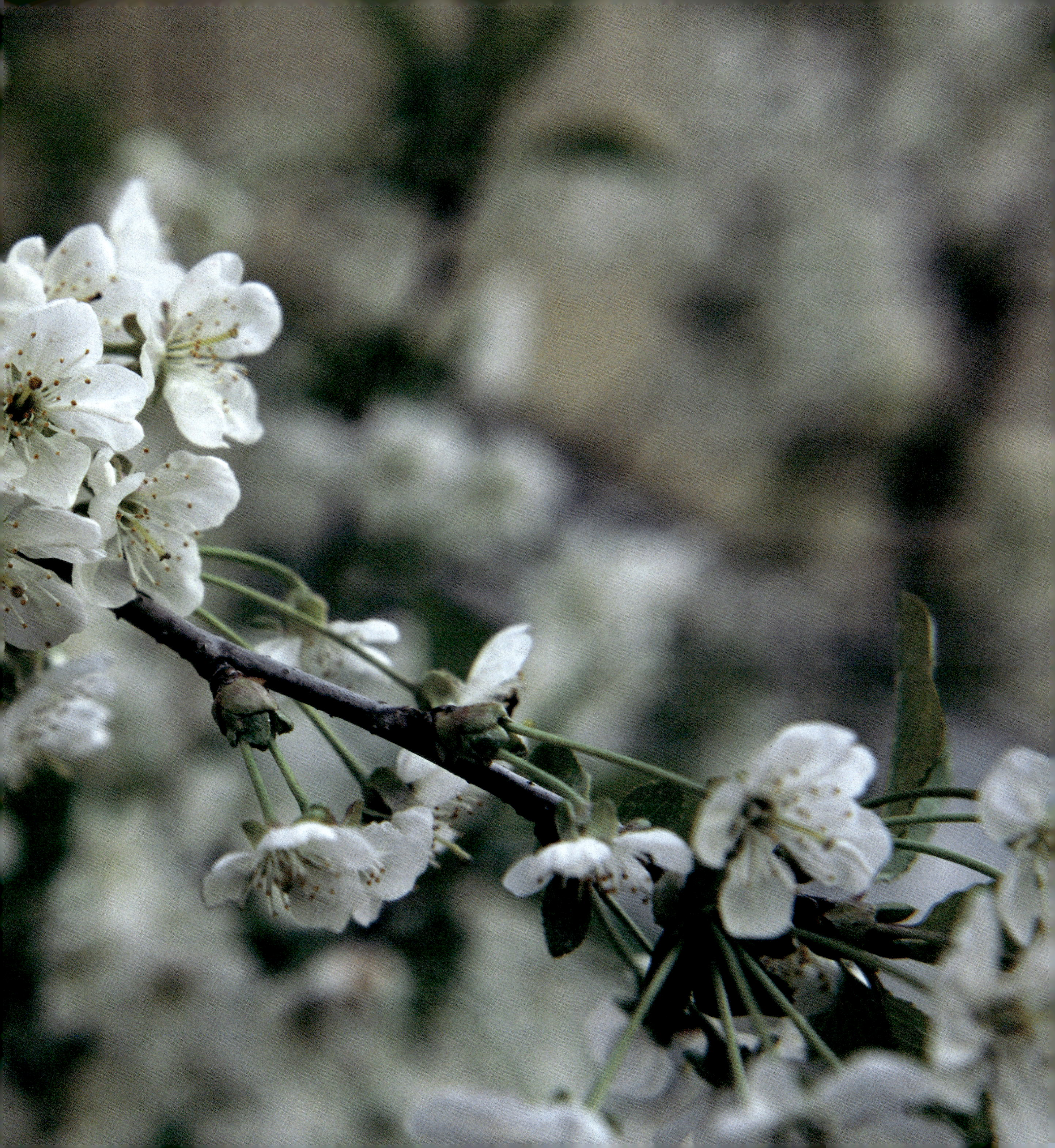

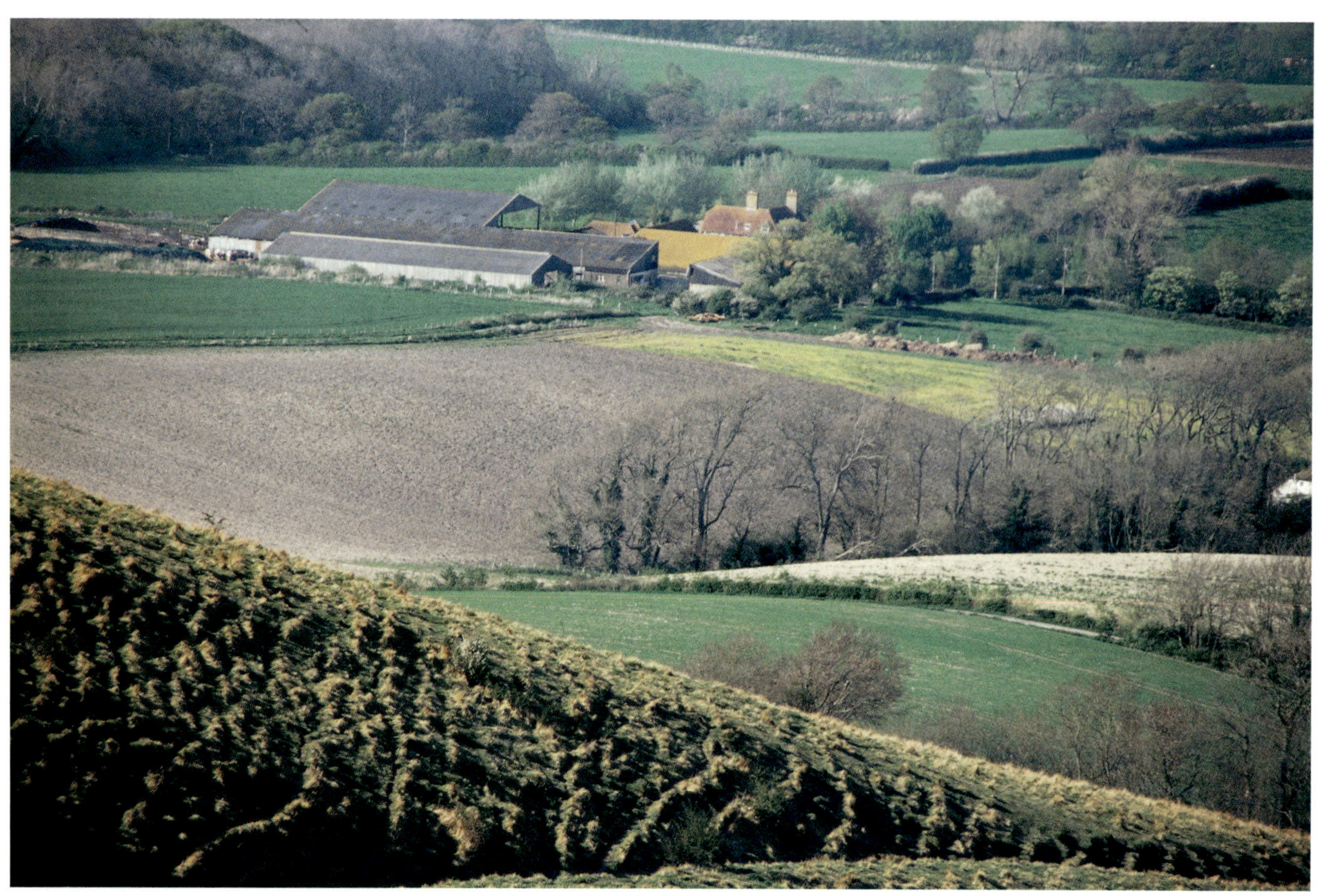

Views of the house and farm

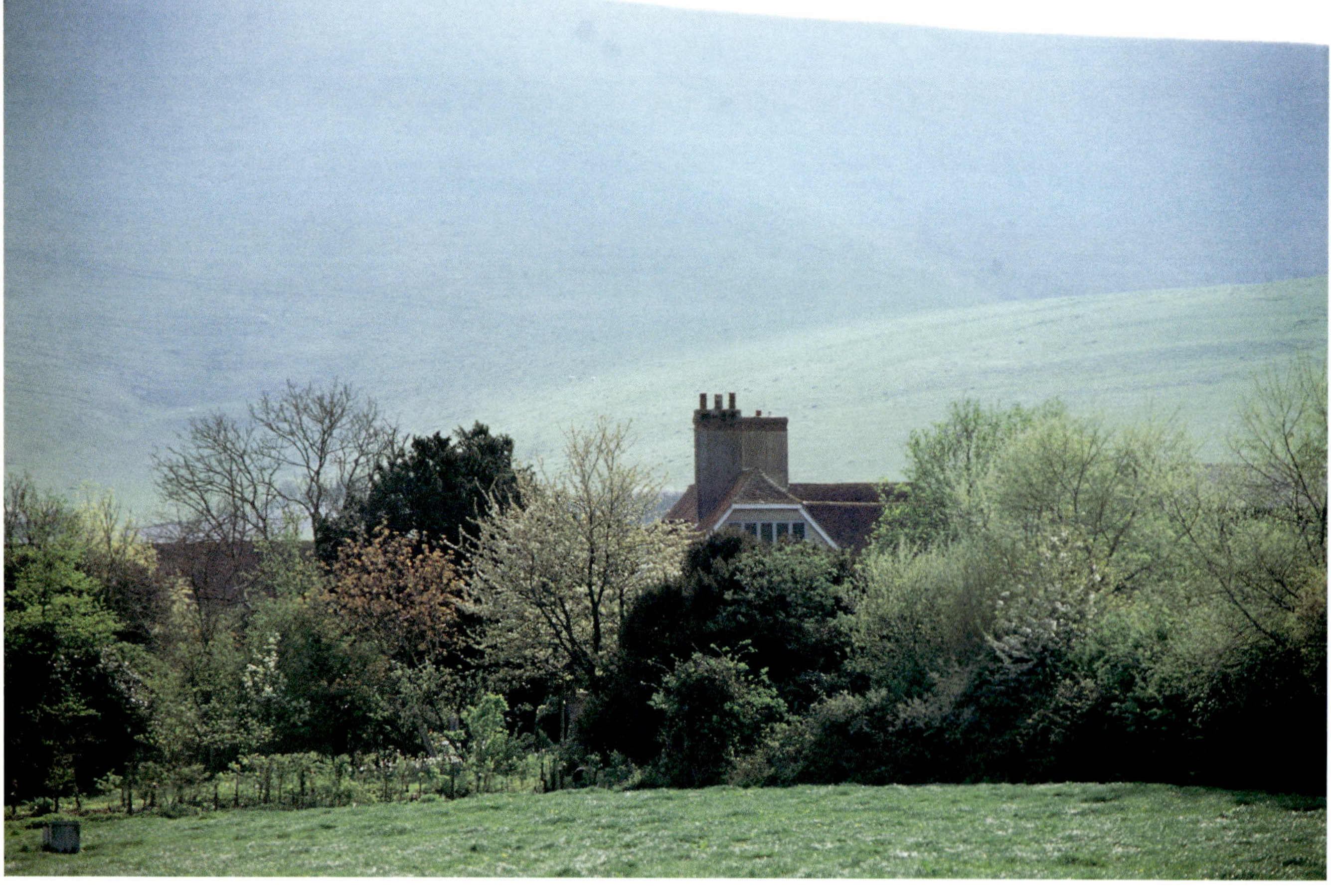

The house from across the pond

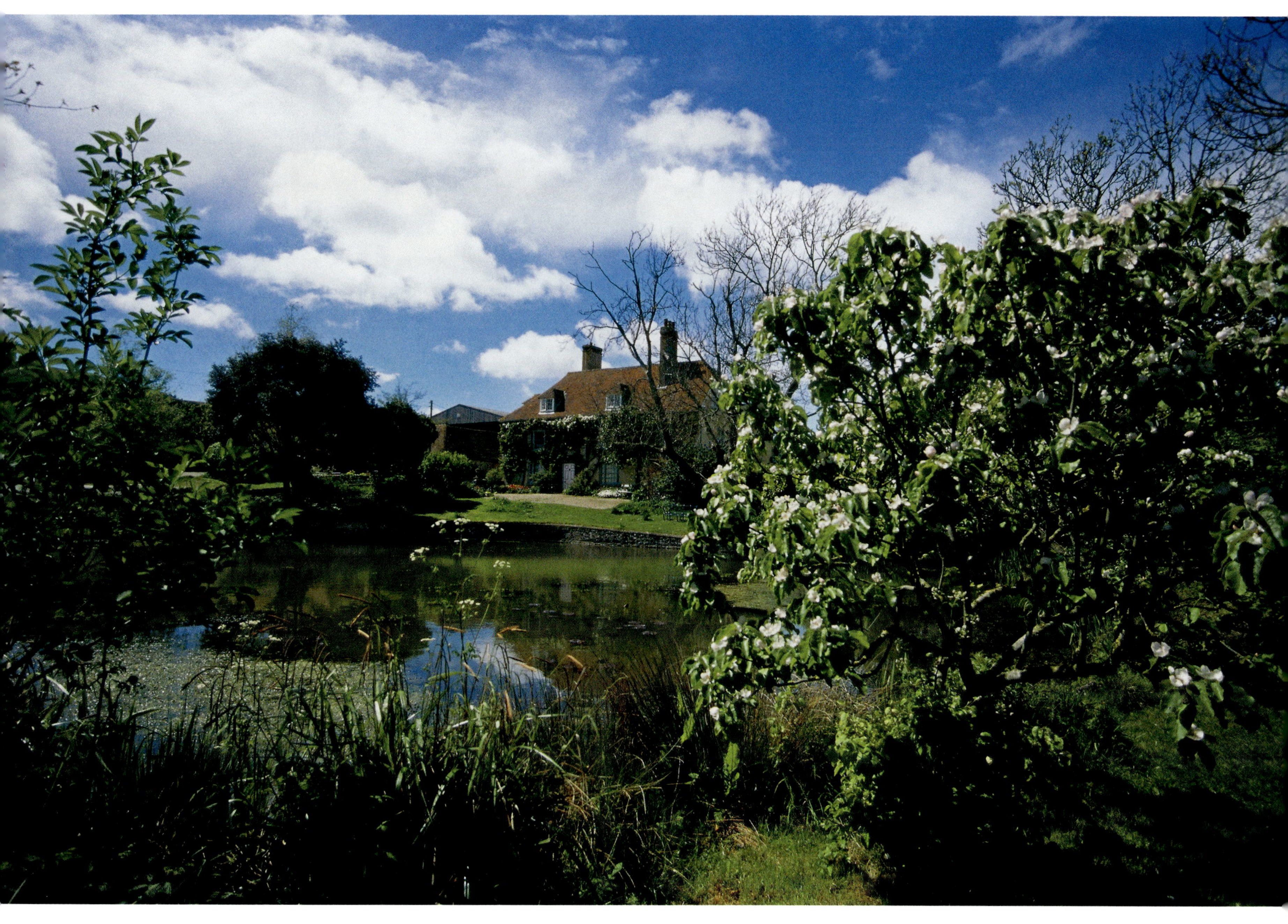

The house and the door to the walled garden

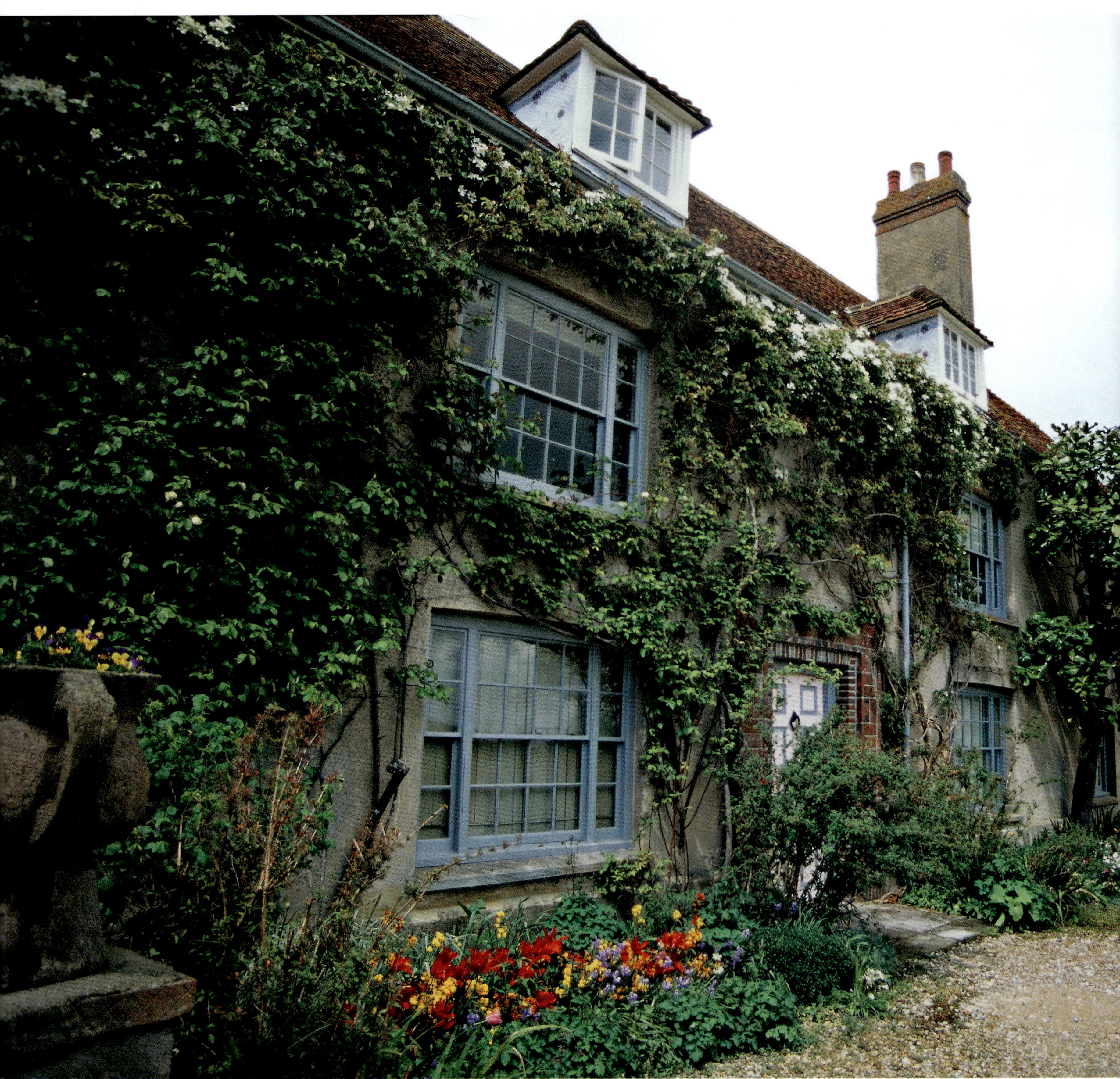

Flowering cherry and the path to *Pomona* by Quentin Bell

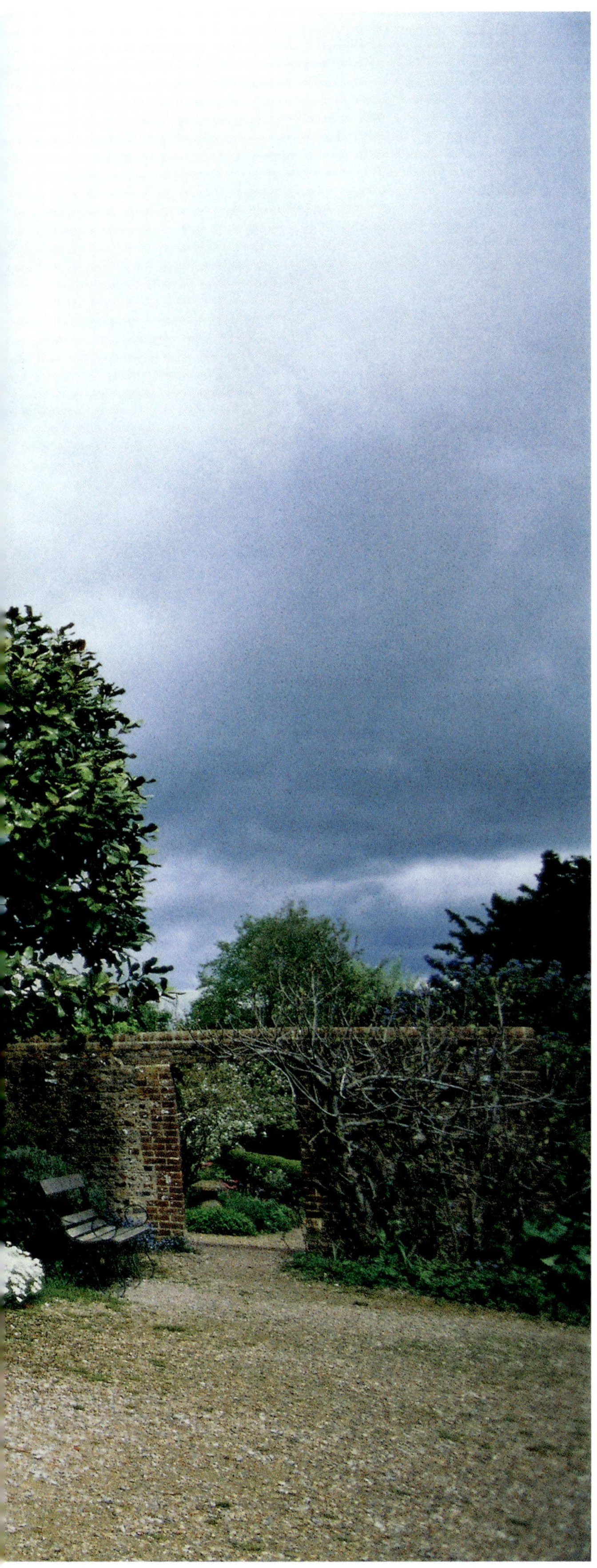

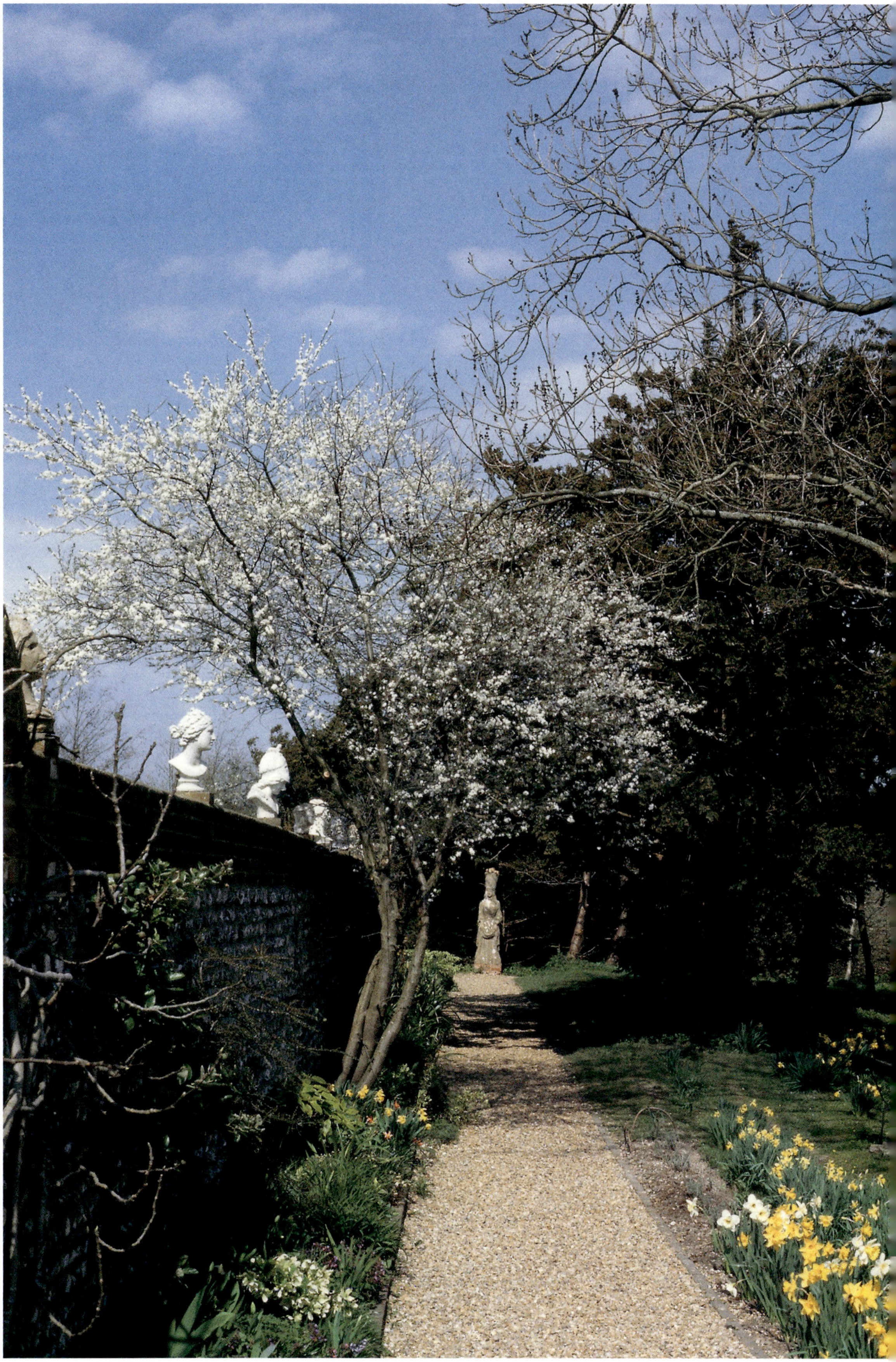

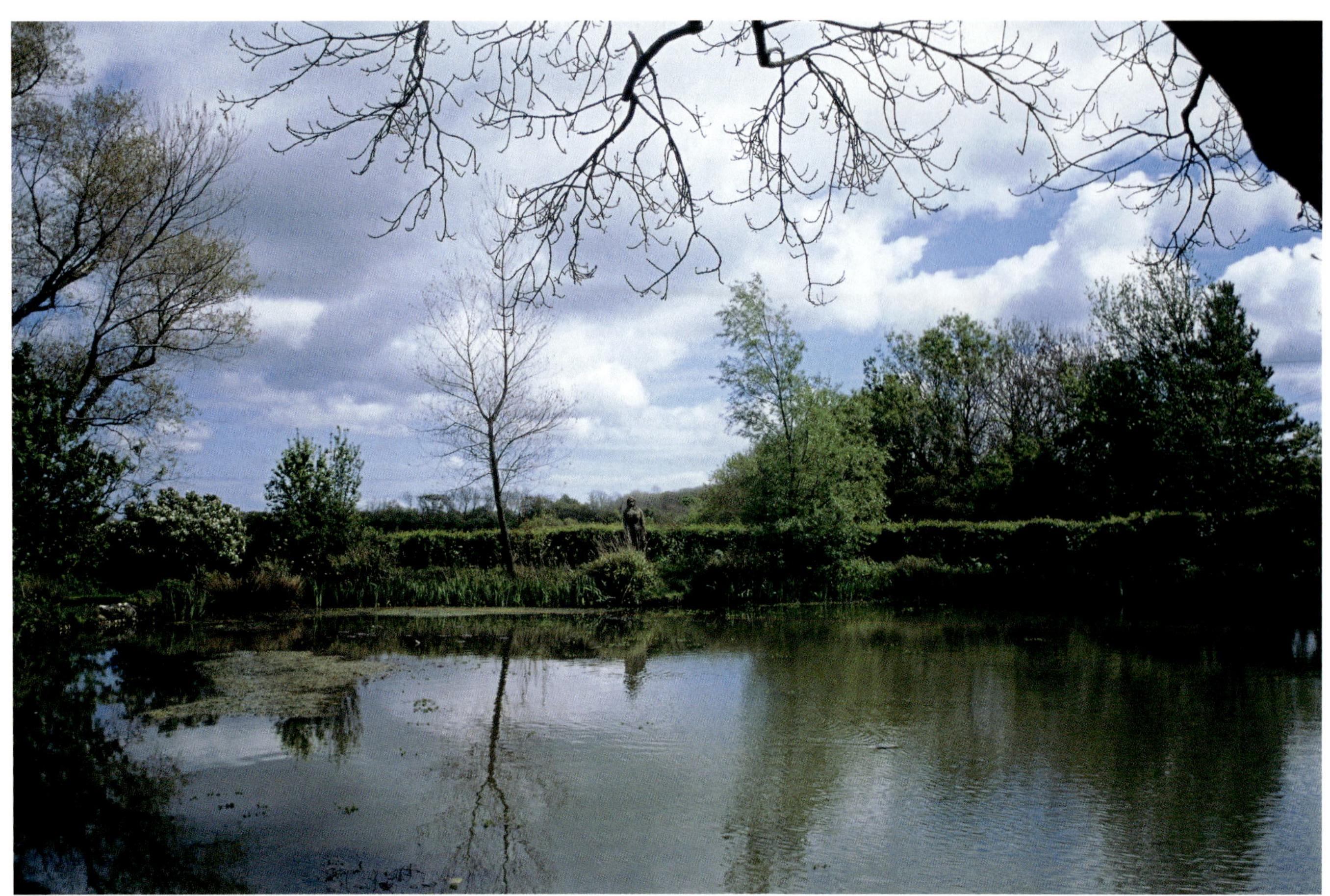

Leaning Female Figure by Quentin Bell

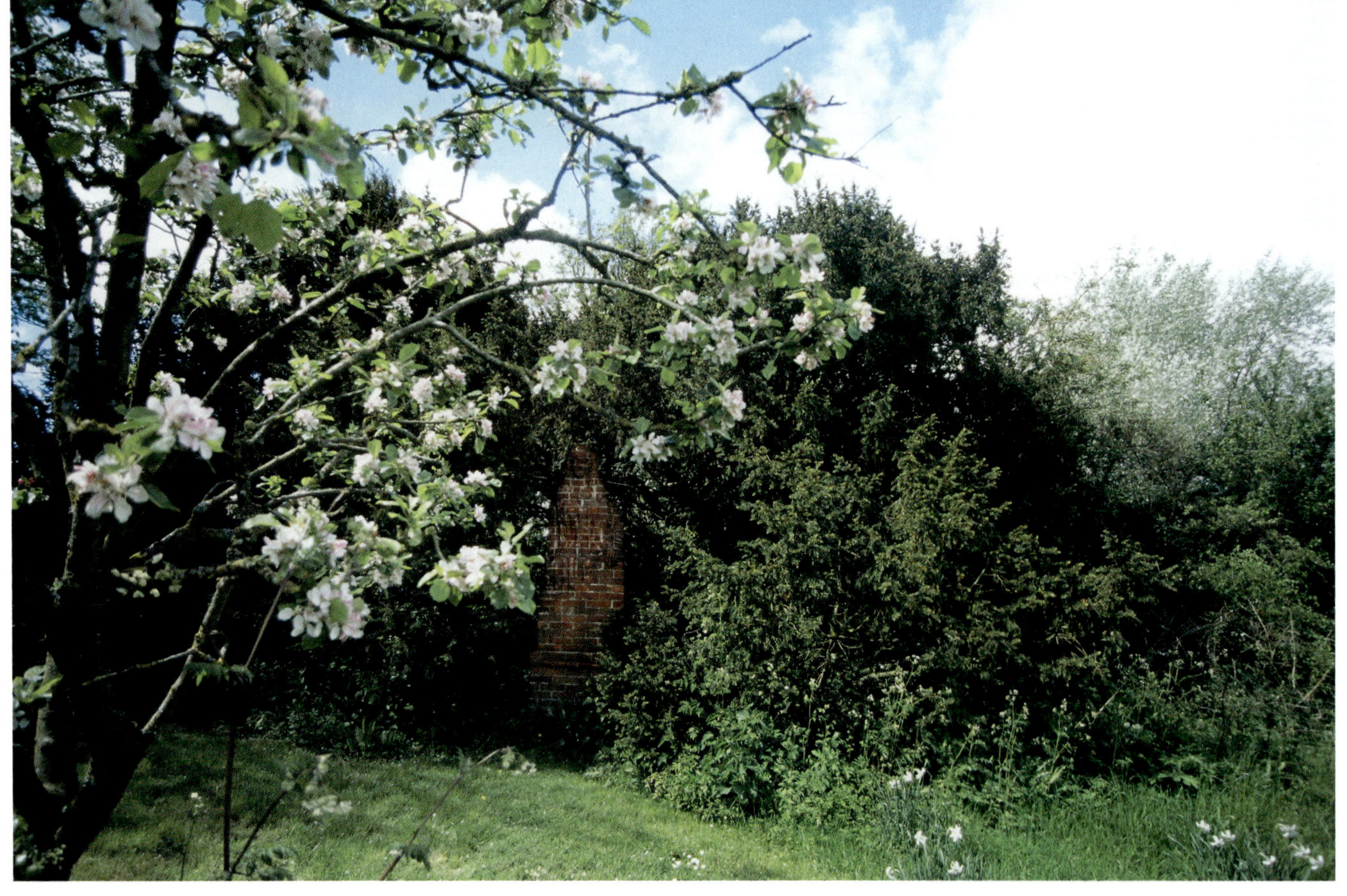

The Spink by Quentin Bell

Cherry blossom

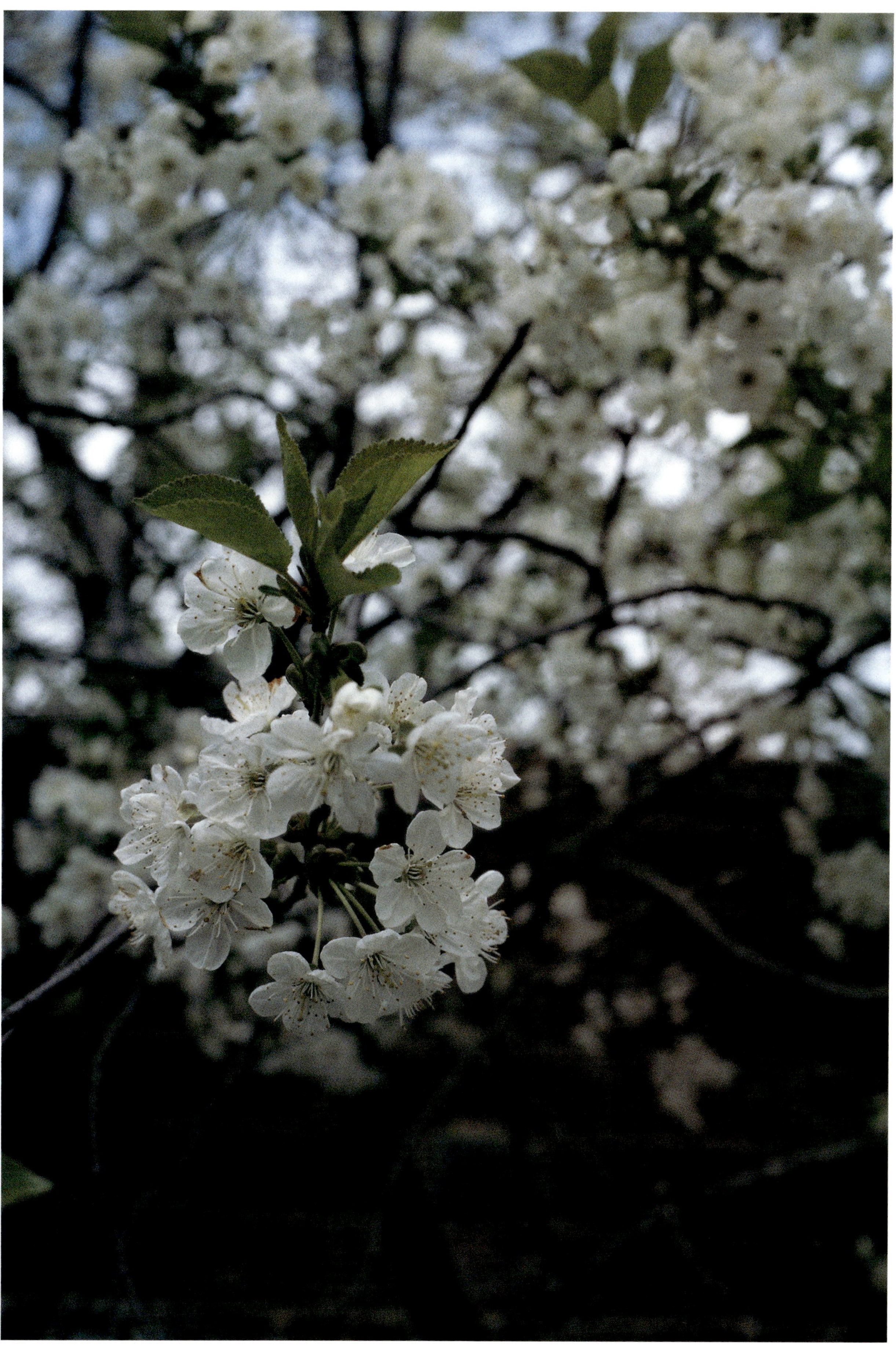

Garden latch

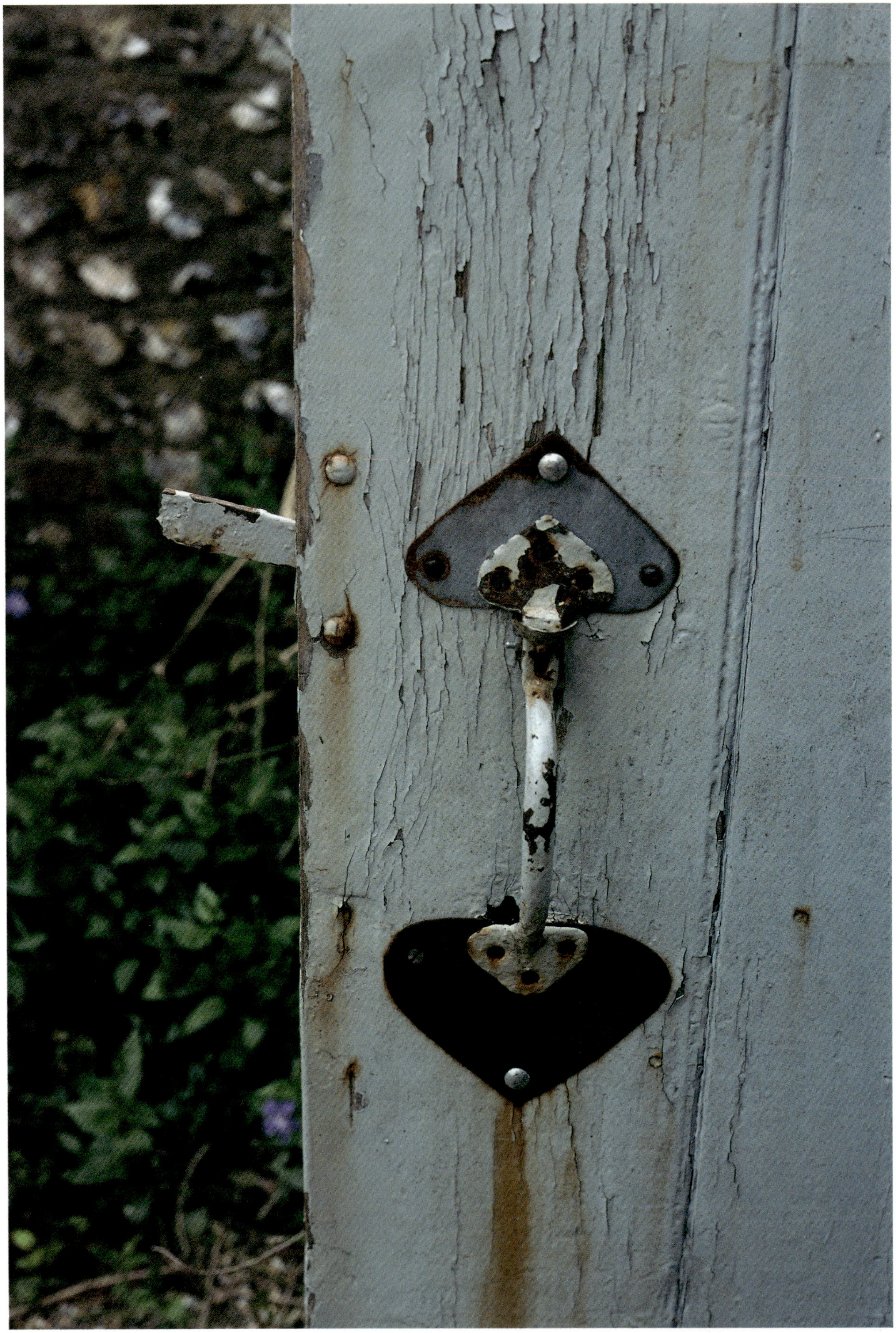

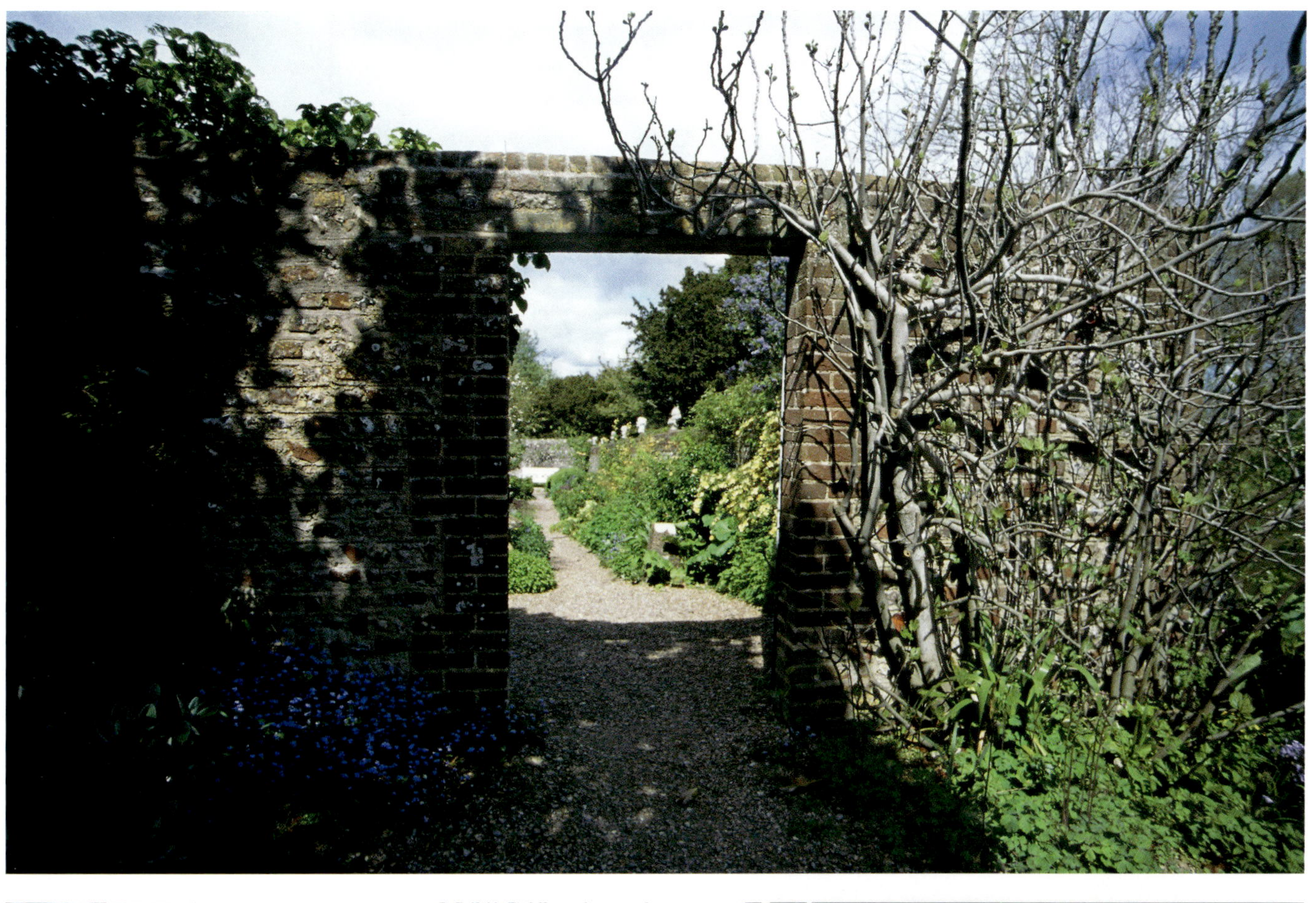

Fig by doorway

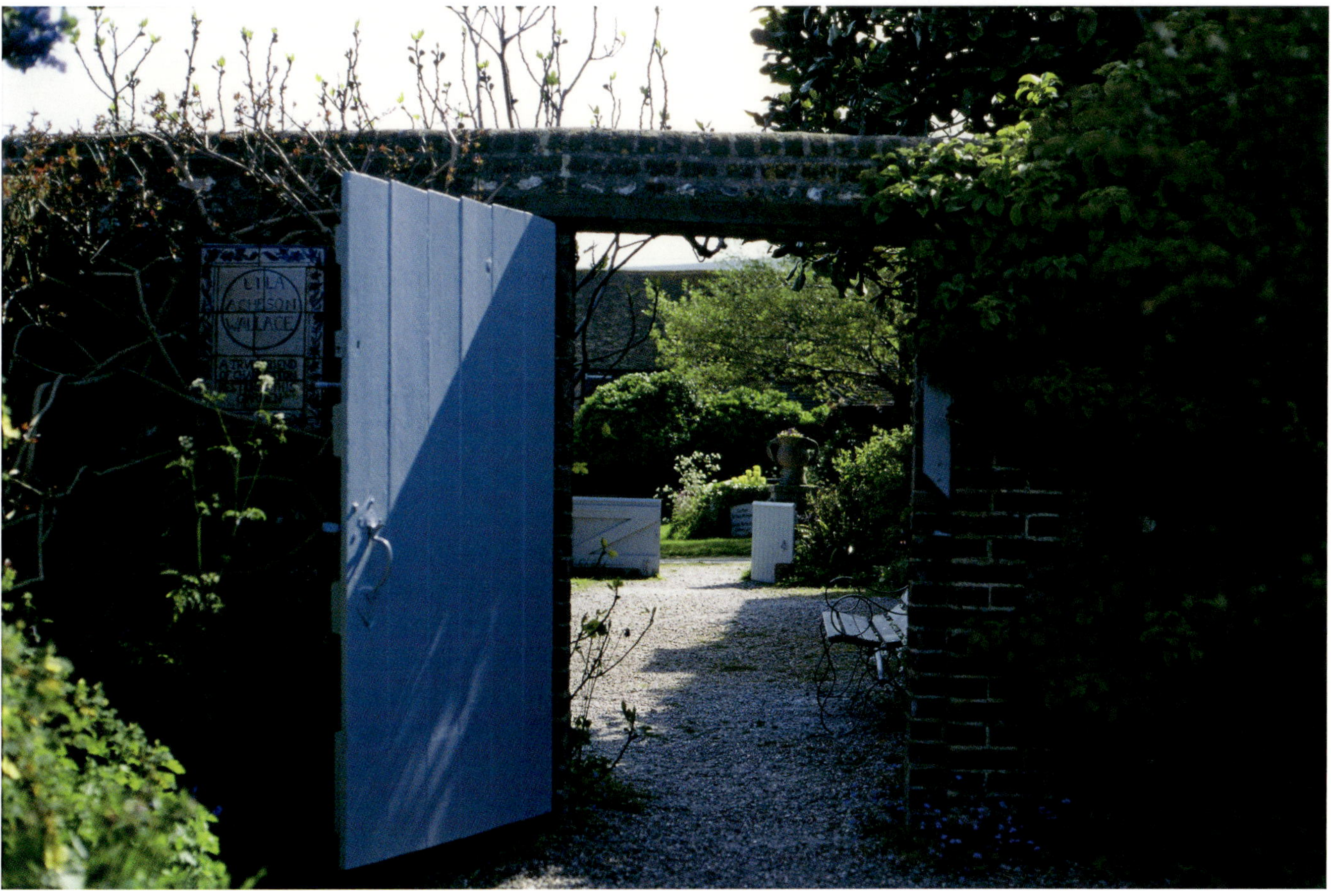

View to the farm

Storm approaching the walled garden

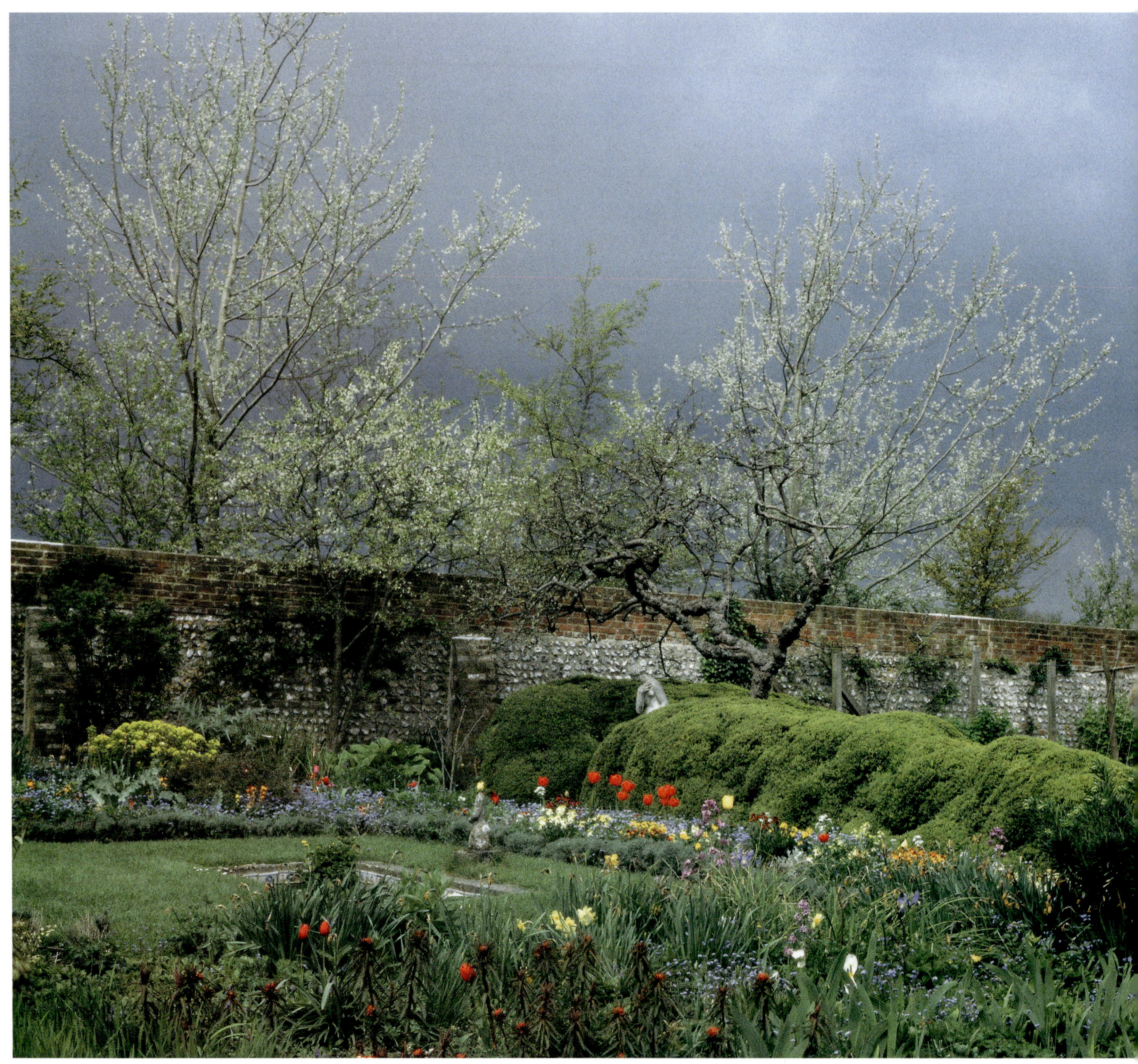

Spiraea 'Arguta' and a standing stone

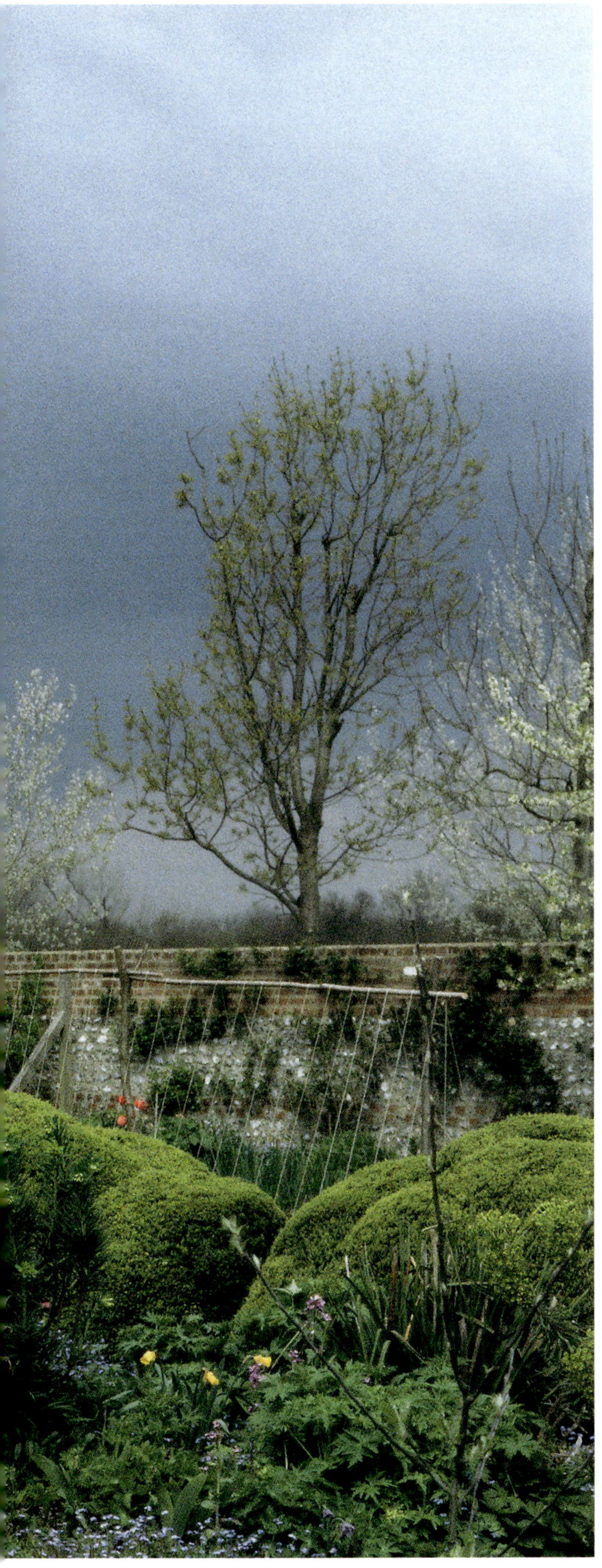

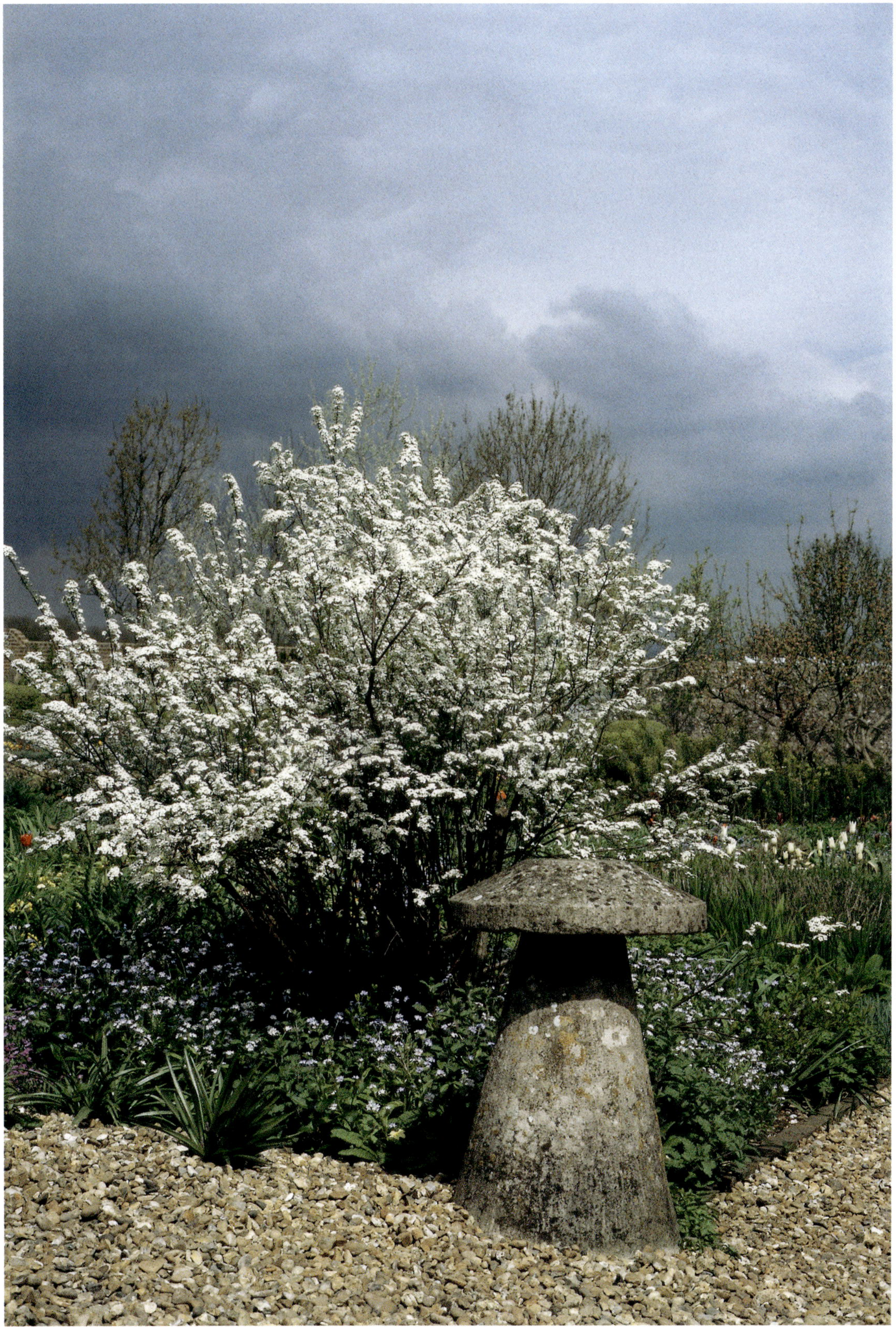

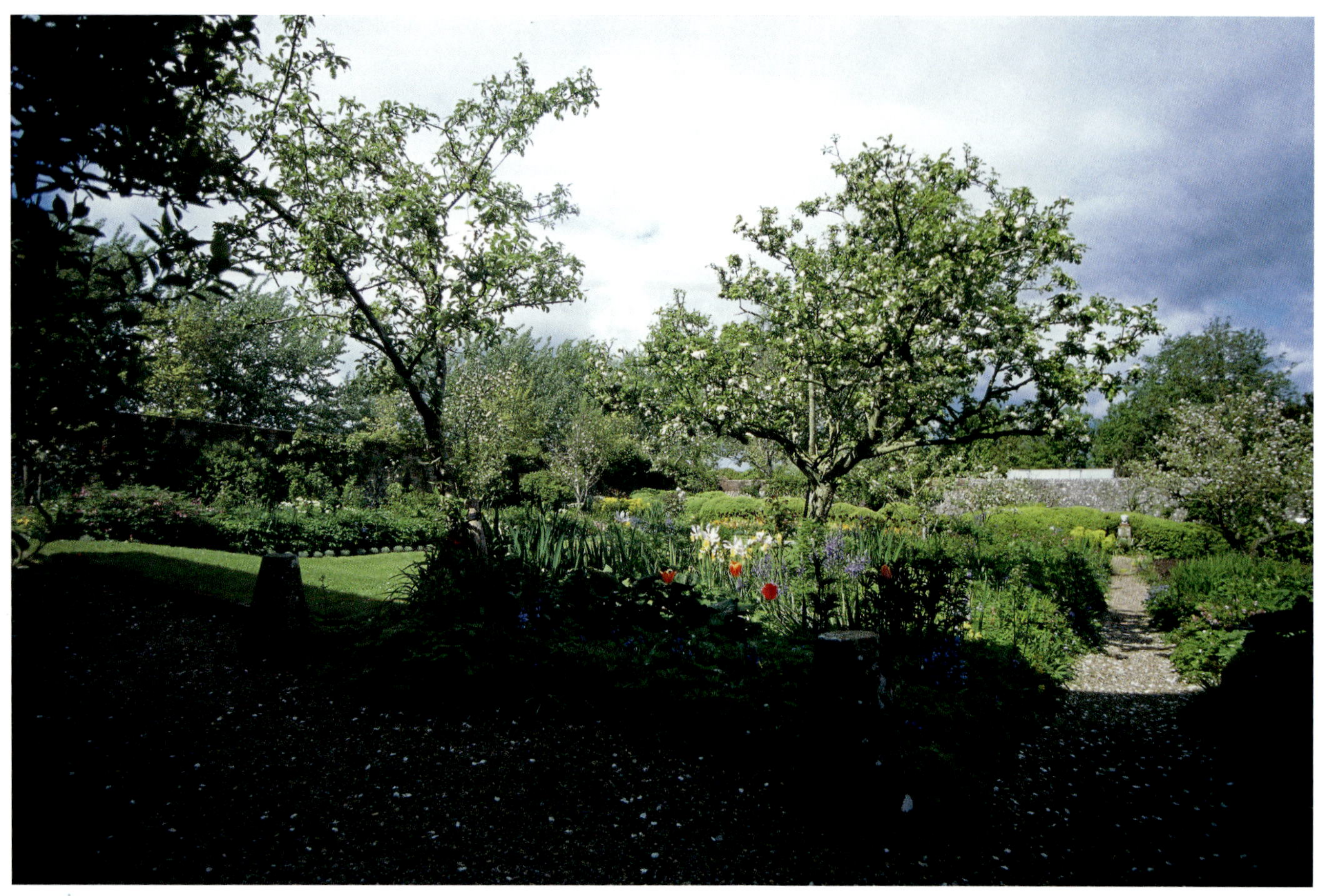

'Devonshire Quarrenden' apple

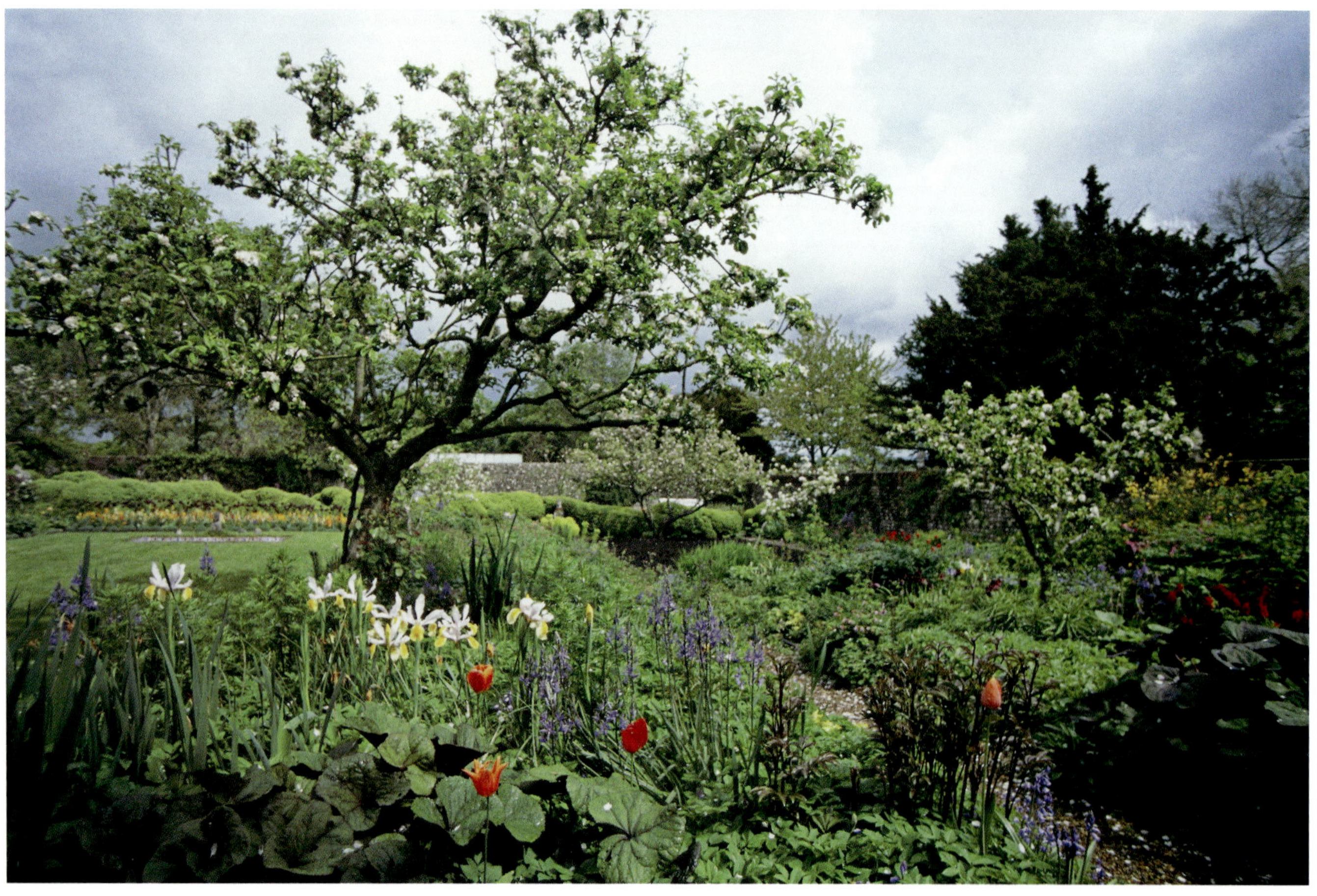

'Beauty of Bath' apple

'Egremont Russet' apple

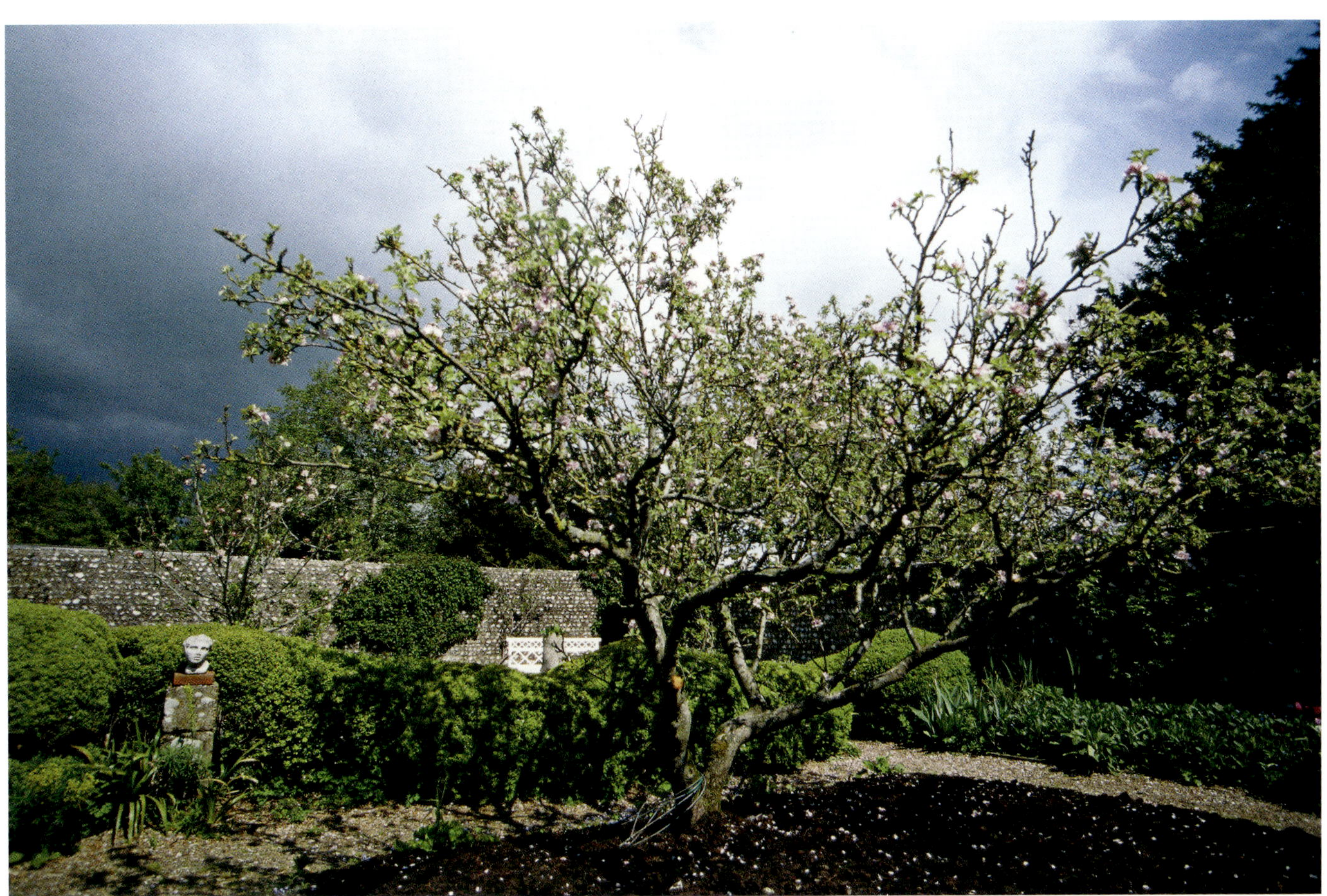

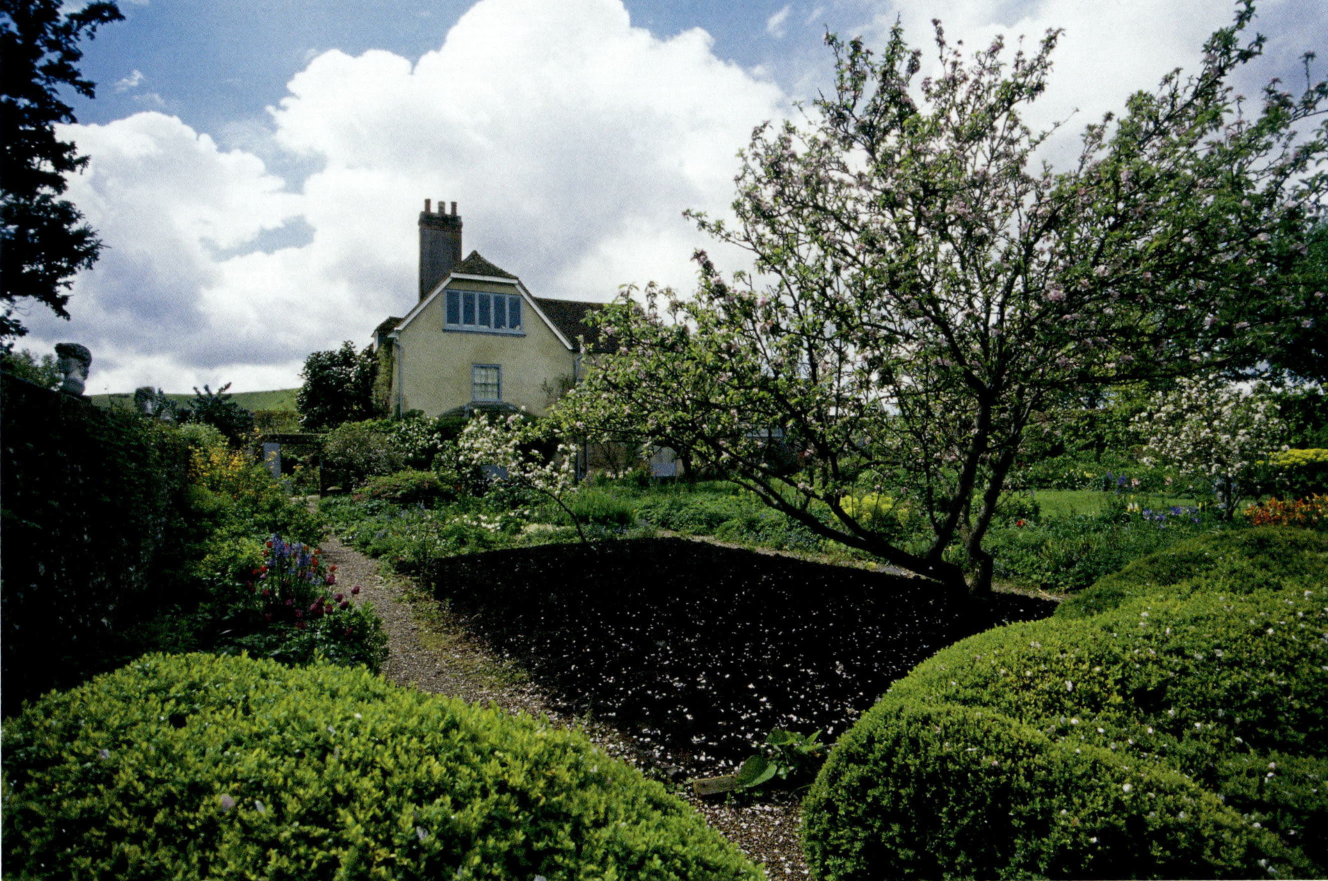

FOLLOWING PAGES
CLOCKWISE FROM LEFT
Cowslip; pheasant's eye narcissi; 'Canary Bird' rose, Parrot tulip; tulip

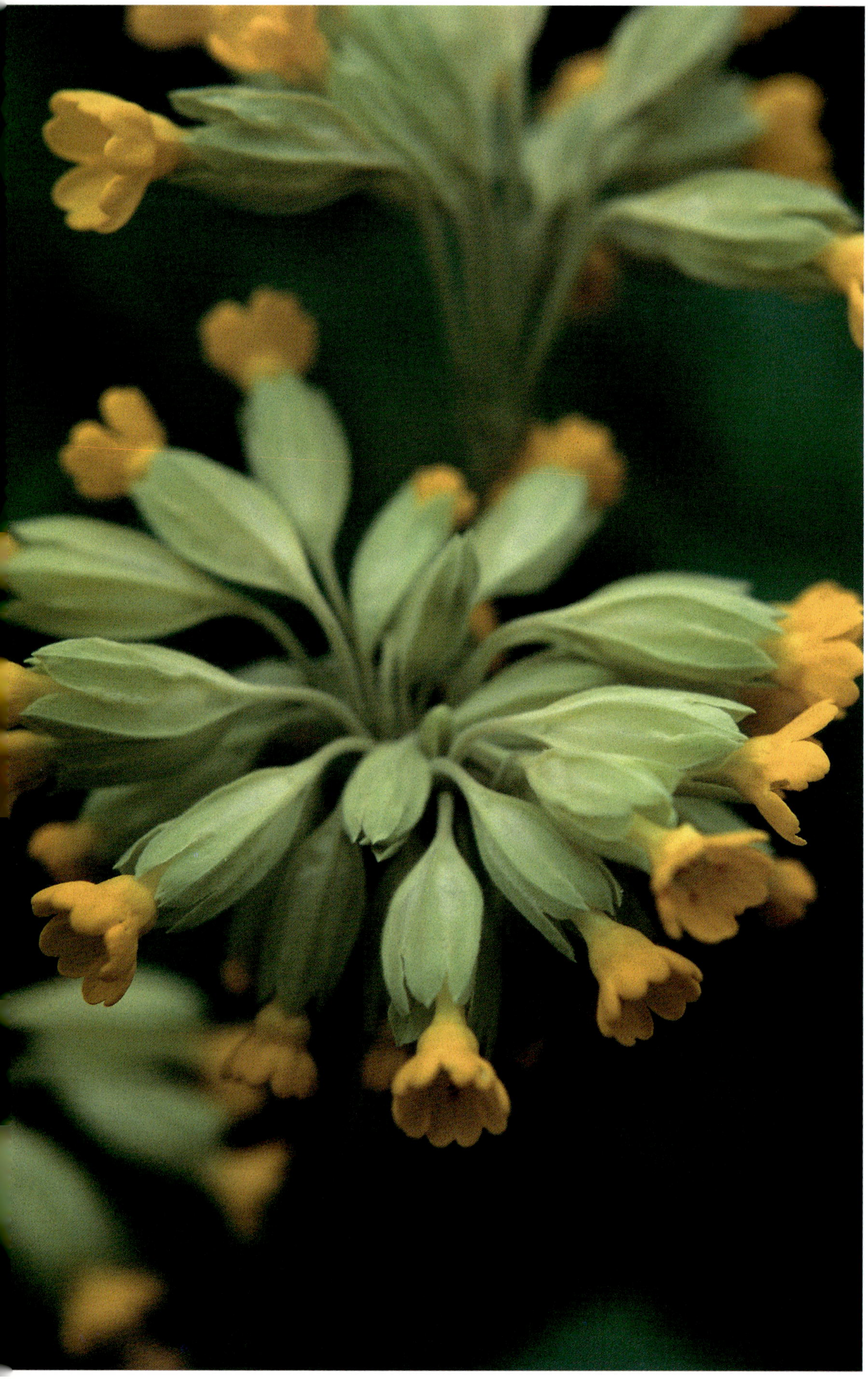

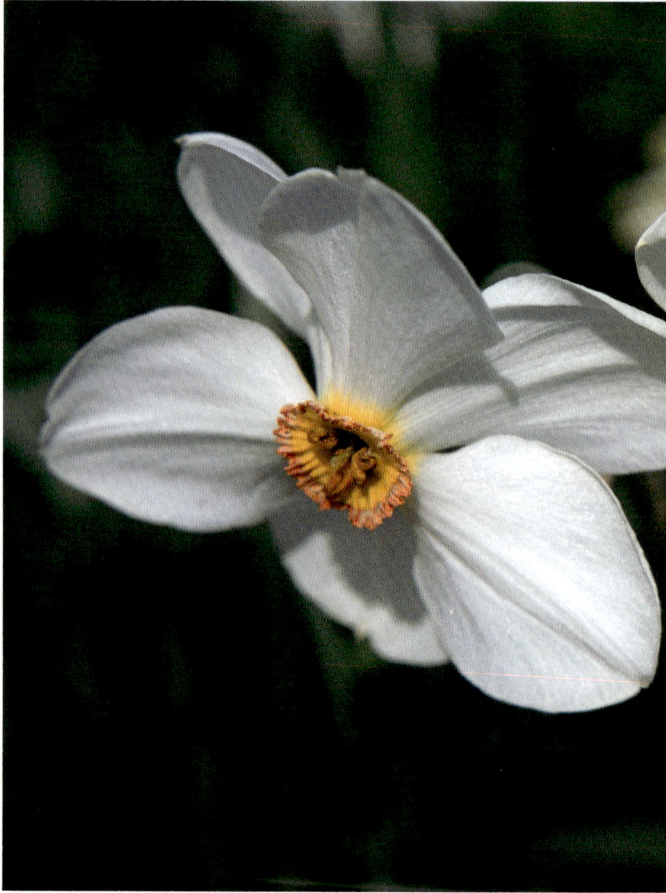

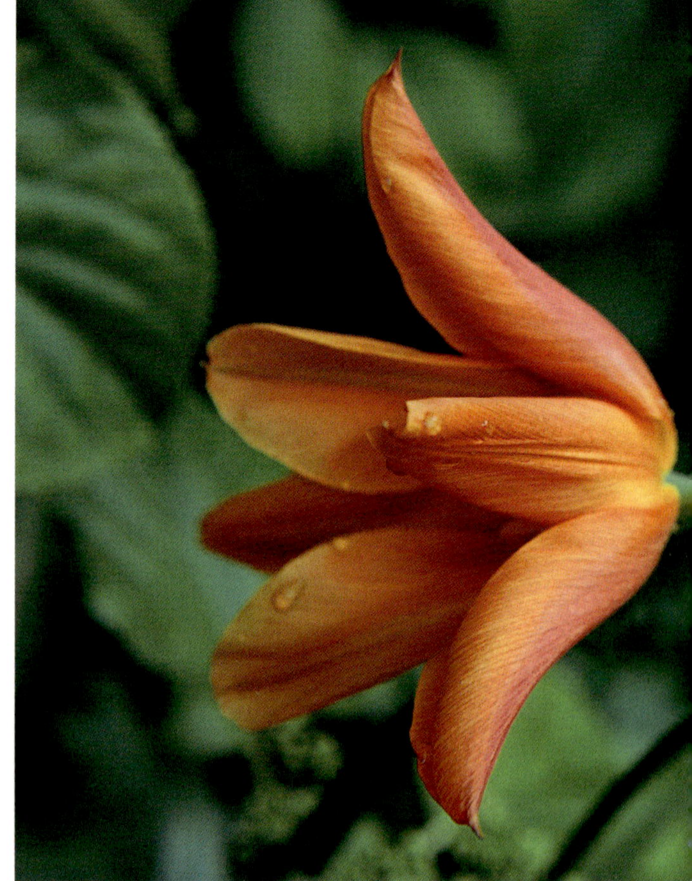

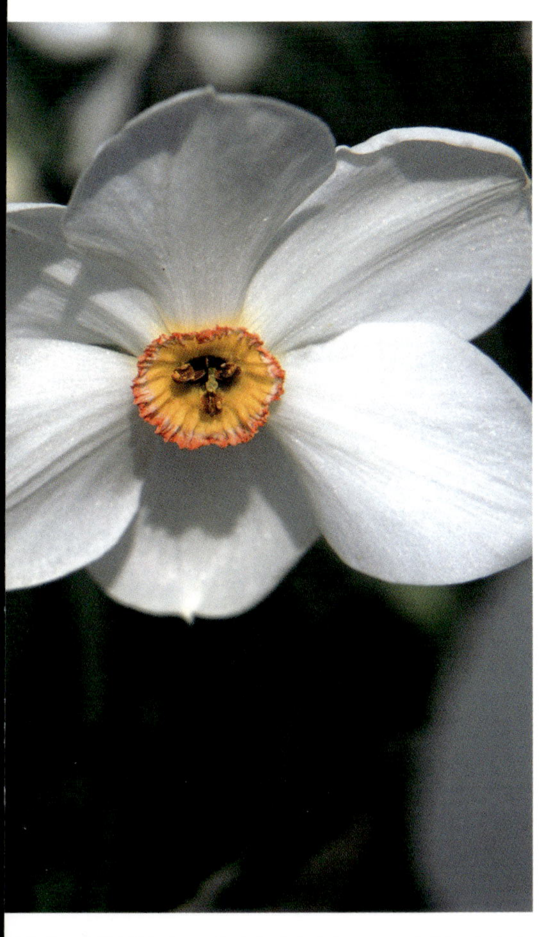

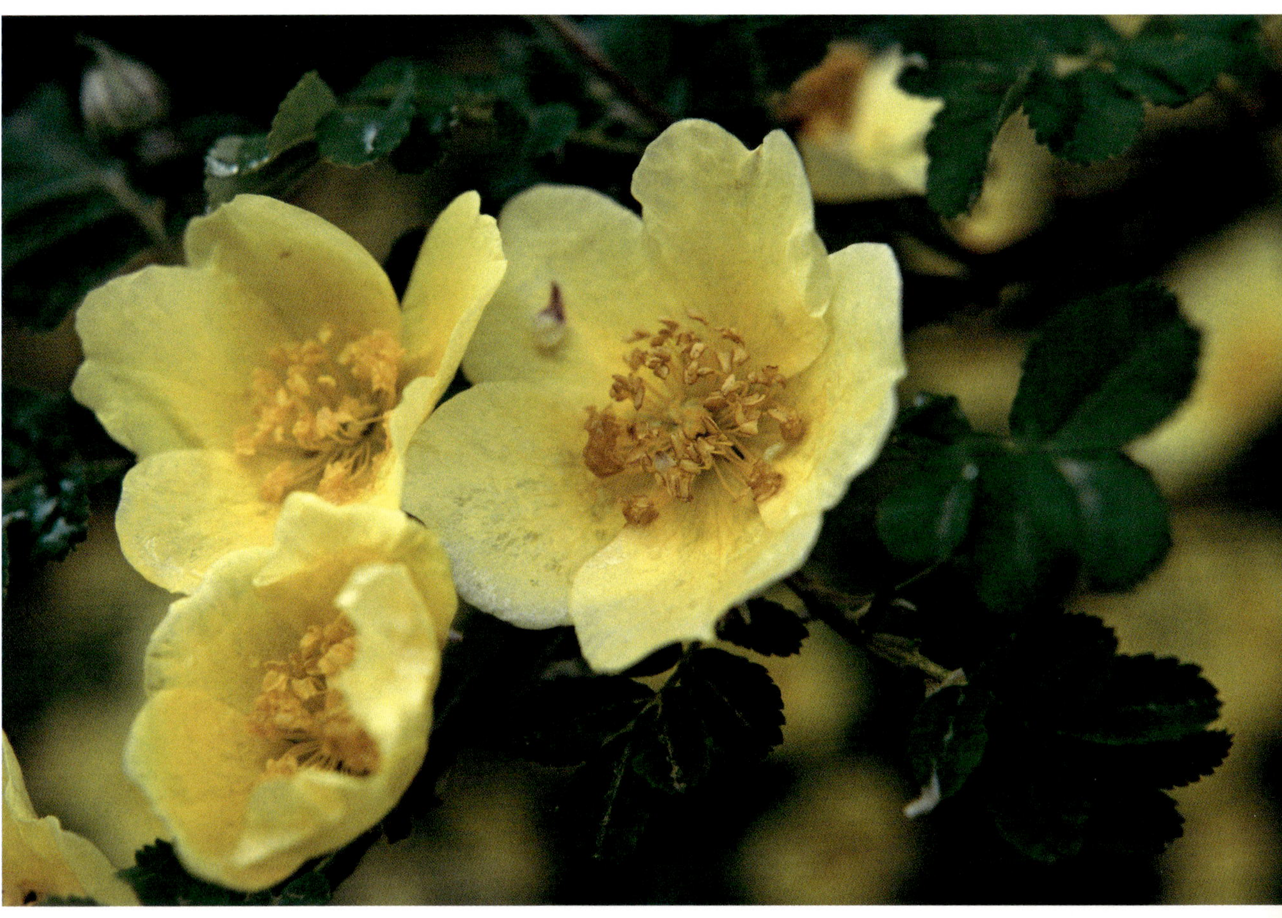

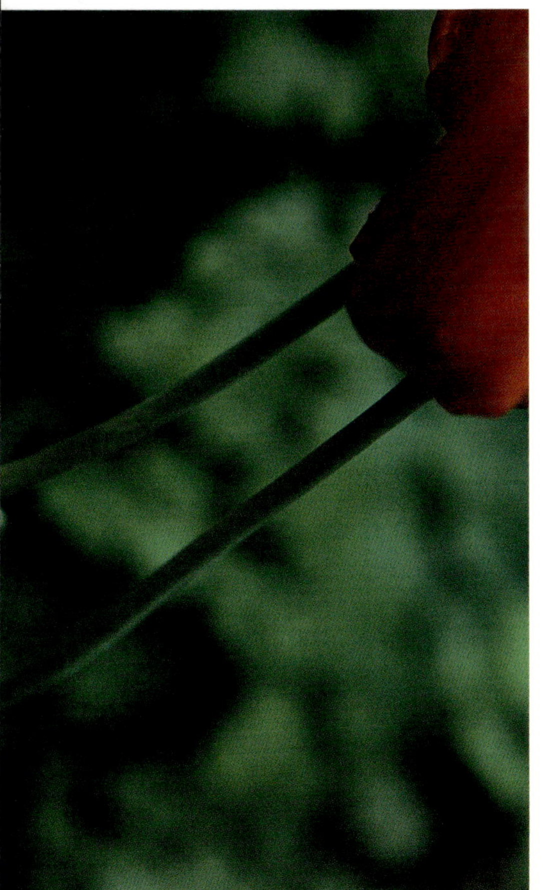

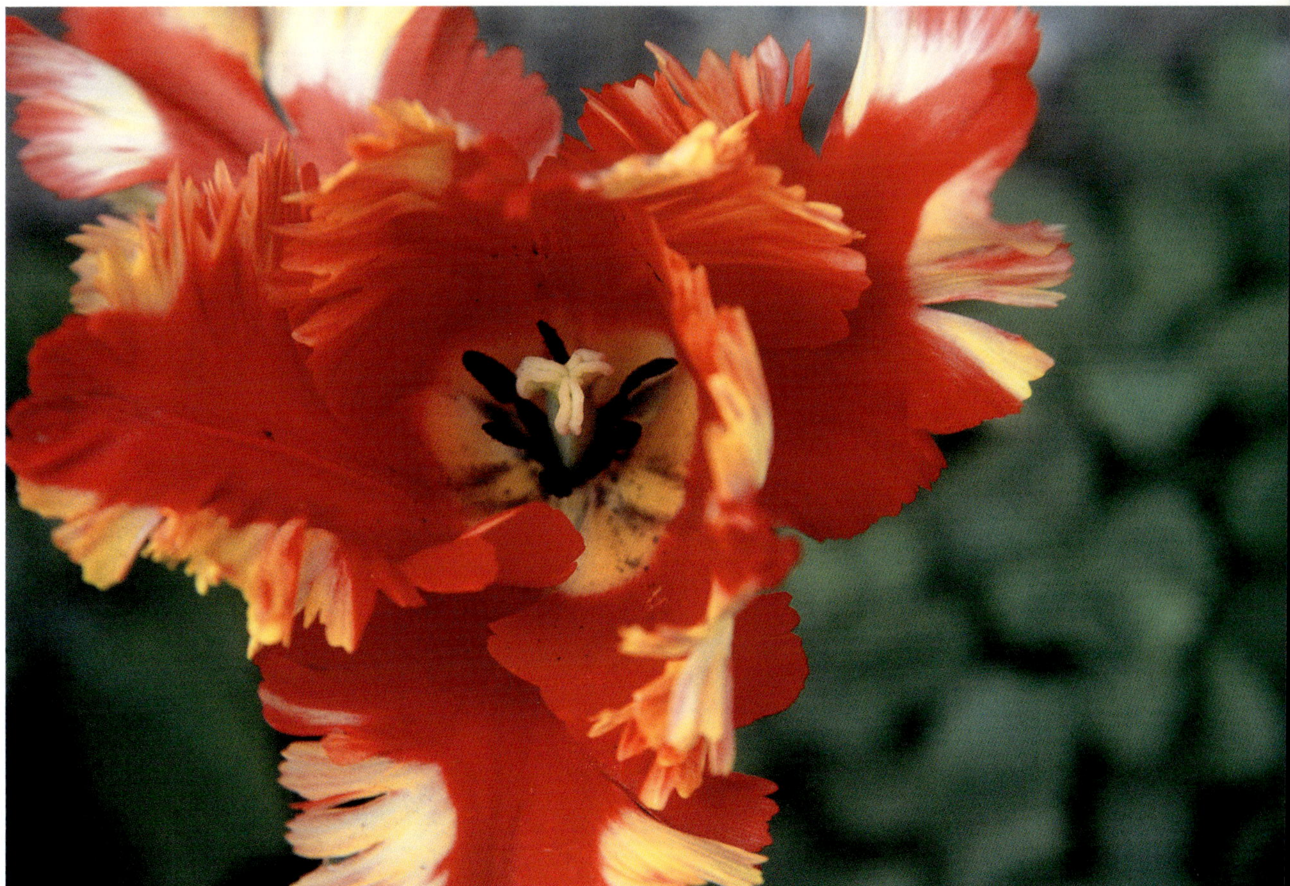

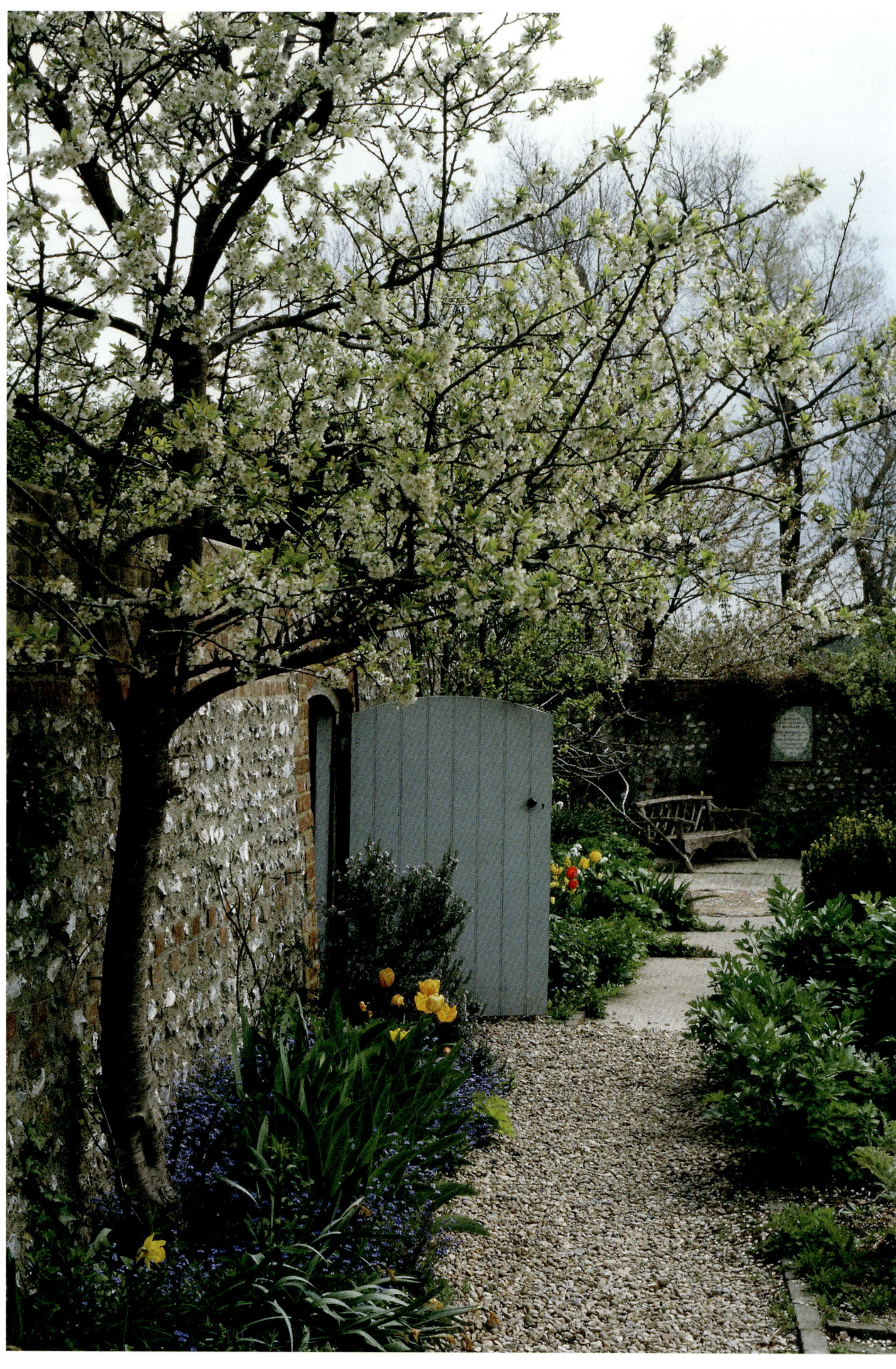

Plum blossom

Cast after a Venus by Giovanni da Bologna

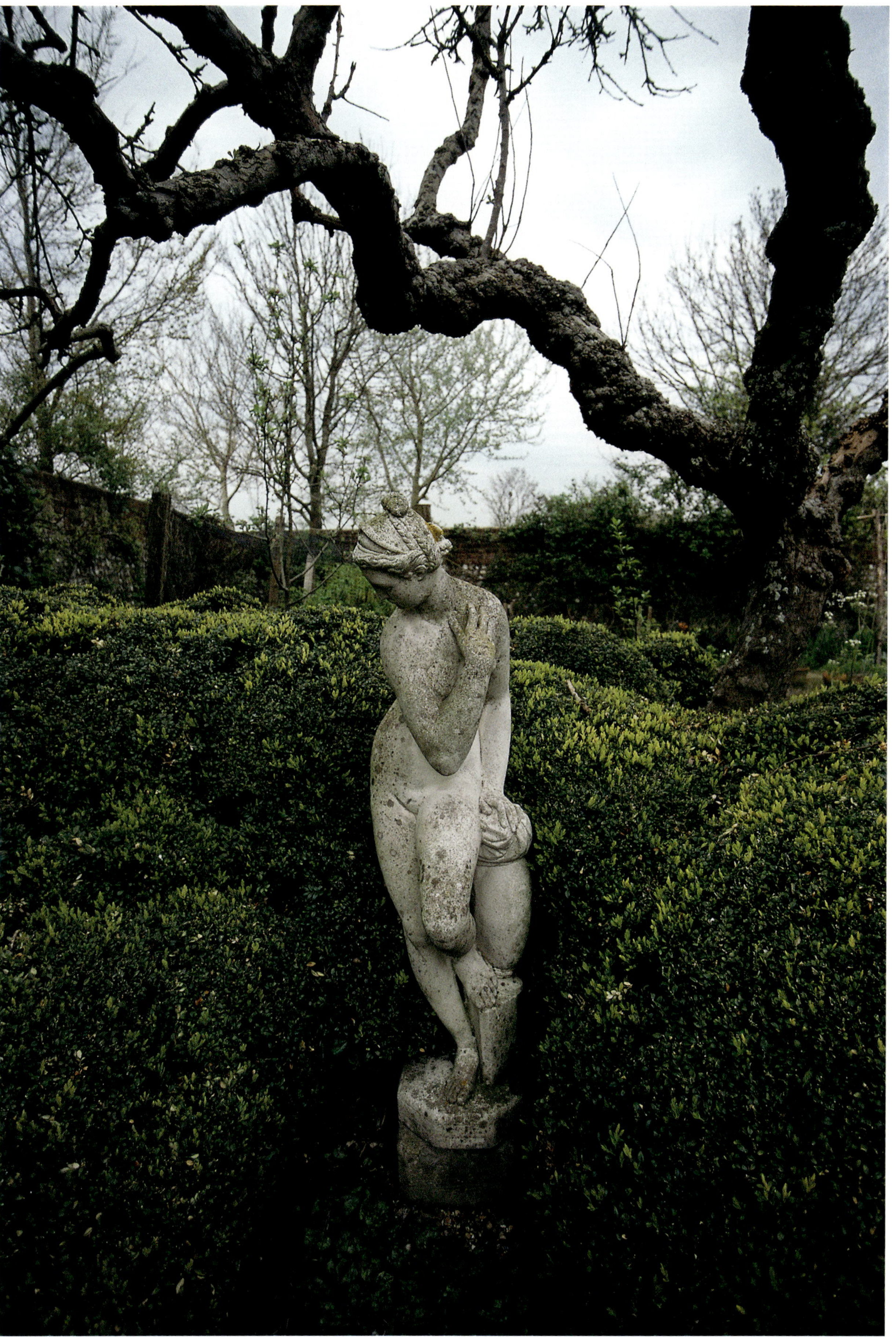

Torso by John Skeaping with shells, wallflowers and 'Queen of Night' tulips

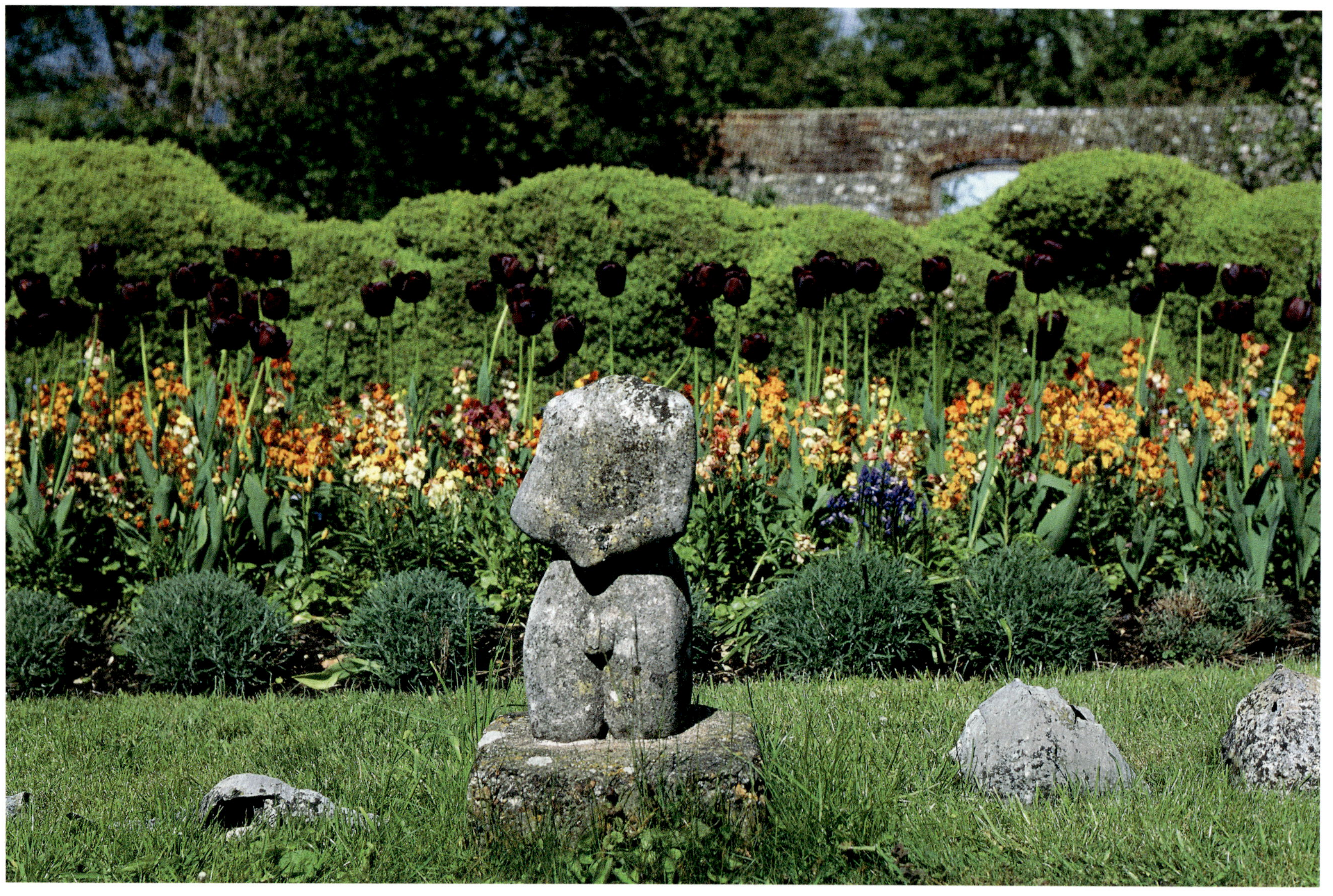

Asparagus fern

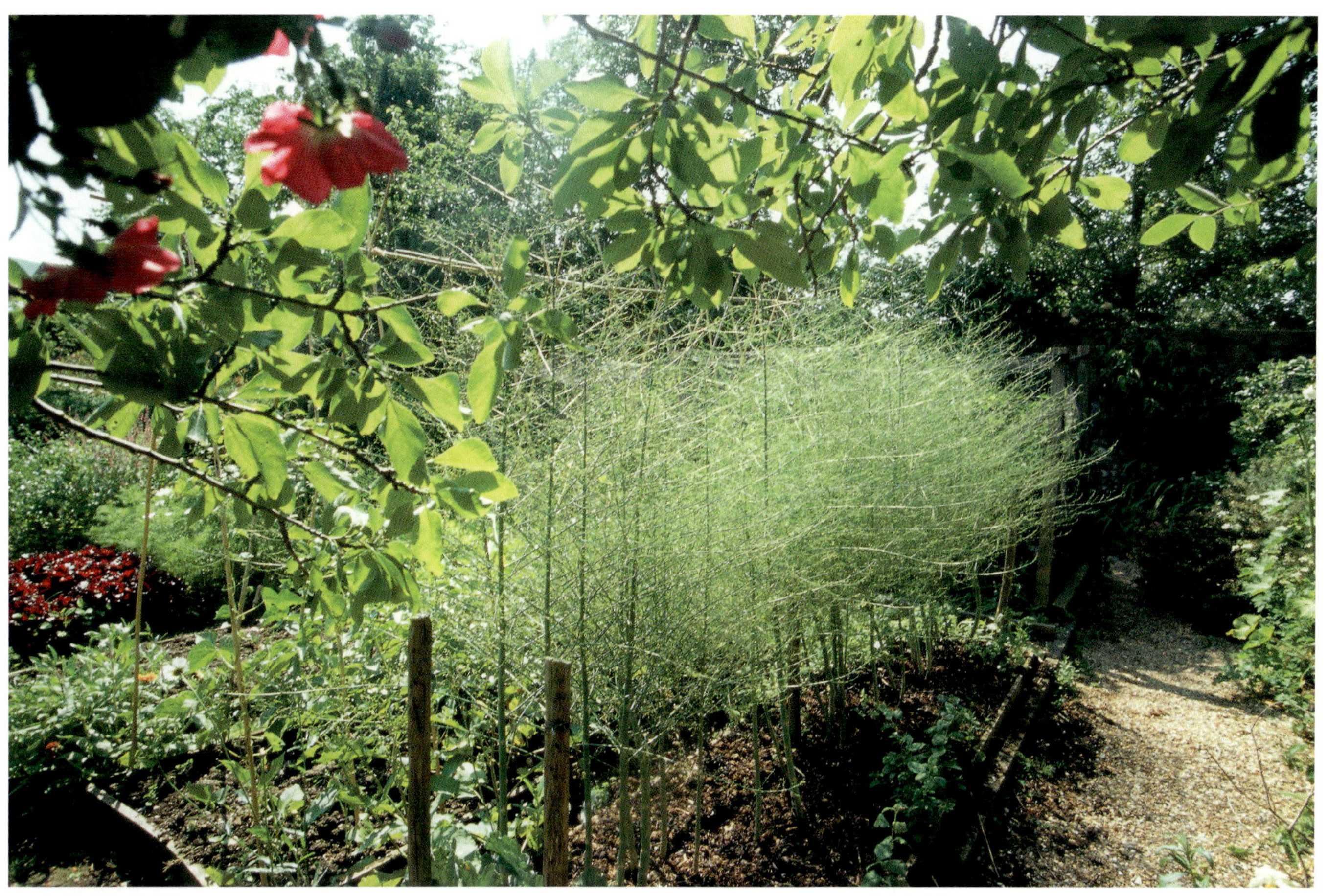

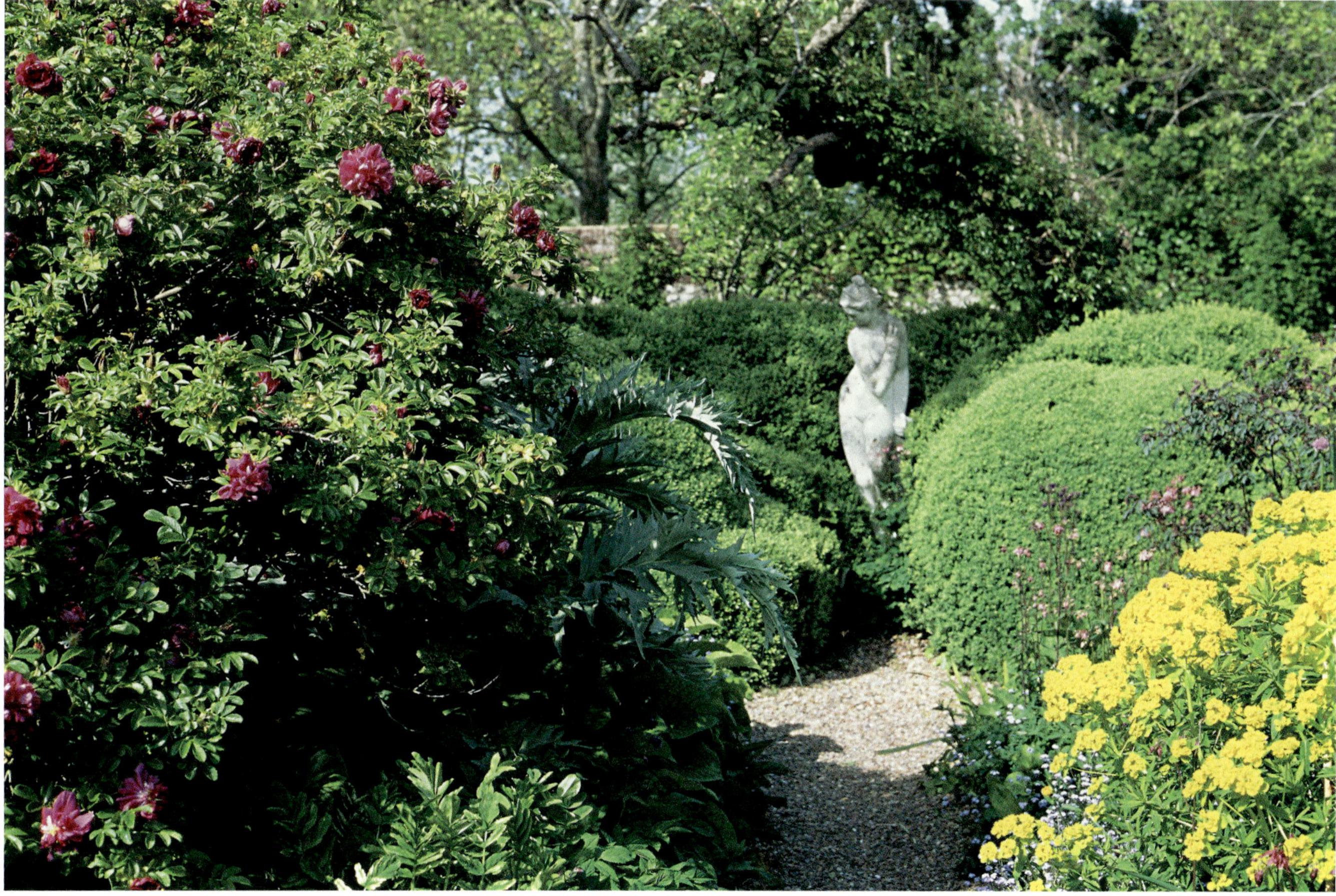

Cast after a Venus by Giovanni da Bologna with 'Roseraie de l'Haÿ' roses

Phaeum geranium (left) and white alium bud (right)

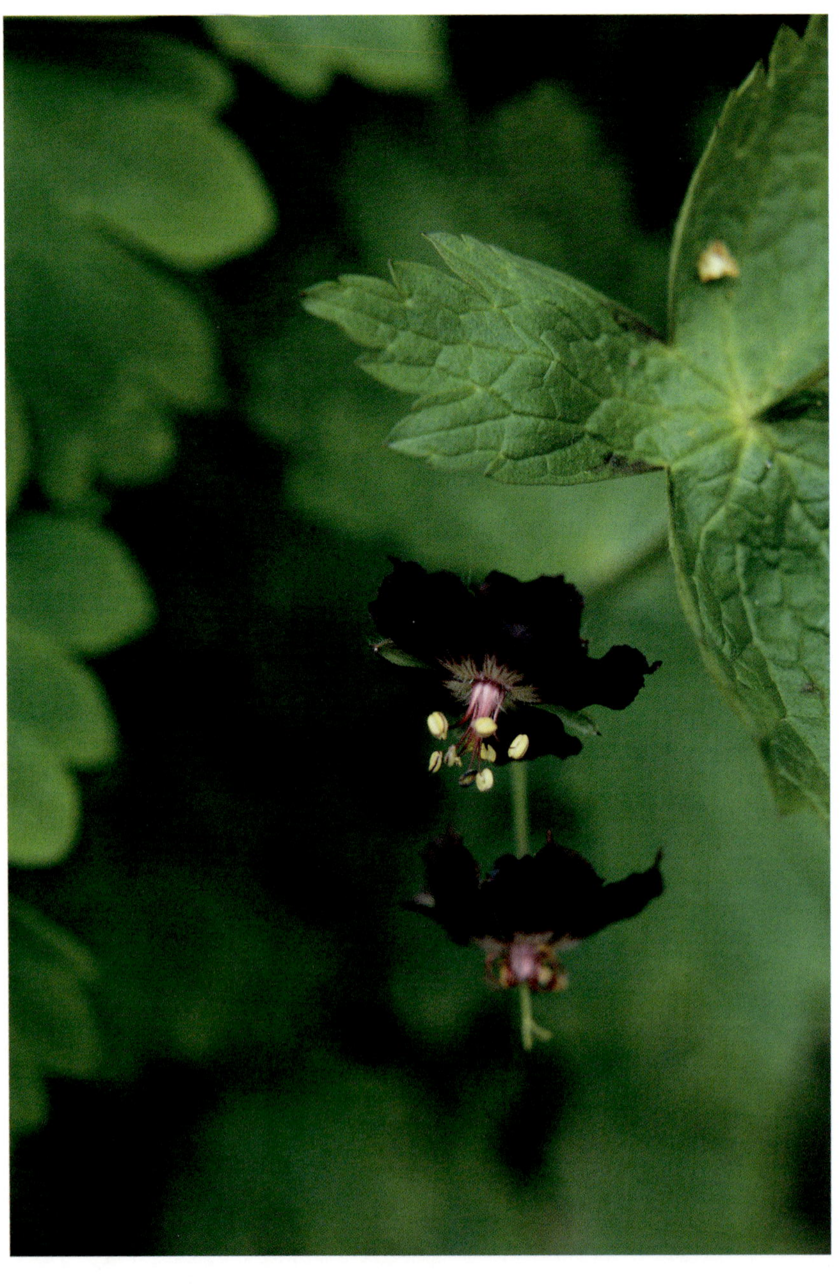

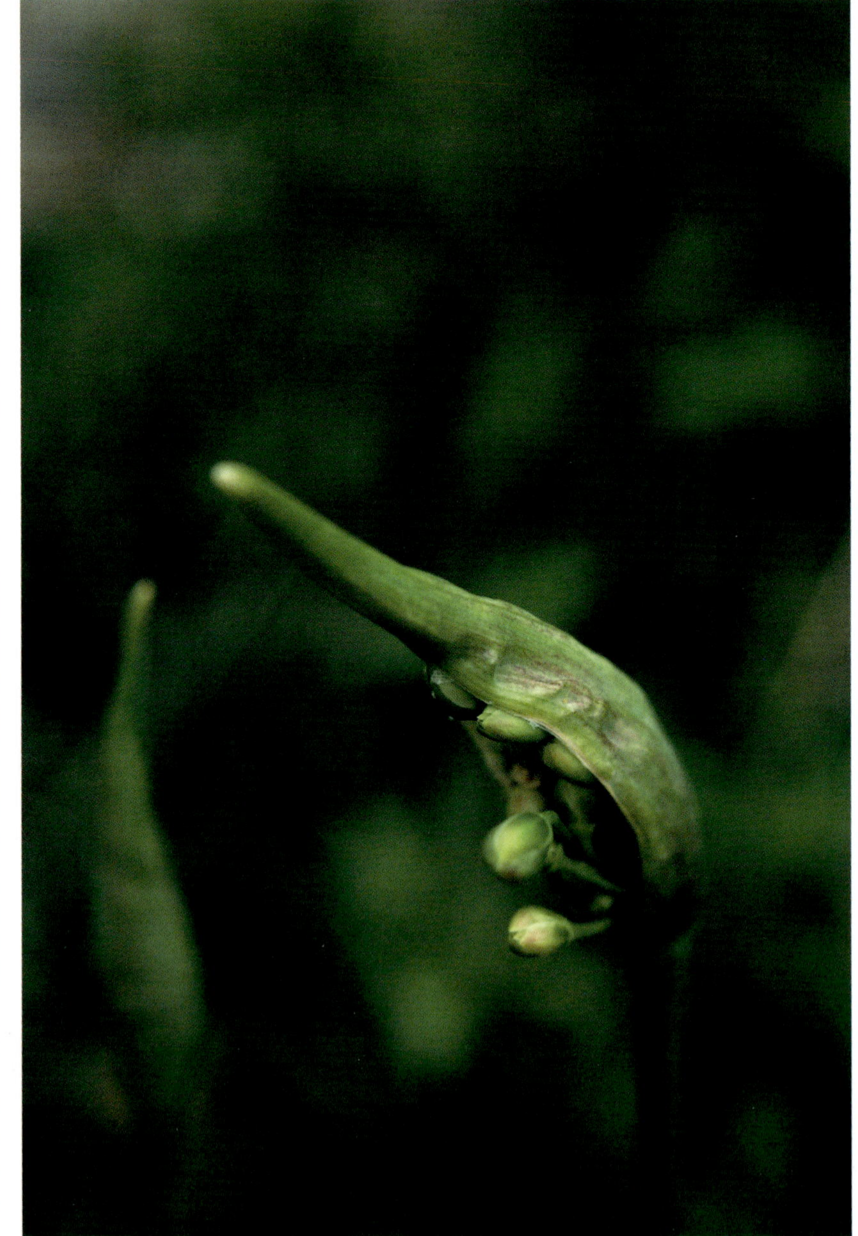

‘Queen of Night’ tulip

FOLLOWING PAGES CLOCKWISE FROM LEFT
Curled cat; ceramic crockery circle; small pond with fountain head by Quentin Bell; young lettuce; frog on a water lily leaf

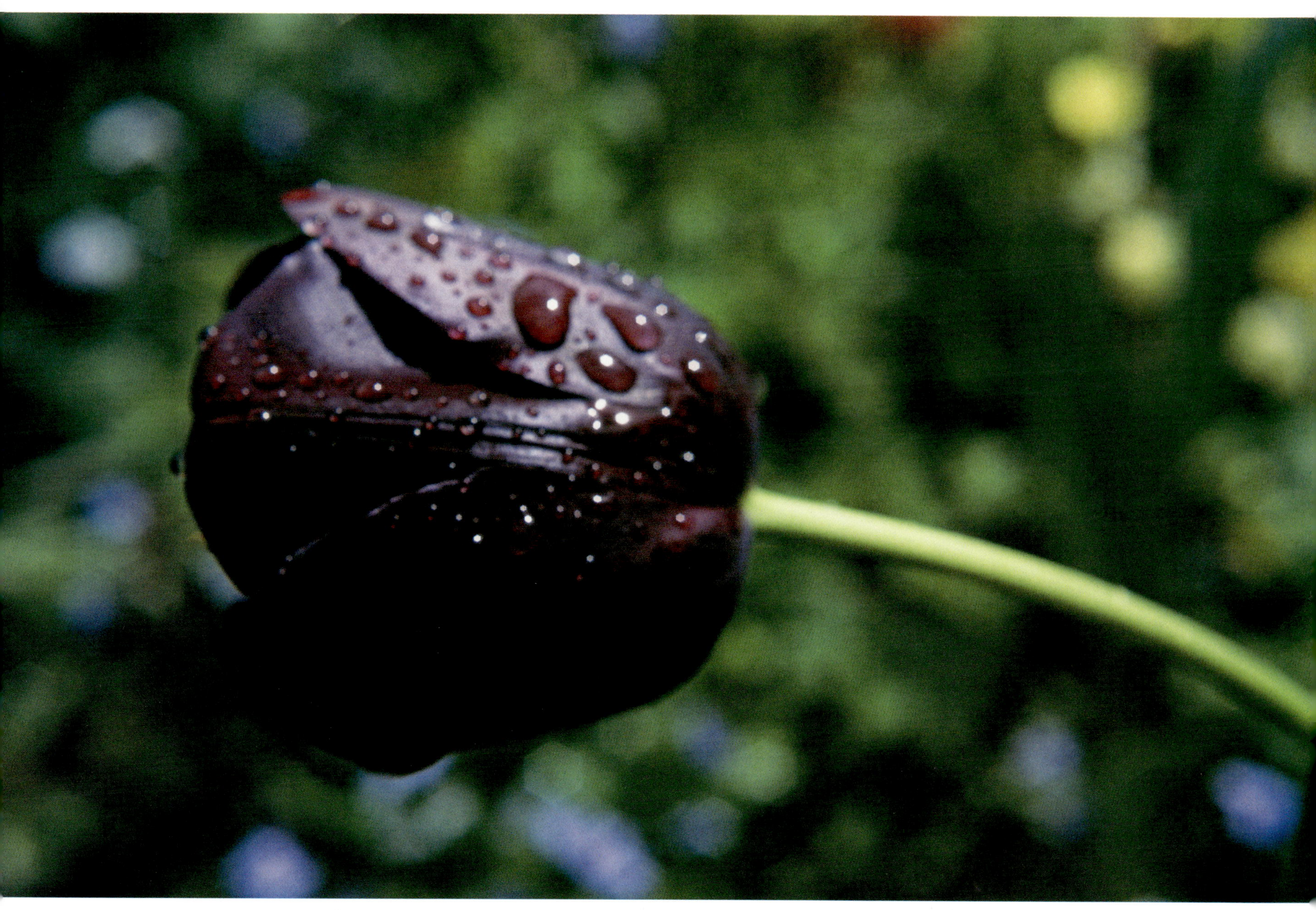

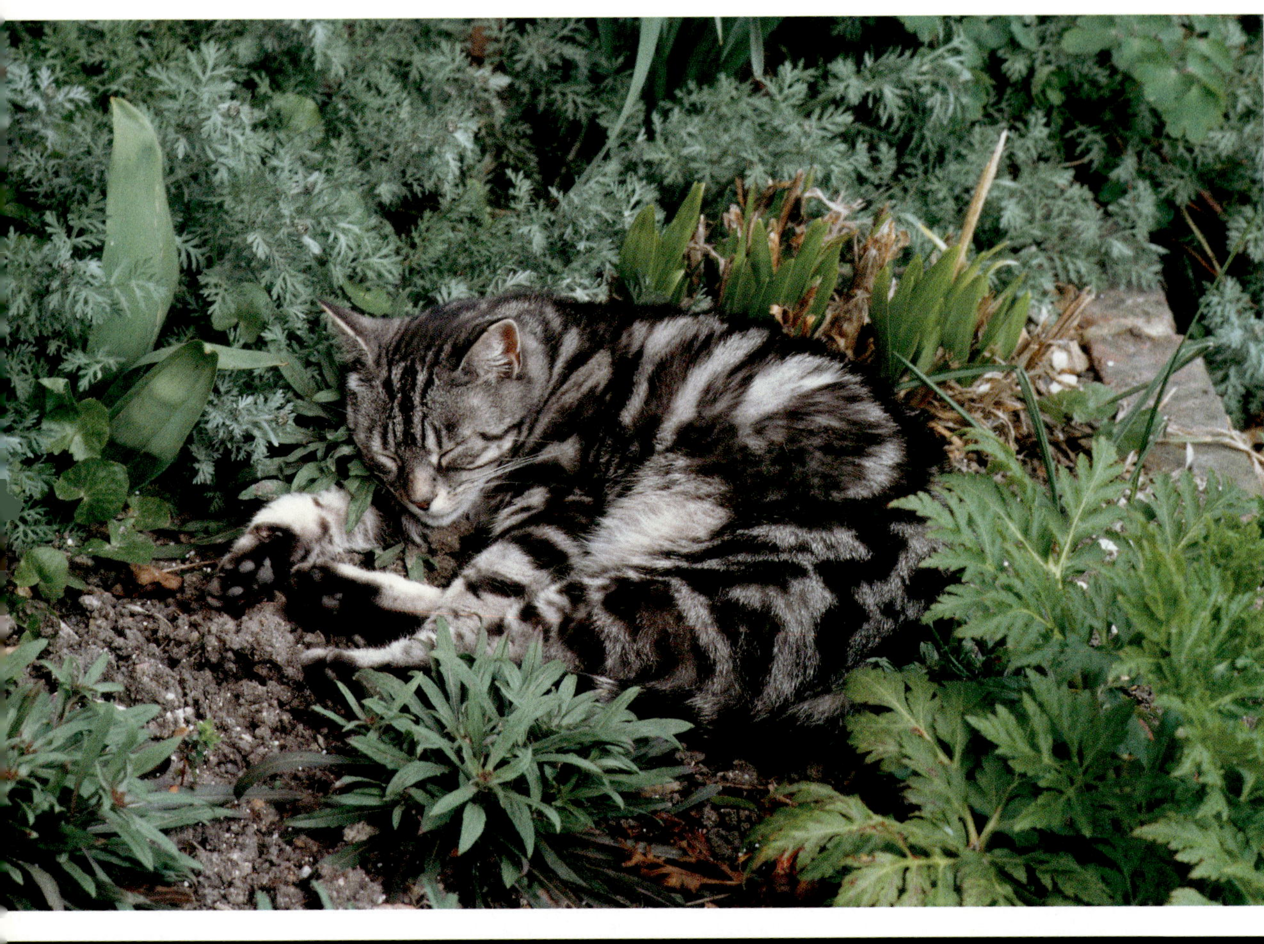

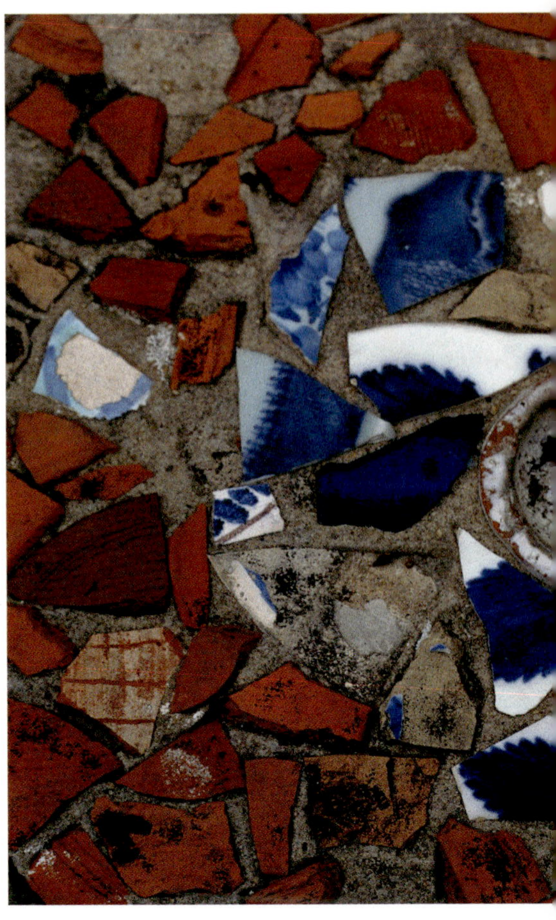

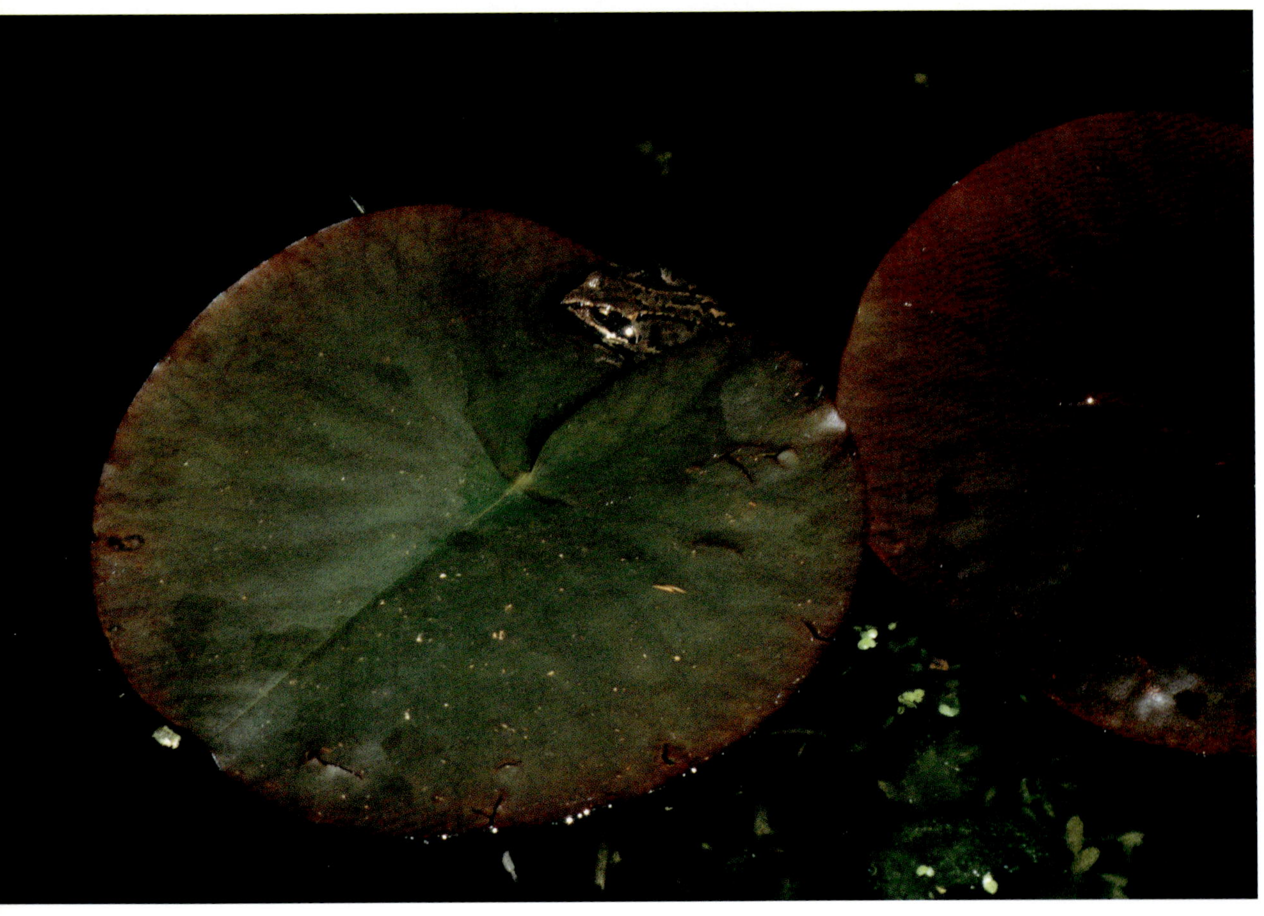

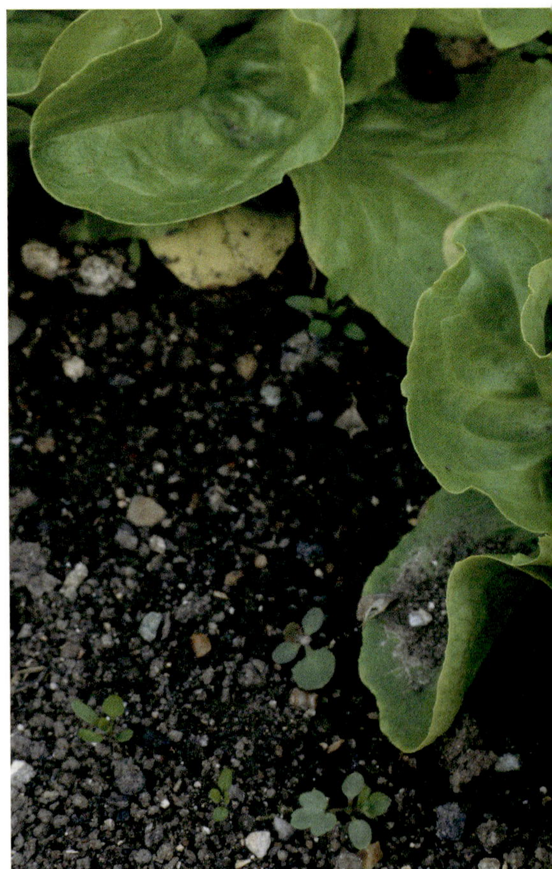

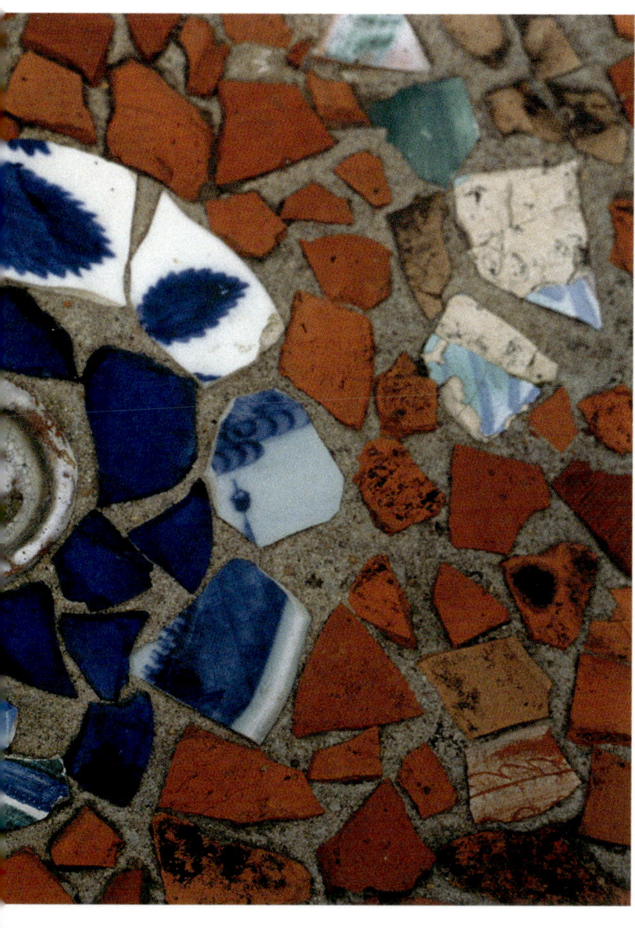

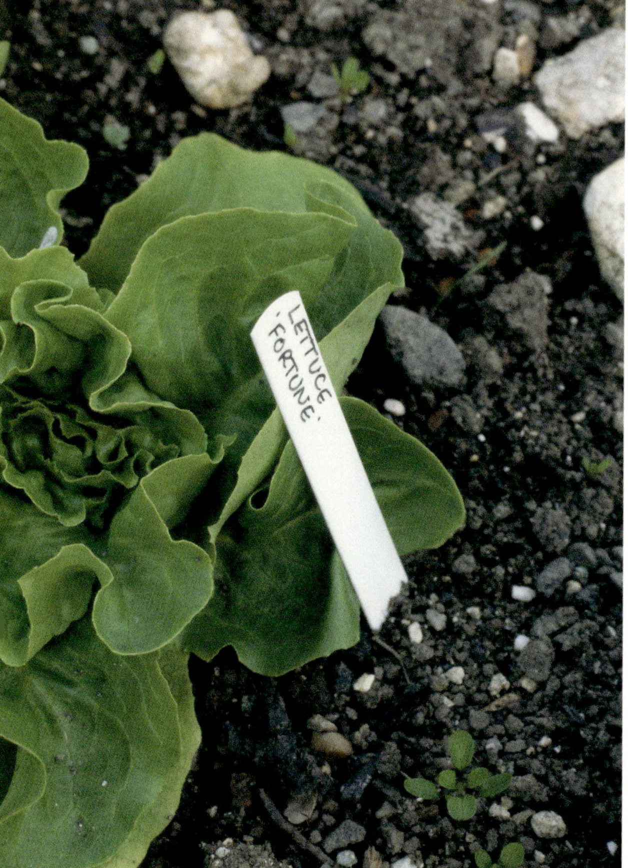
LETTUCE
'FORTUNE'

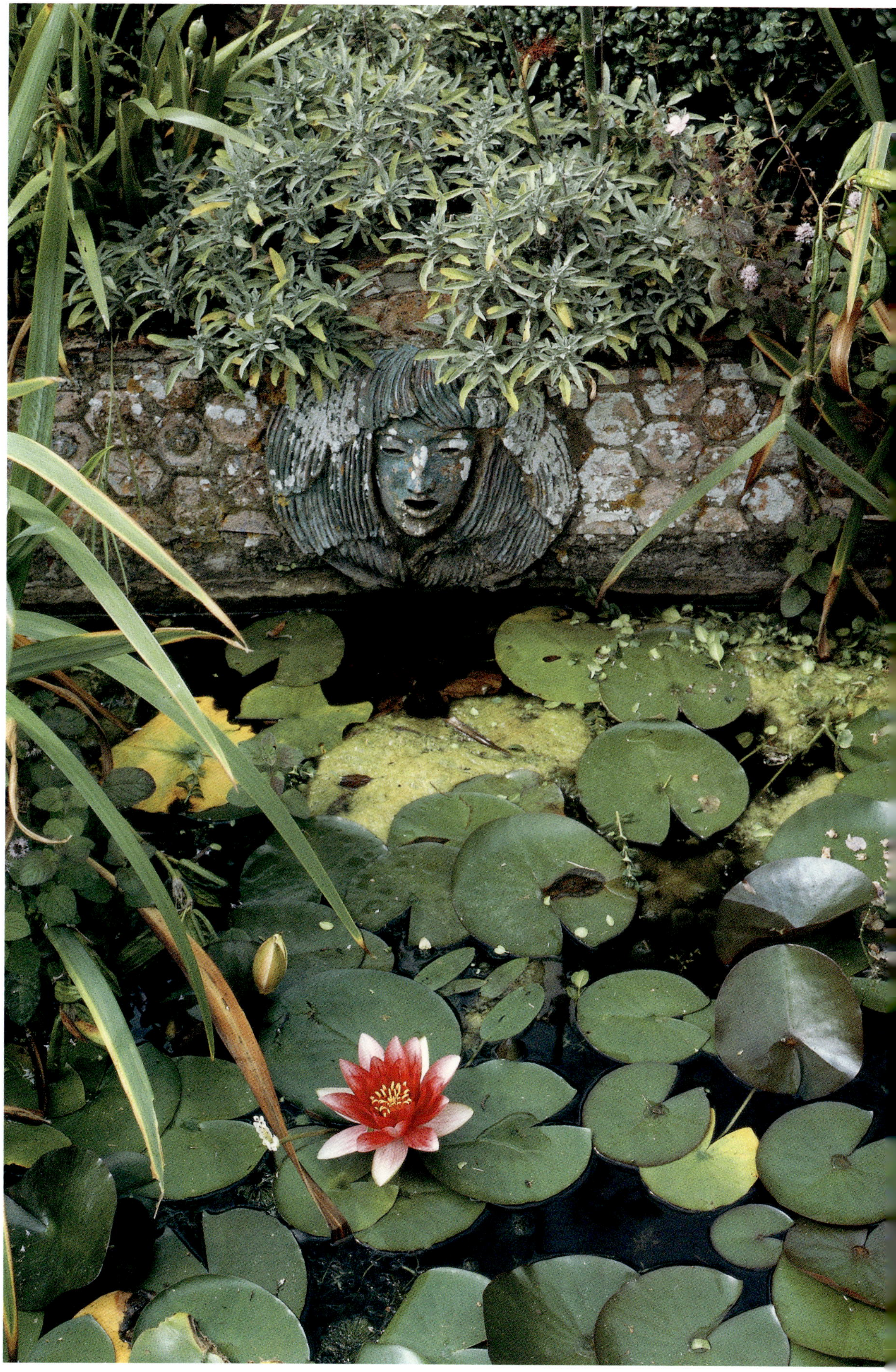

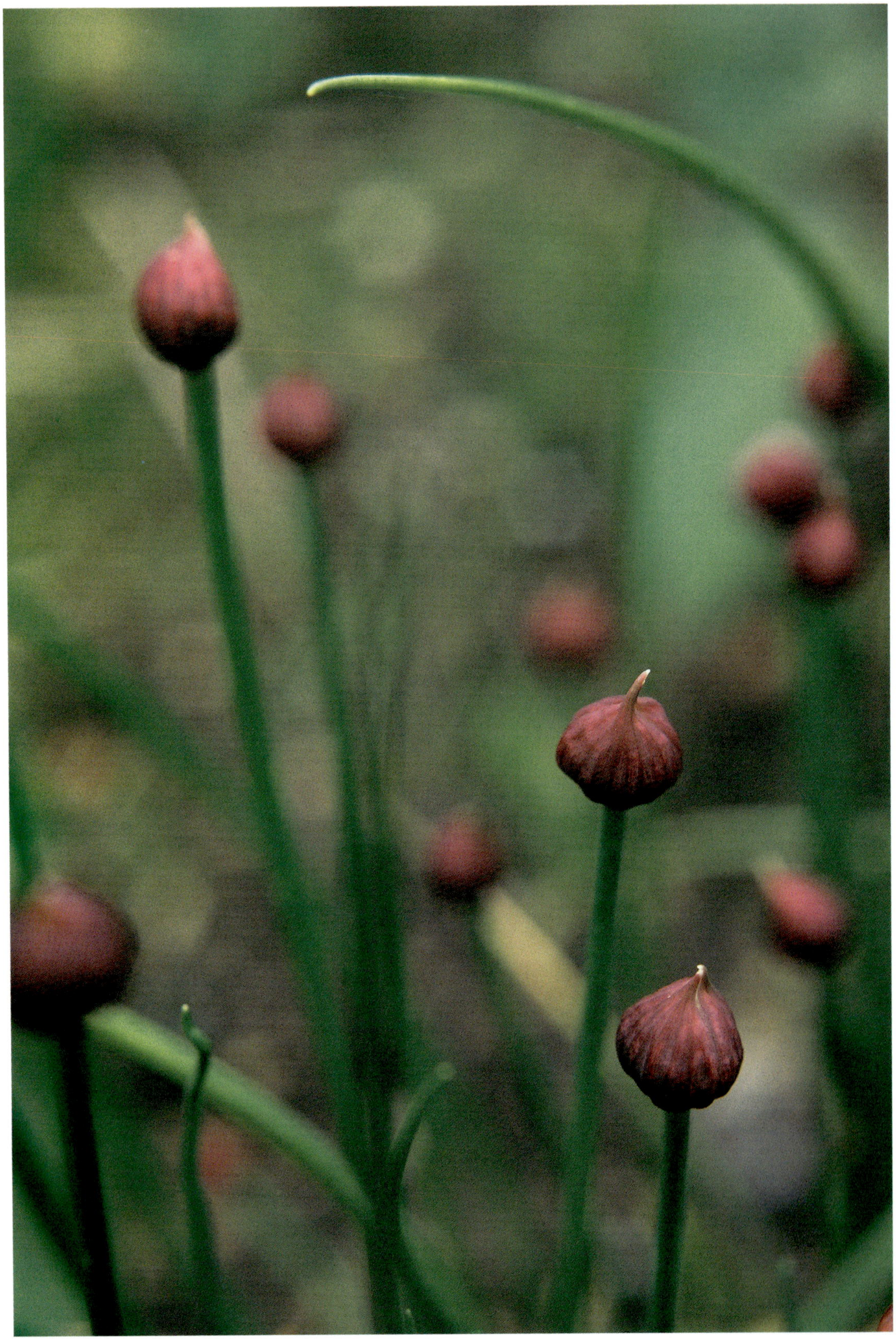

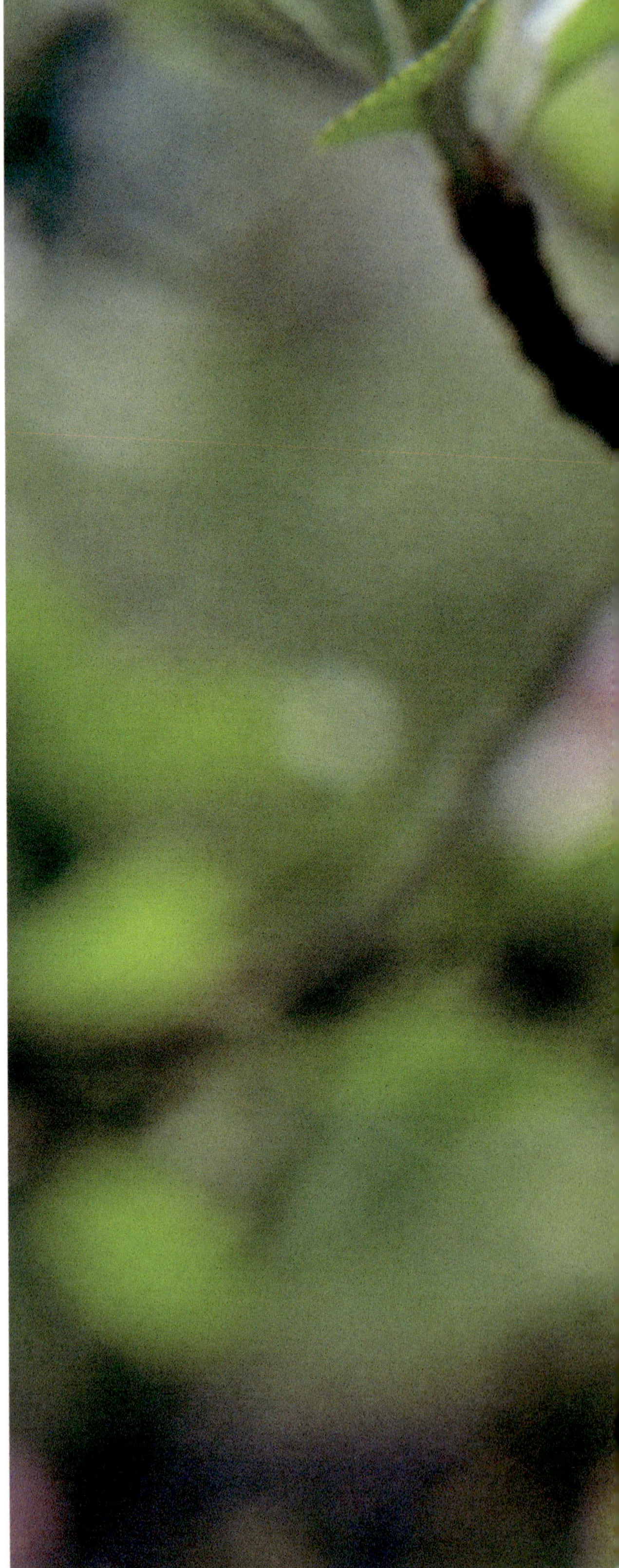

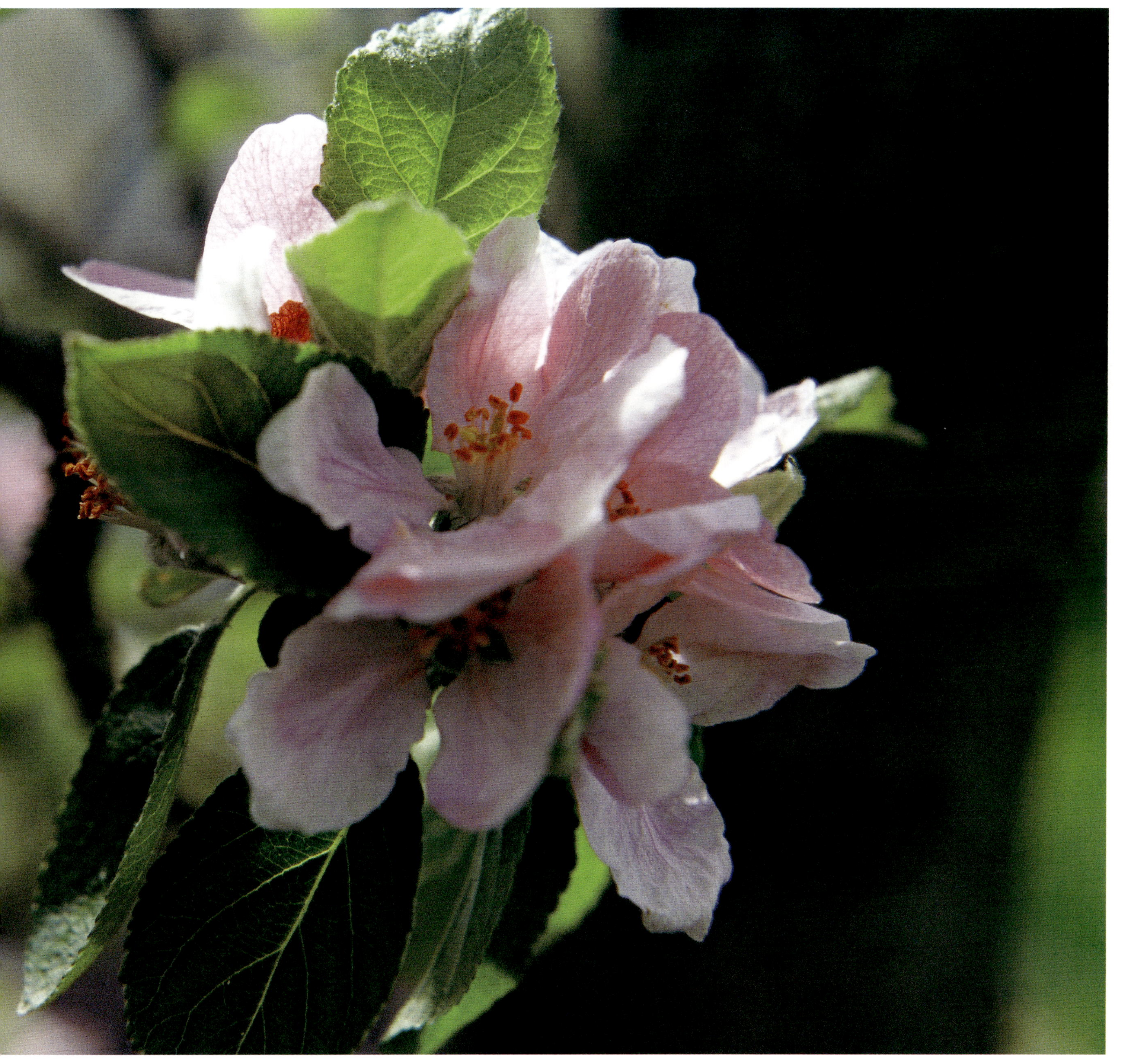

CLOCKWISE FROM TOP LEFT 'Roseraie de l'Haÿ' rose, tulip, bleeding heart

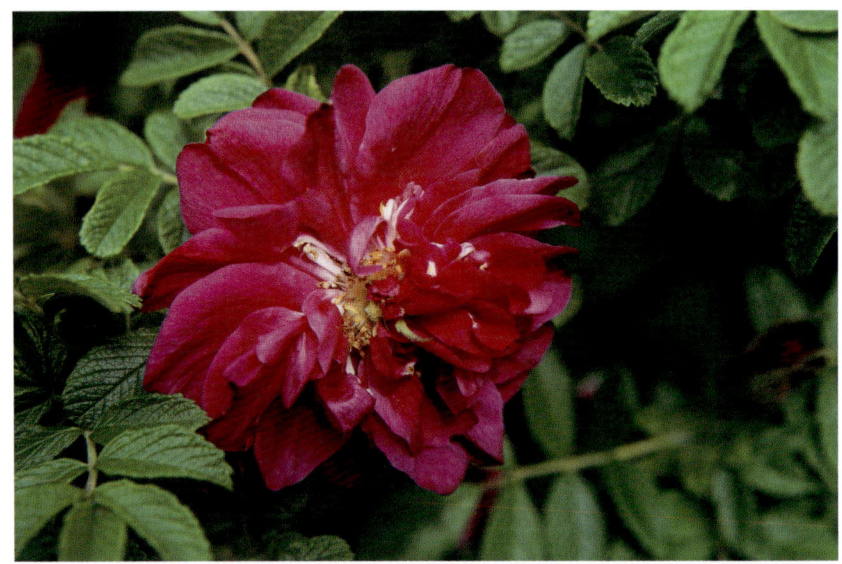

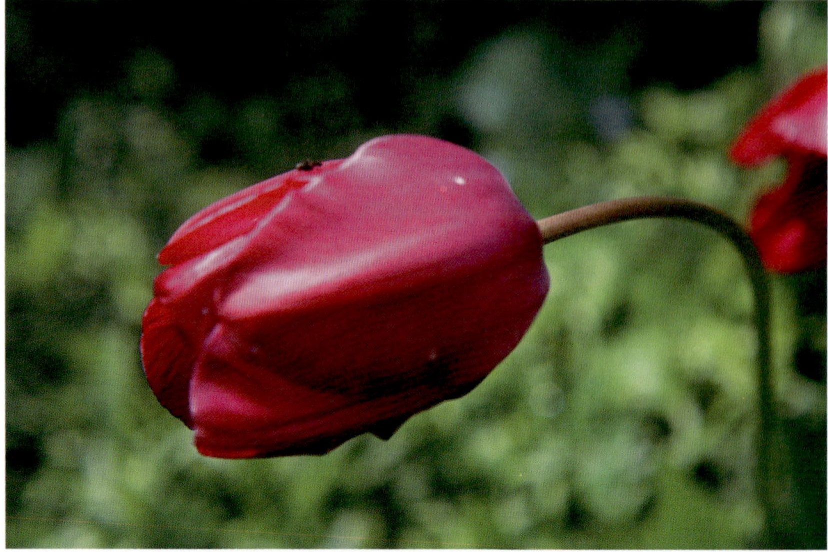

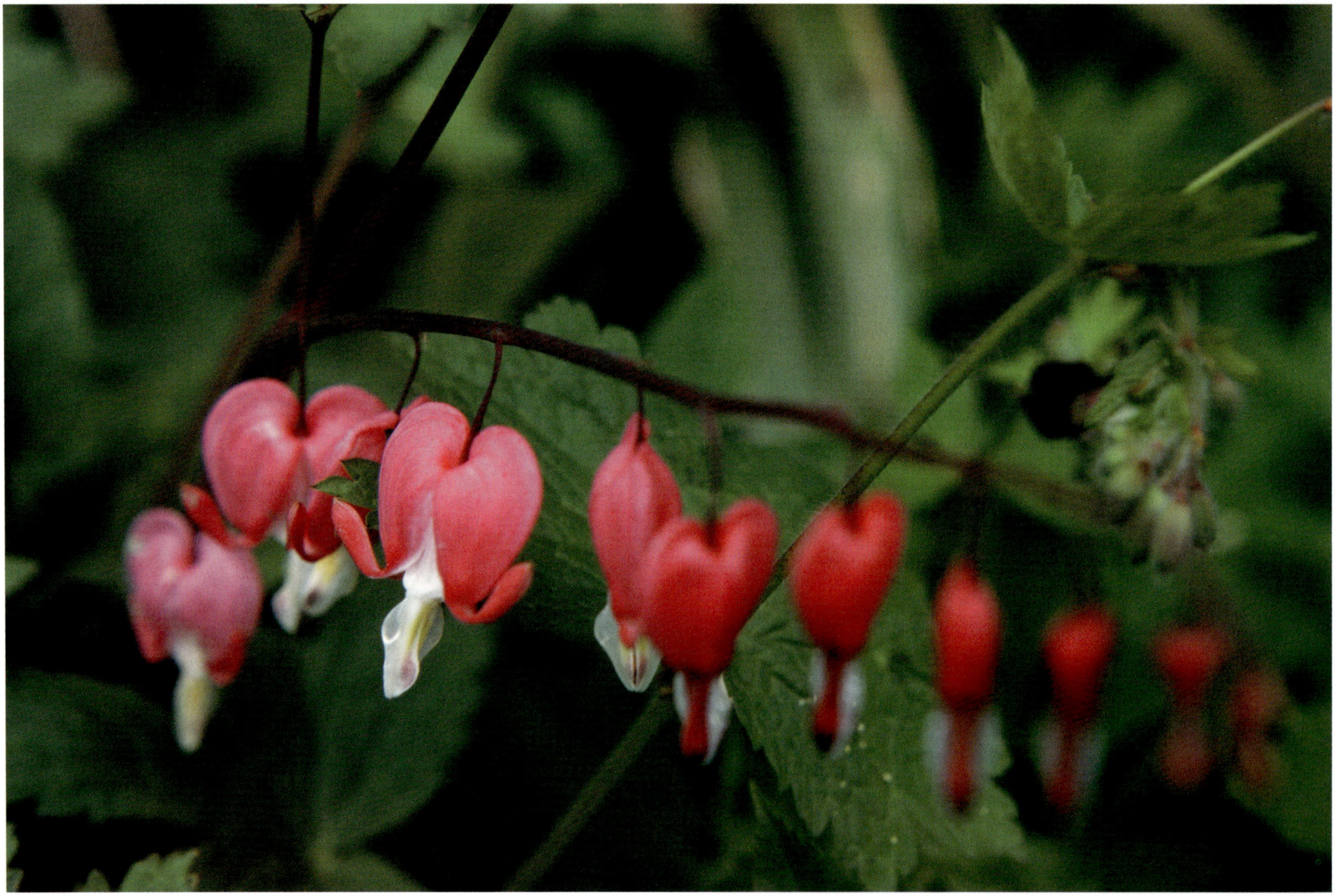

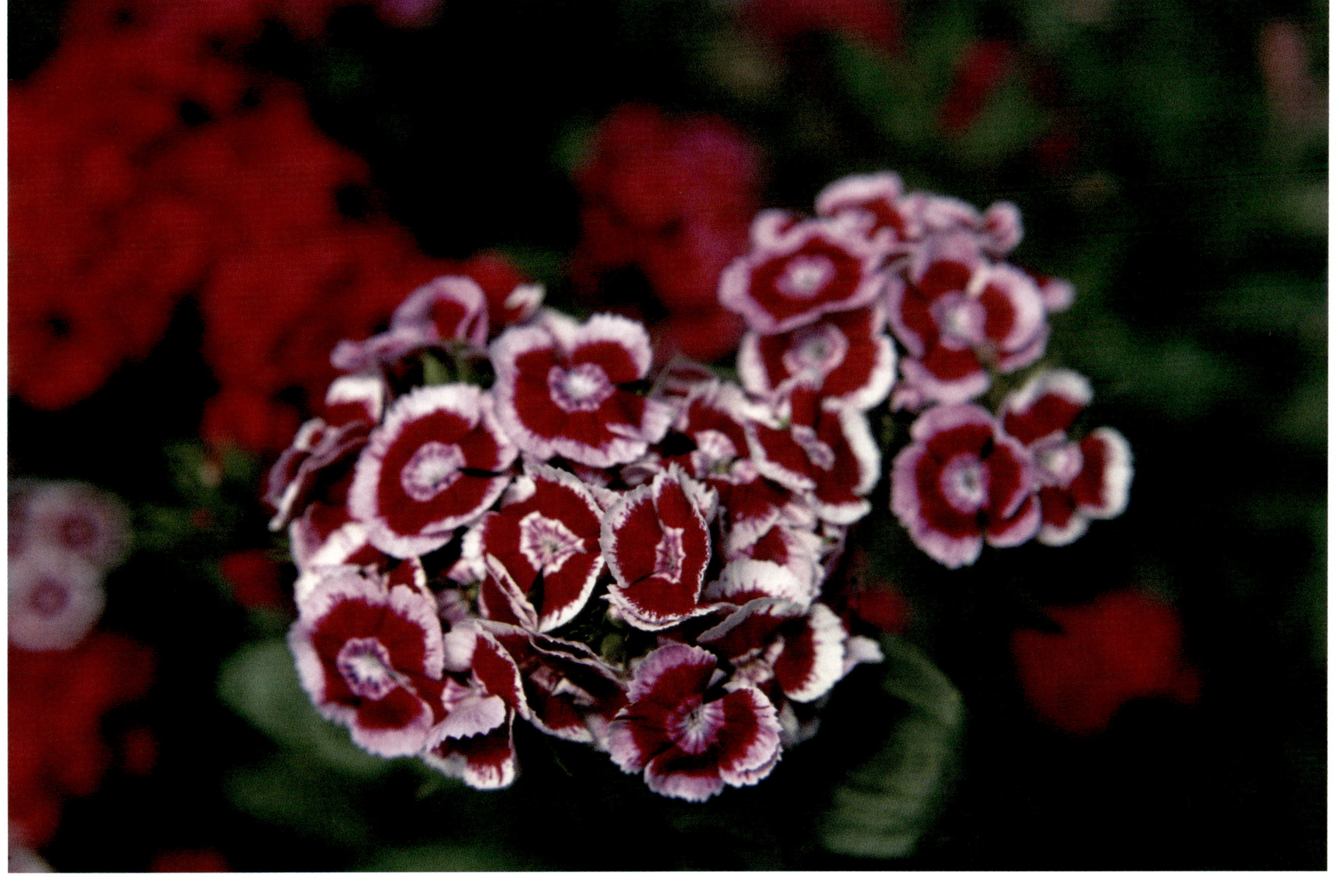

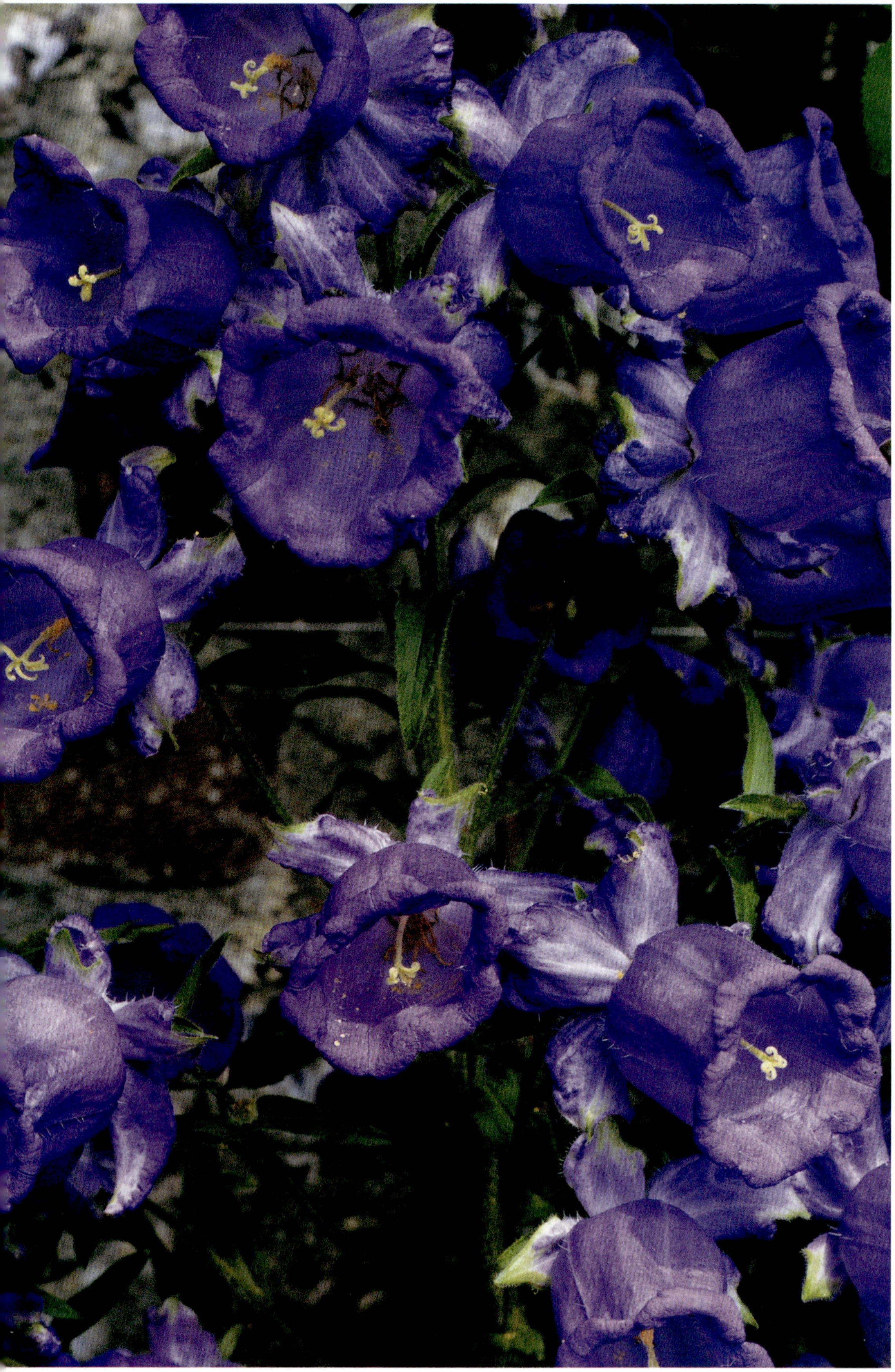

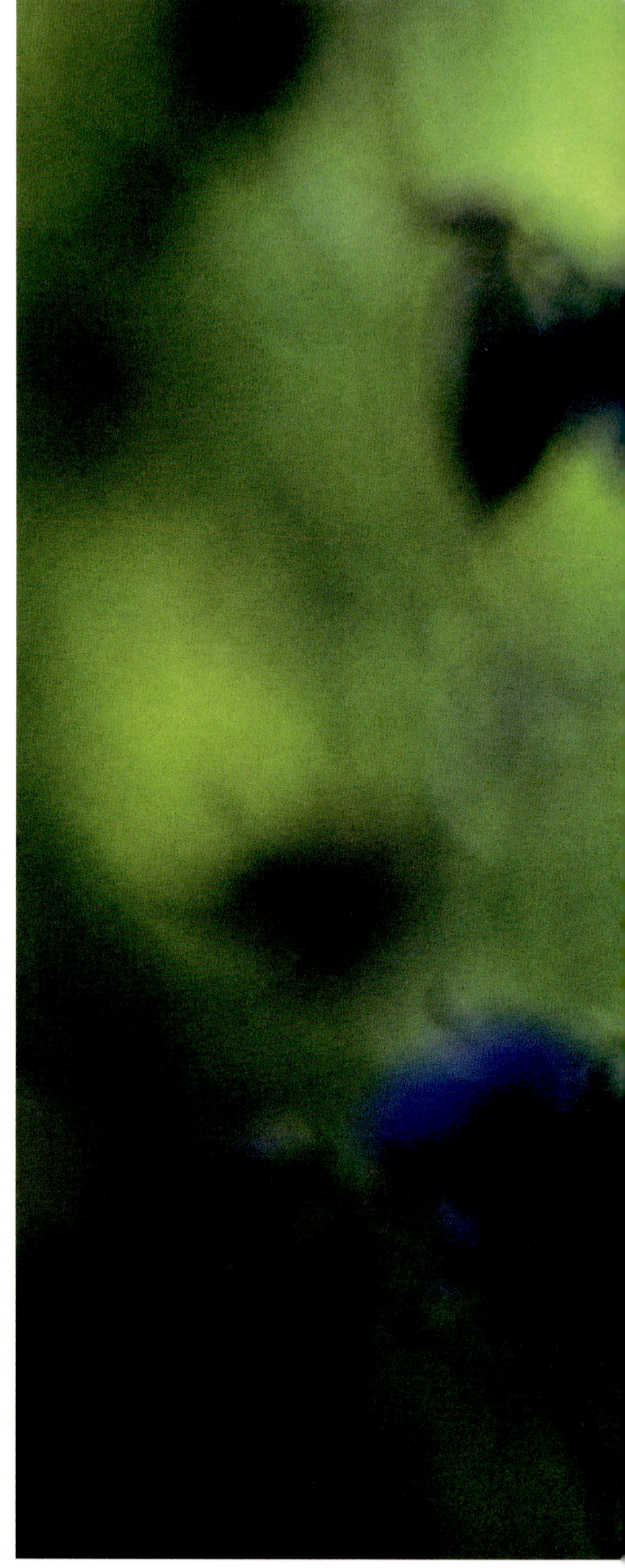

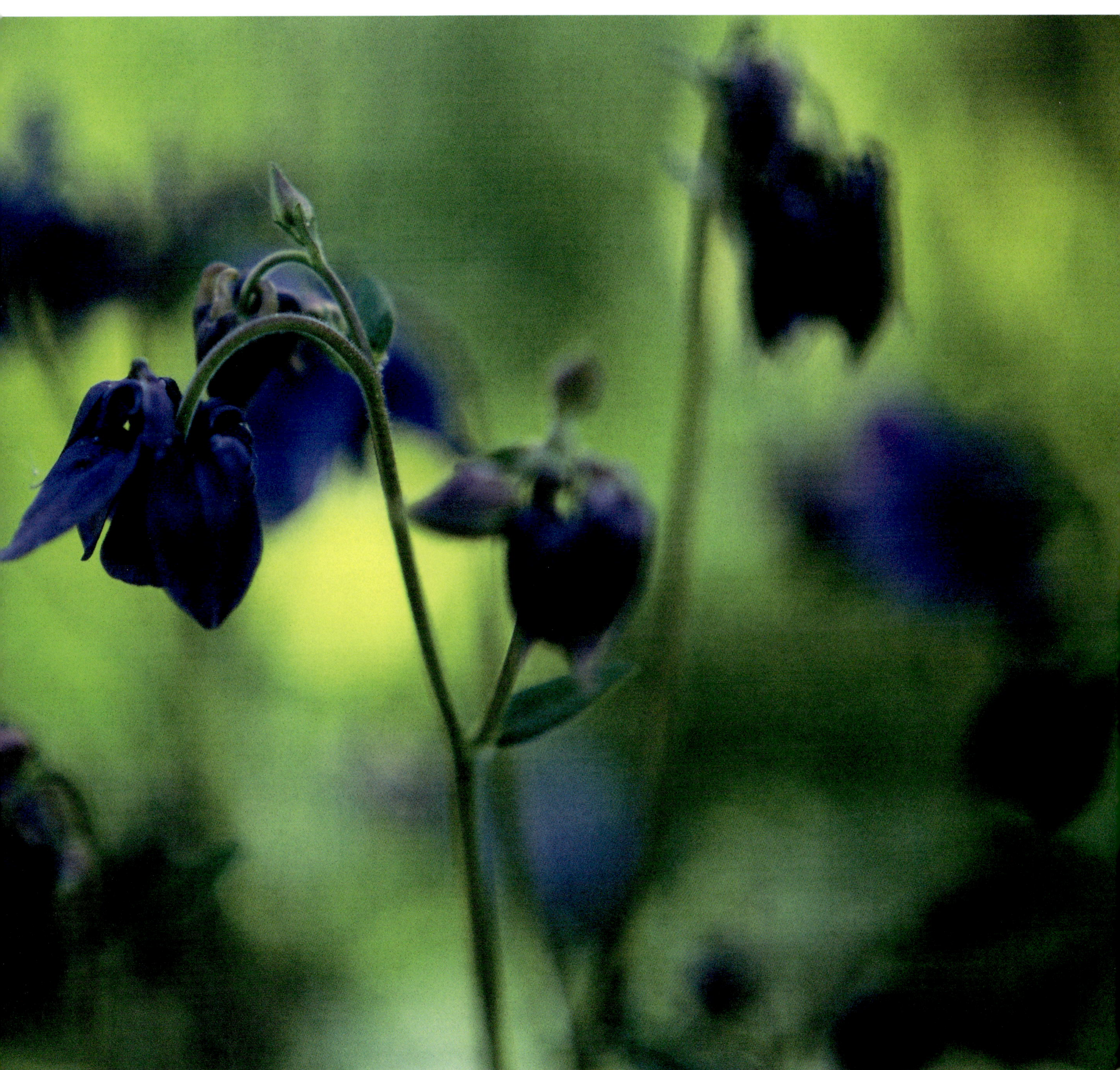

summer

Double poppies

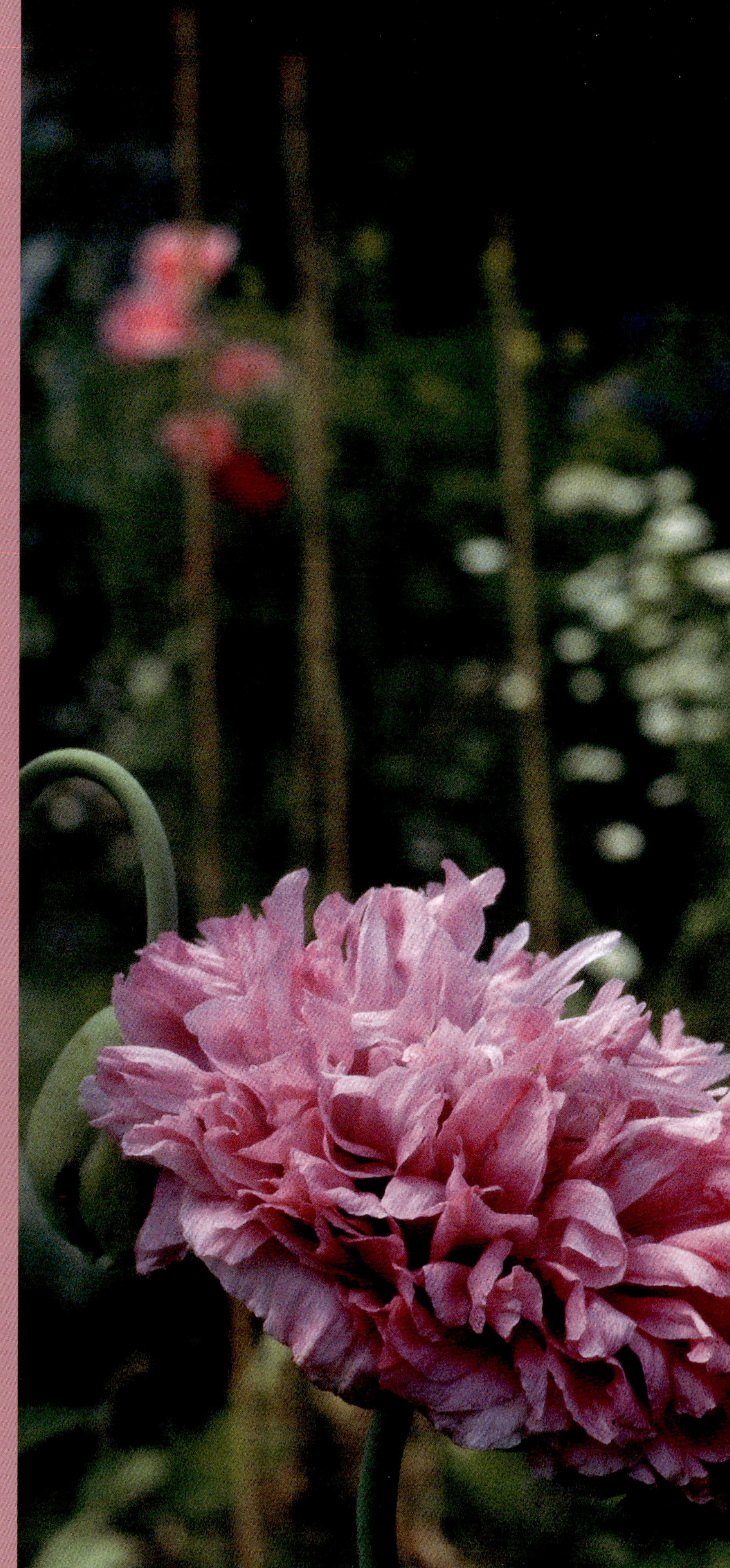

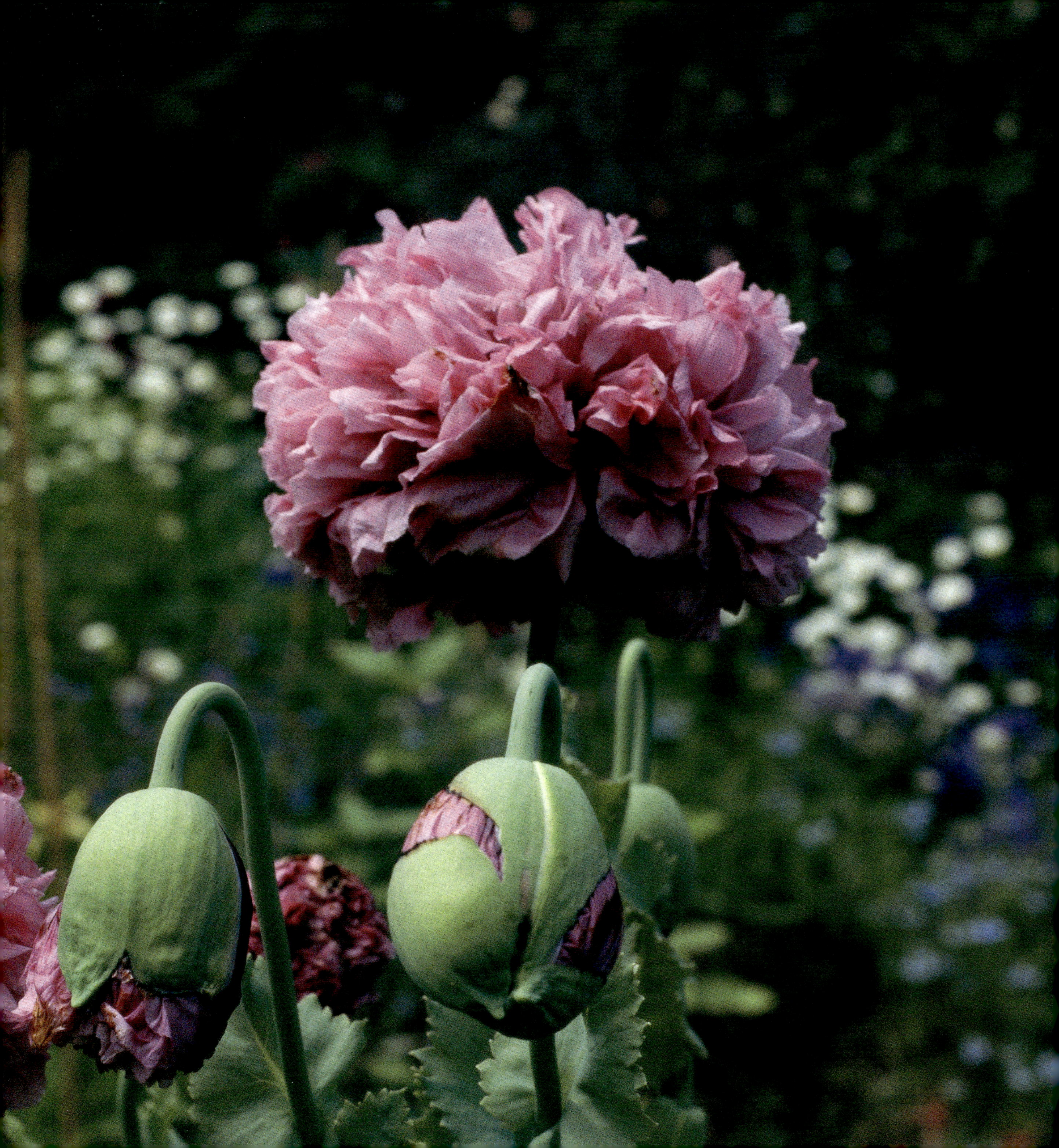

The house, open to visitors

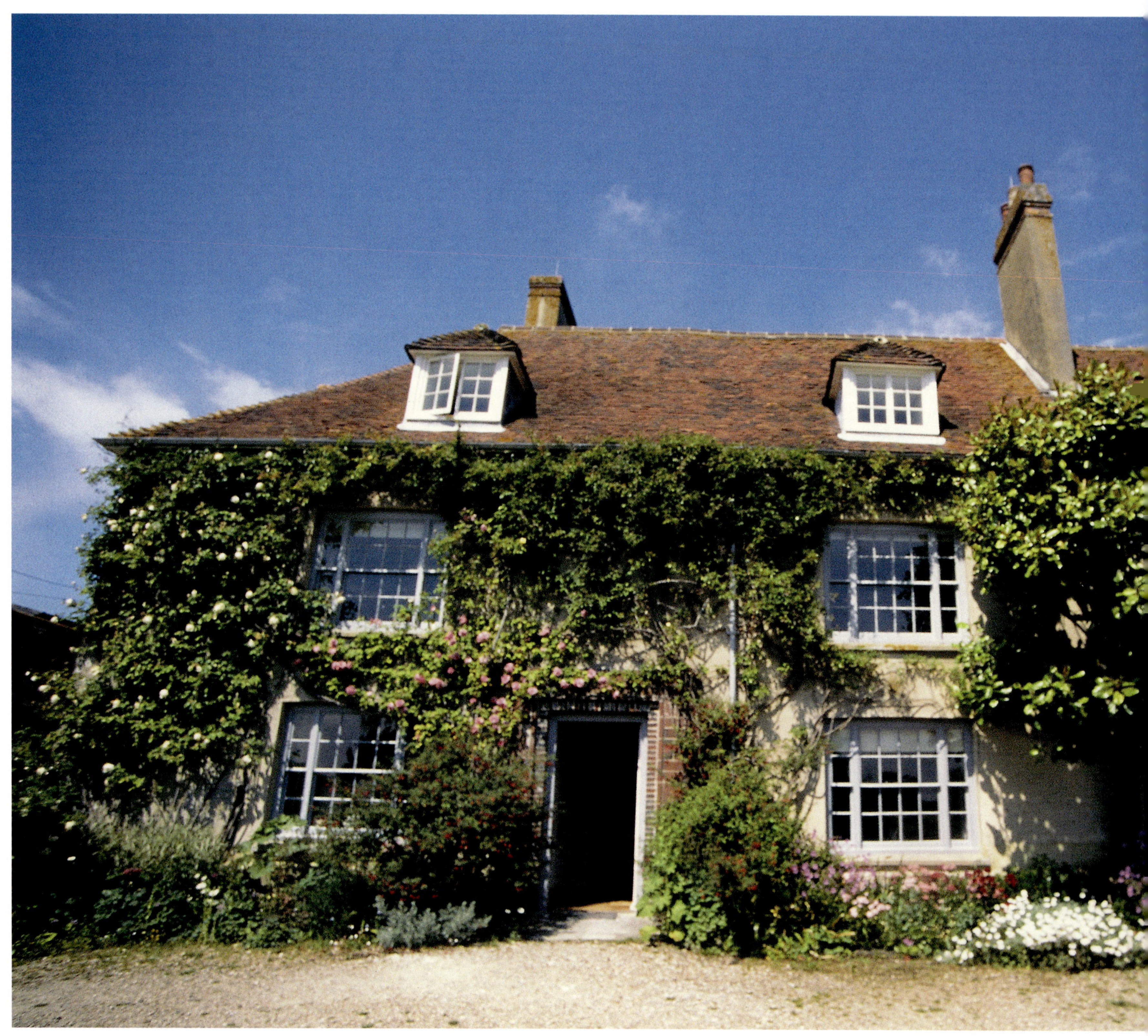

Clematis montana (above) and a climbing rose (below)

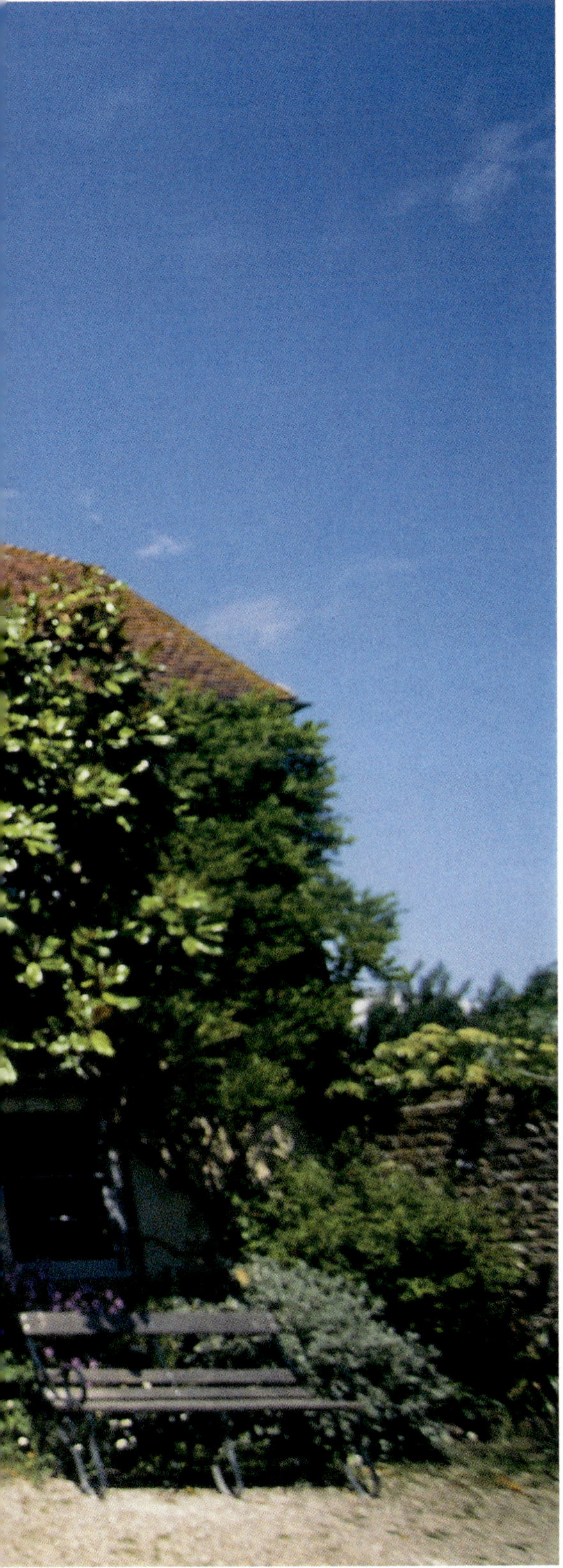

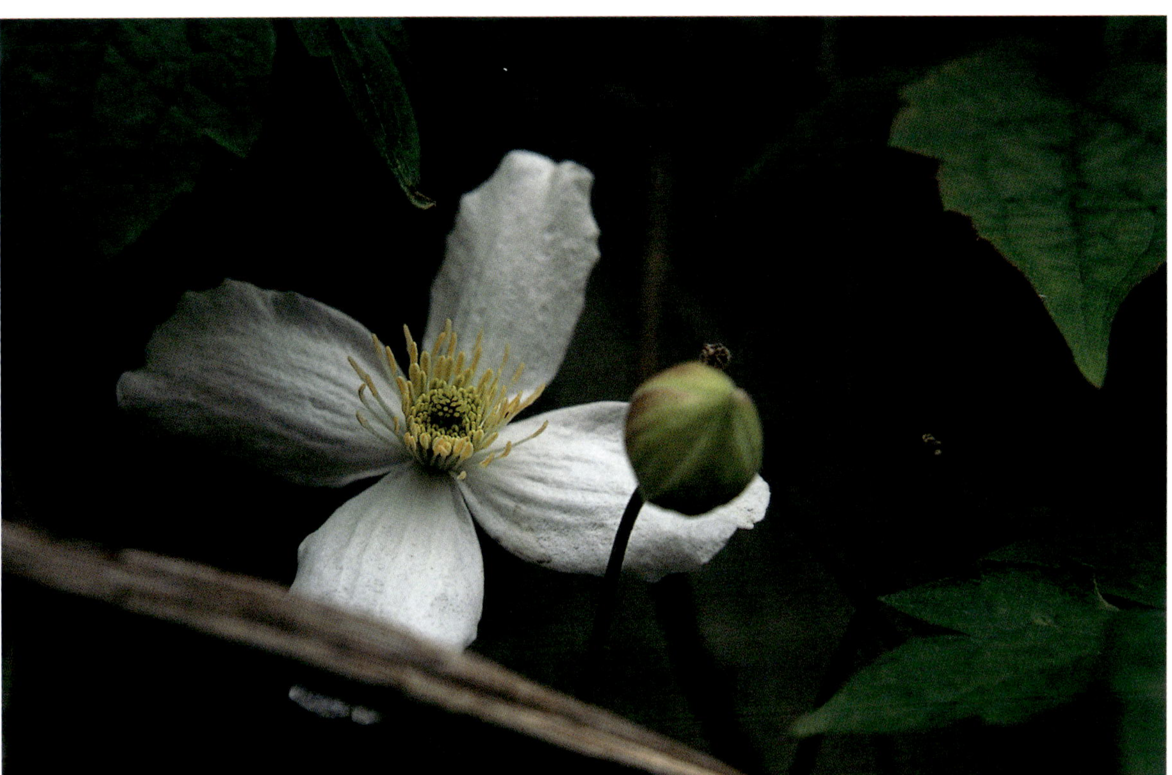

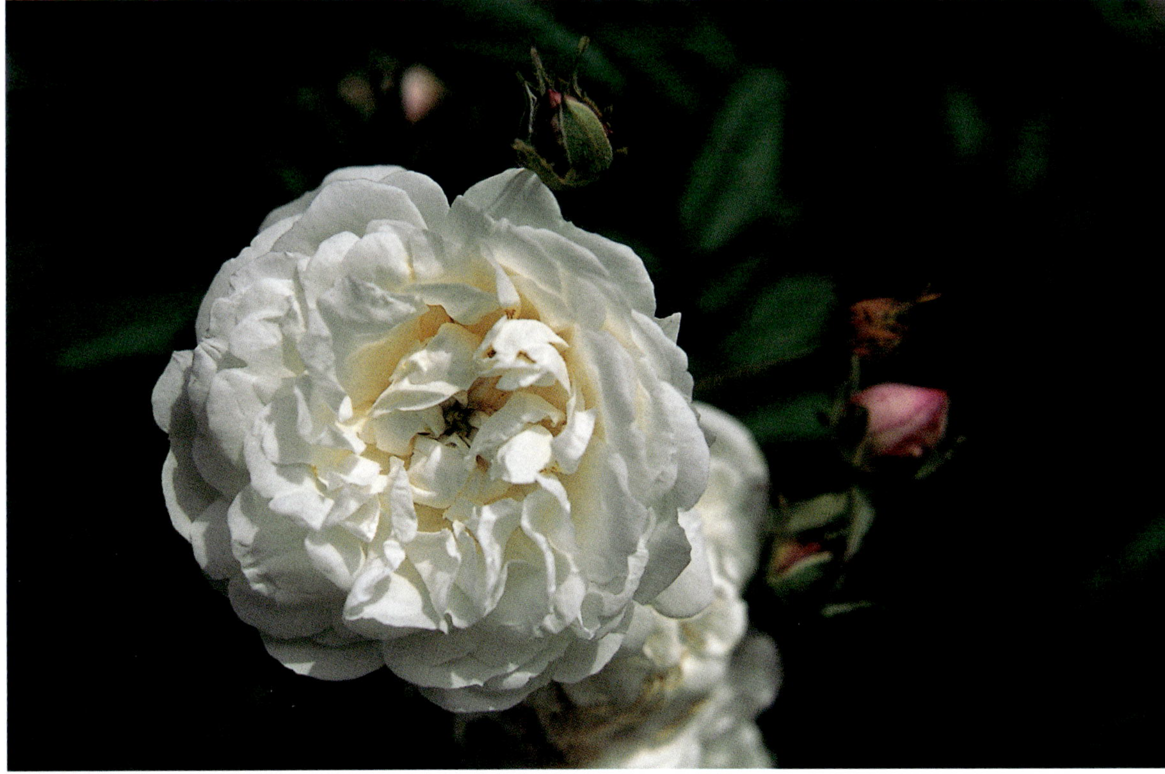

Flint and brick wall with roses

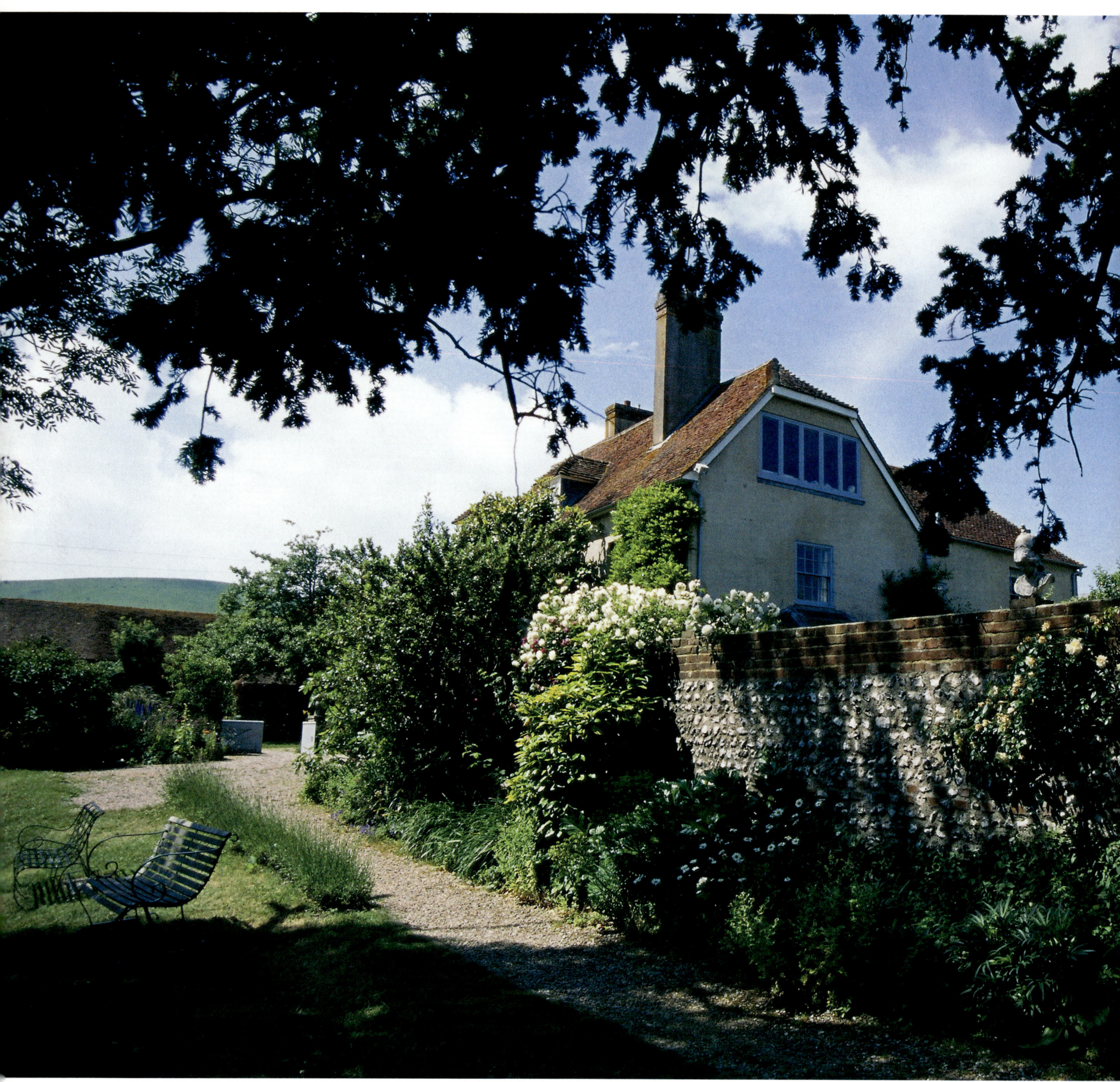

Cast head and 'Iceberg' rose

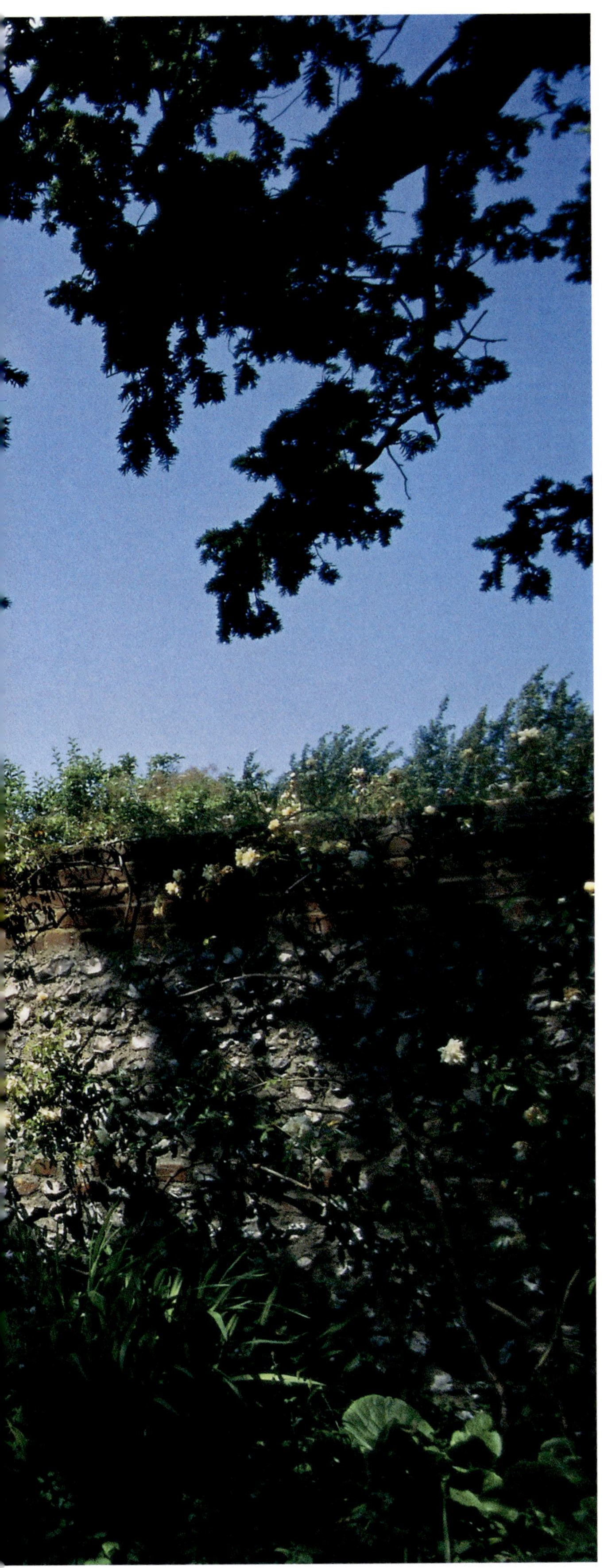

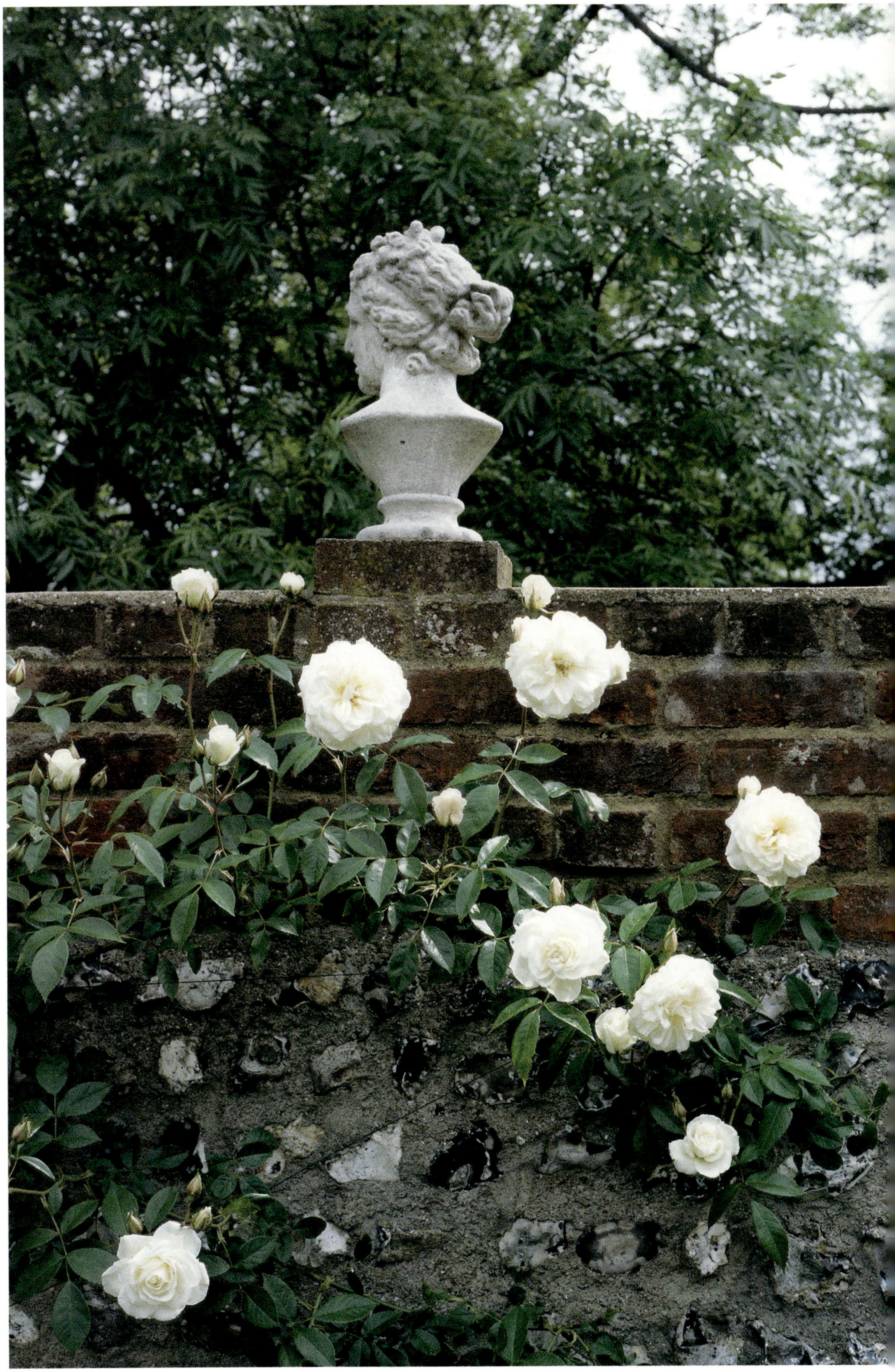

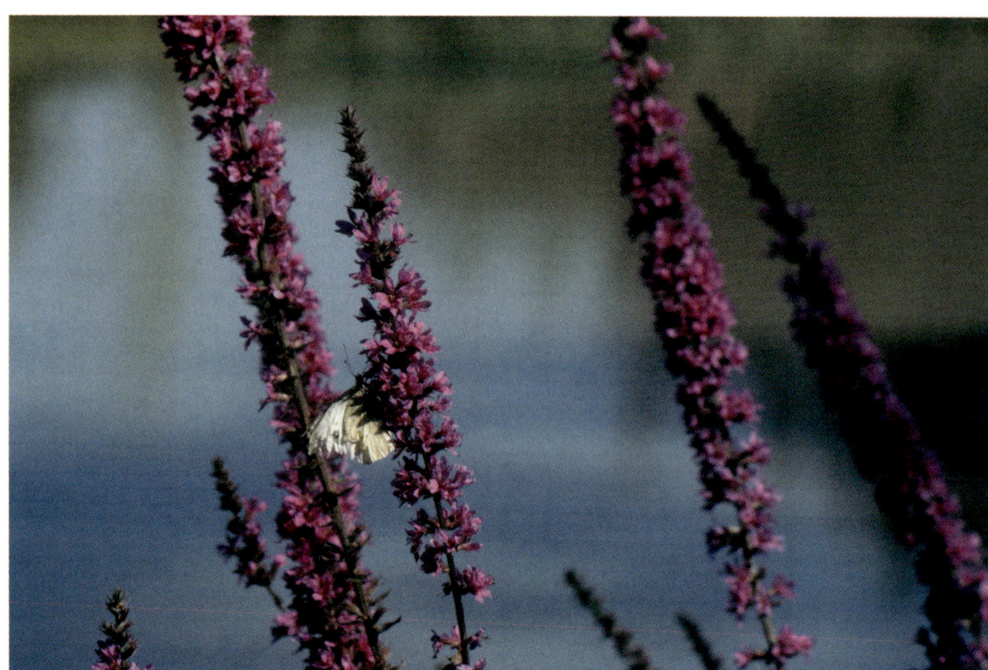

Purple loosestrife beside the pond

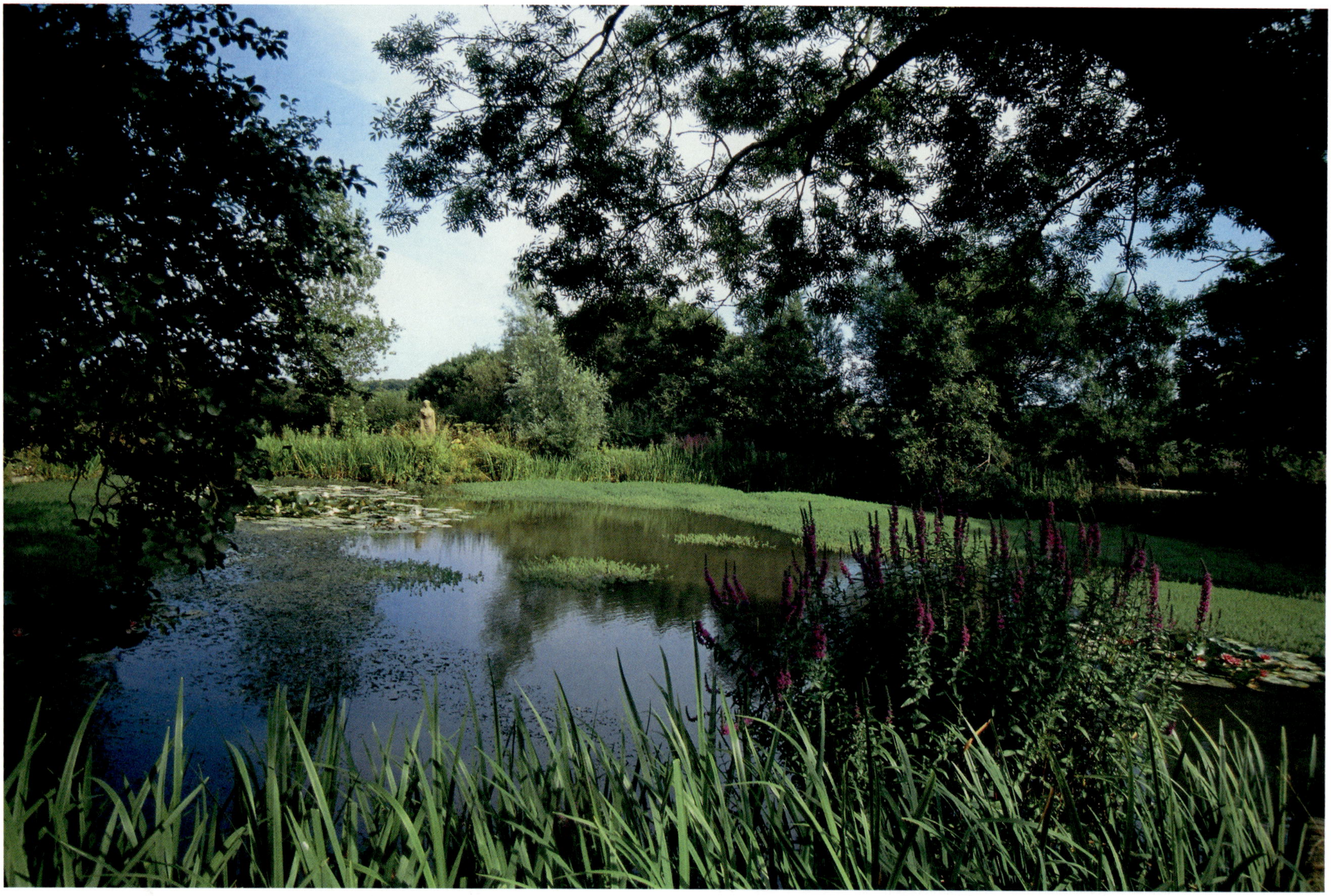

Levitating Lady by Quentin Bell

FOLLOWING PAGES LEFT TO RIGHT
View of the pond from Vanessa Bell's studio;
flag iris; *Leaning Female Figure* by Quentin Bell

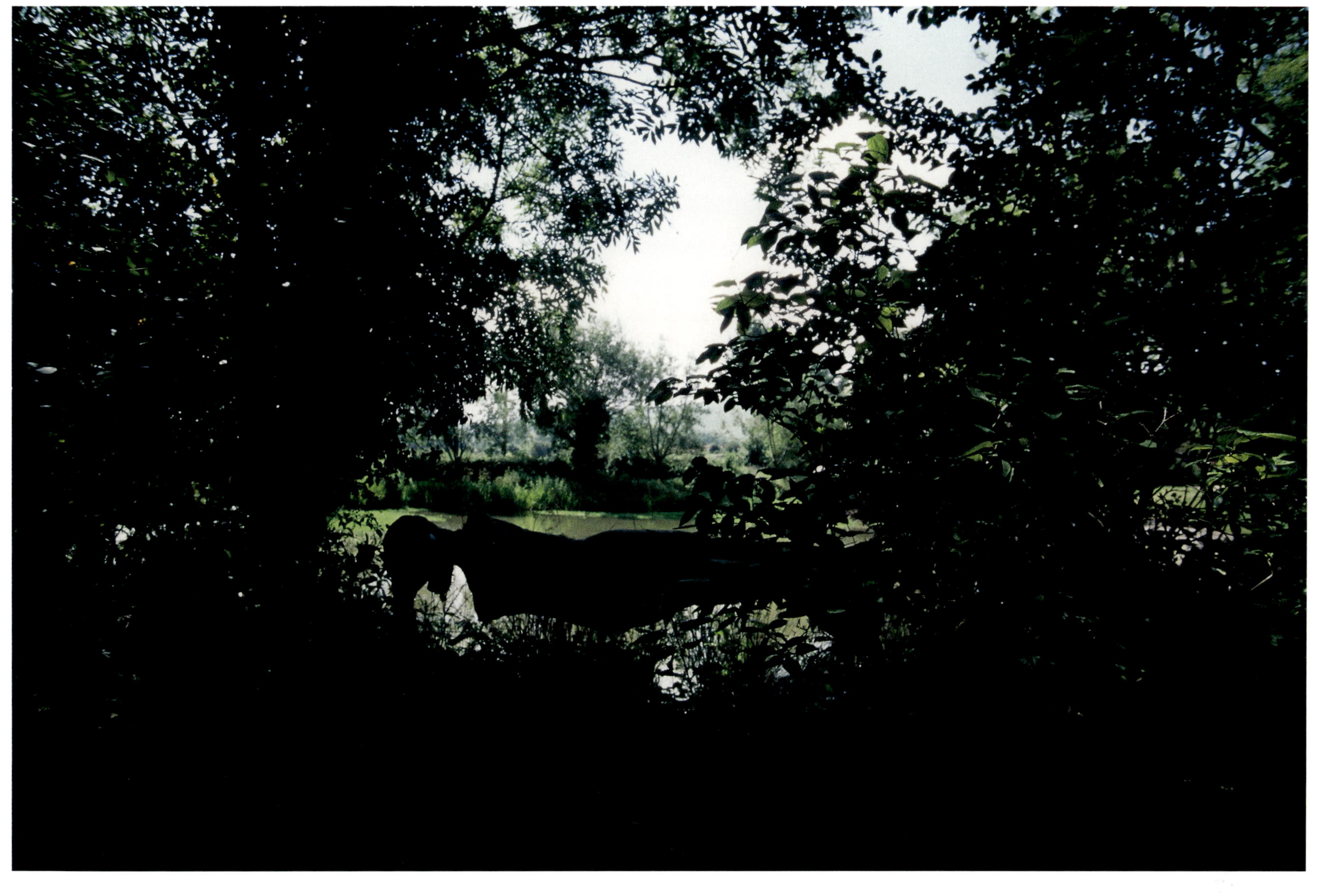

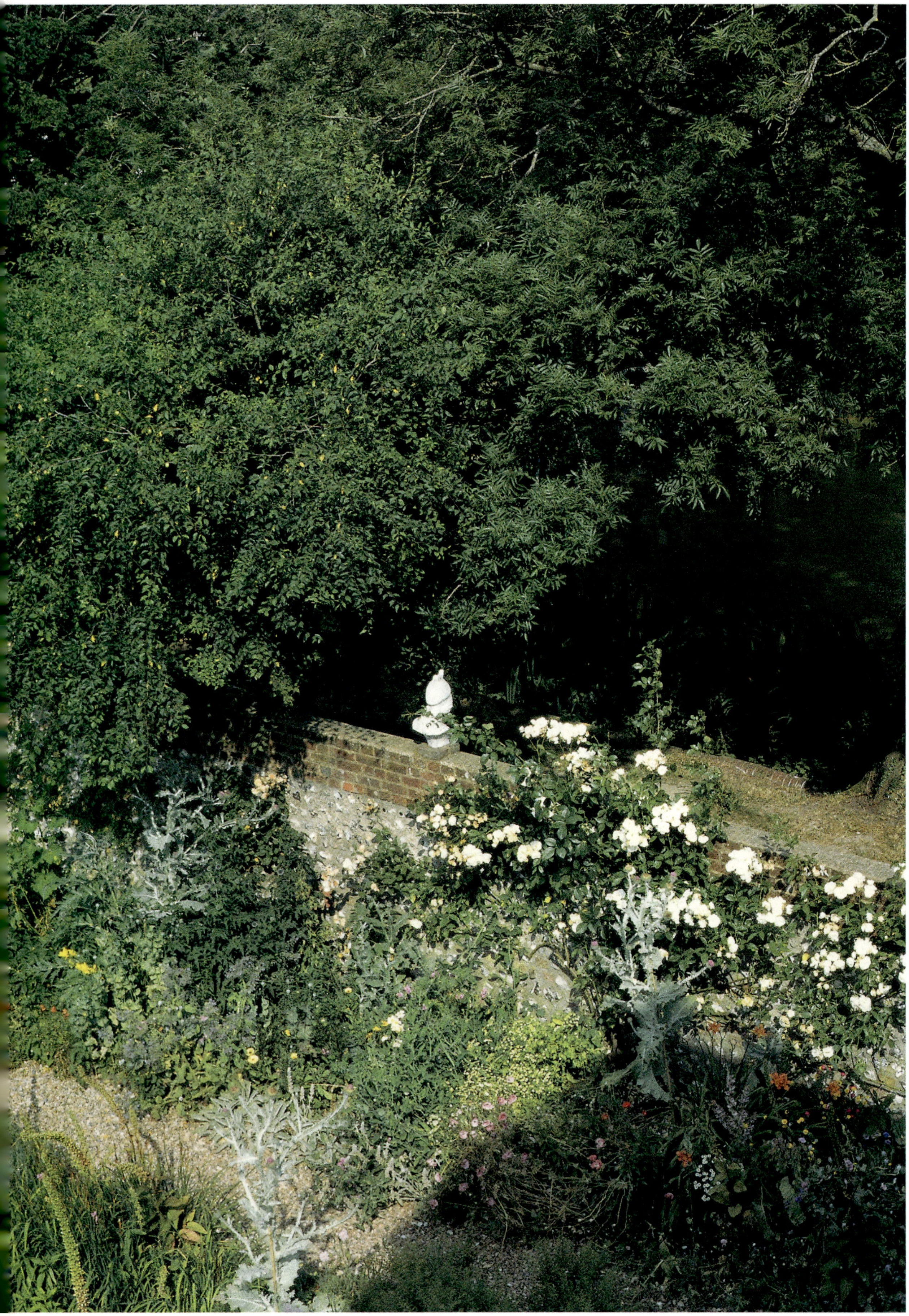

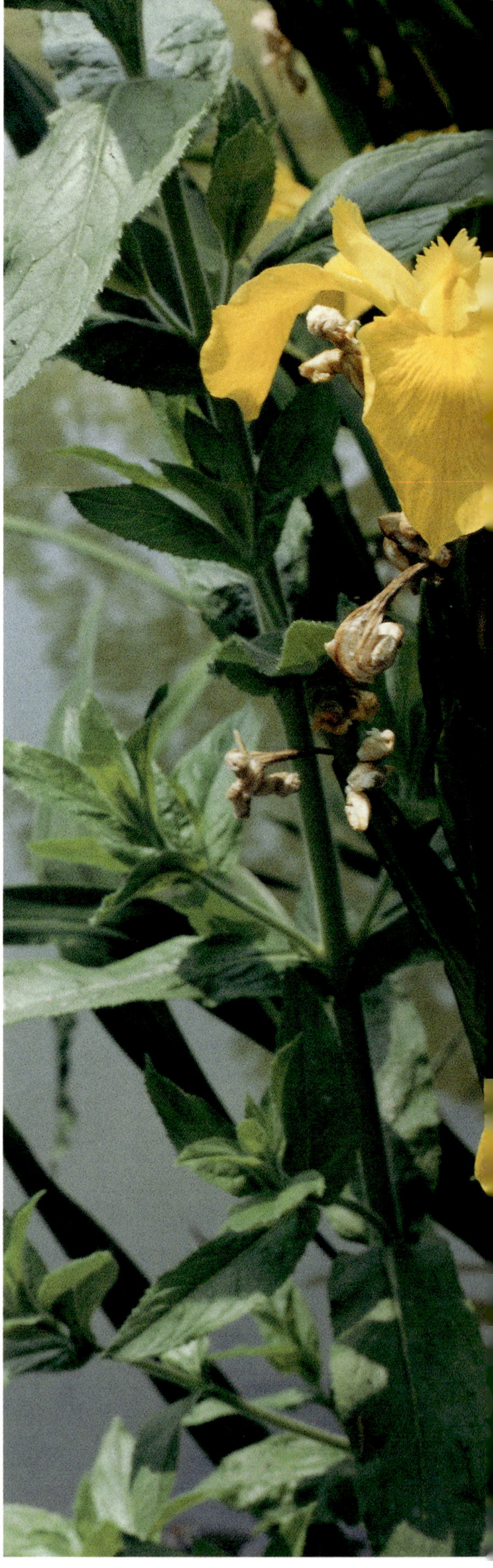

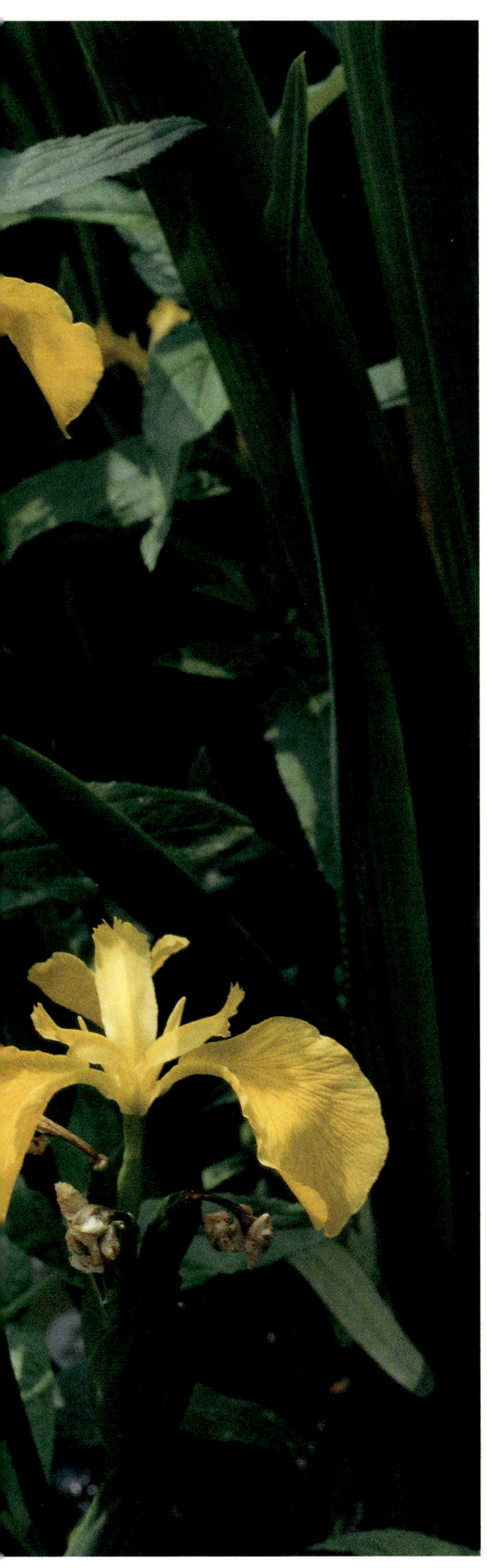

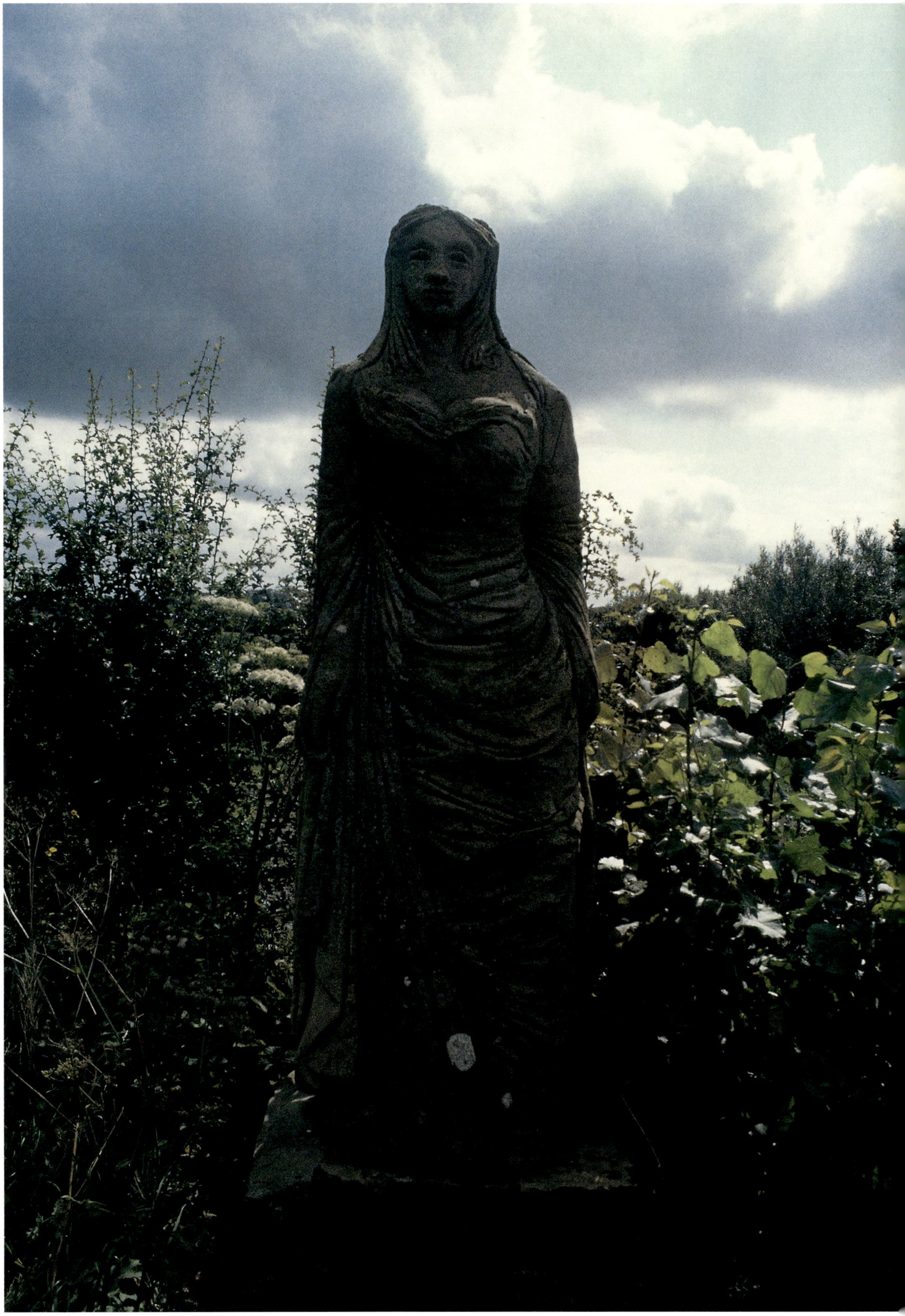

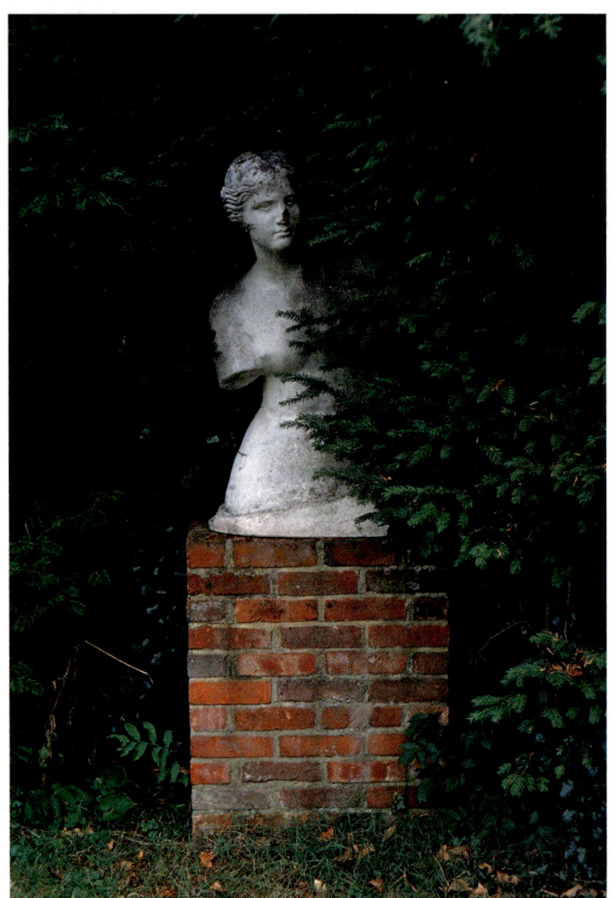

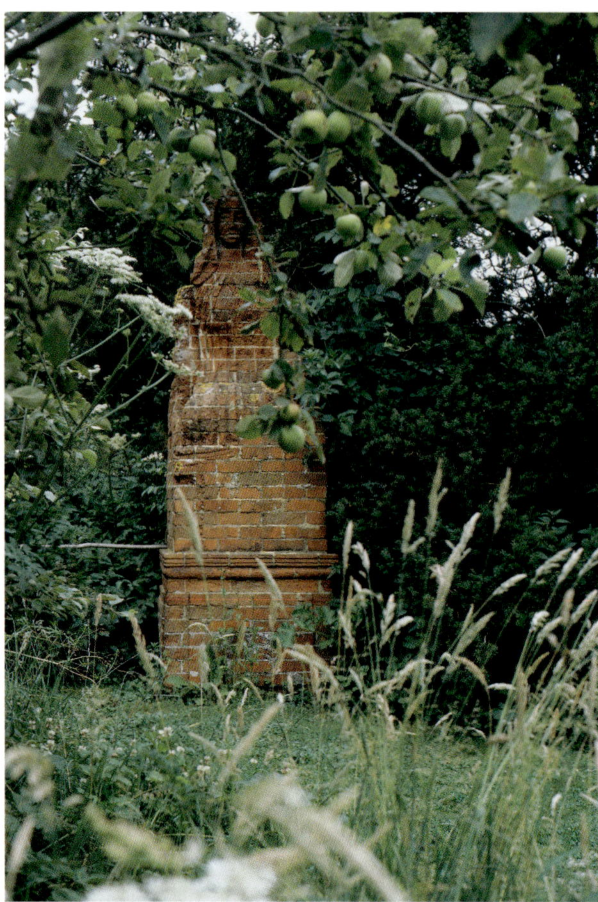

Cast of Venus de Milo (far left) and *The Spink* by Quentin Bell (left)

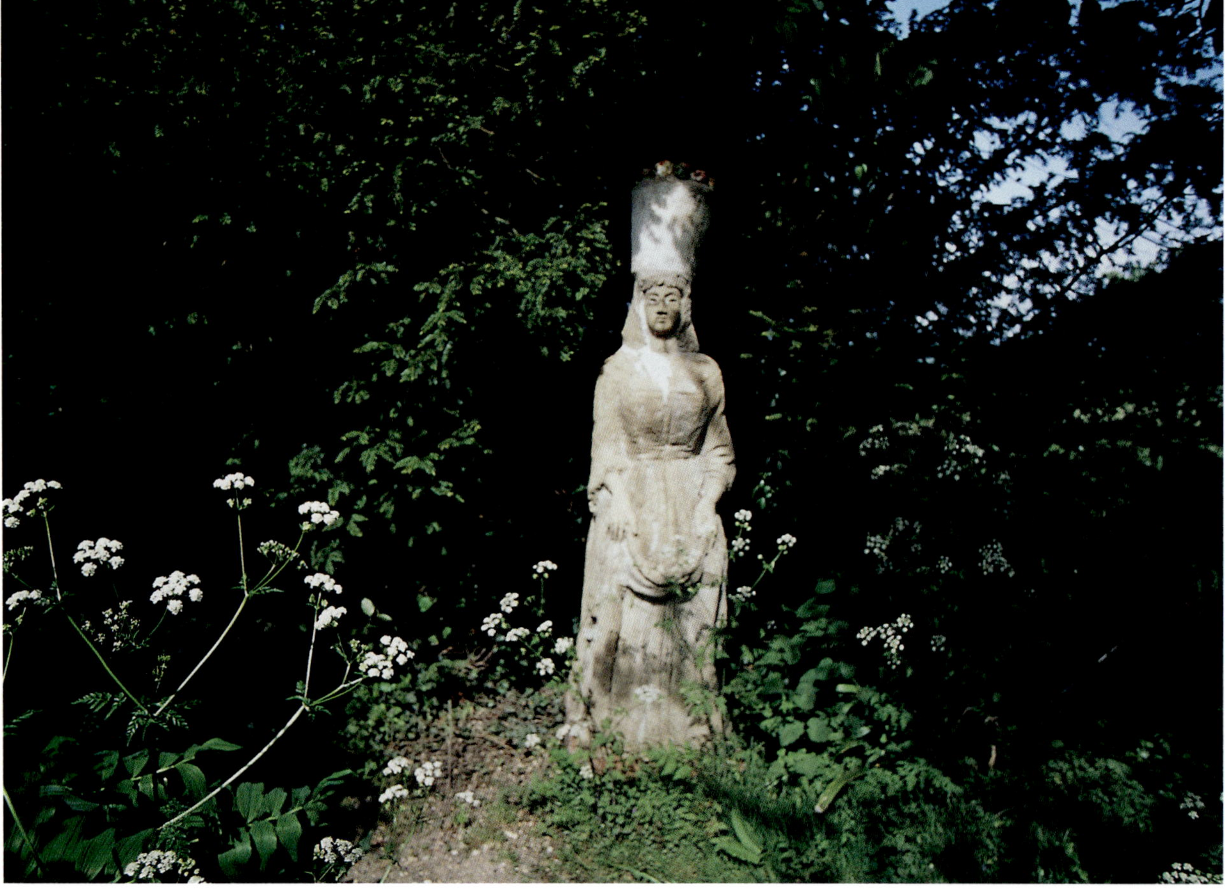

Pomona by Quentin Bell

Spink's hand

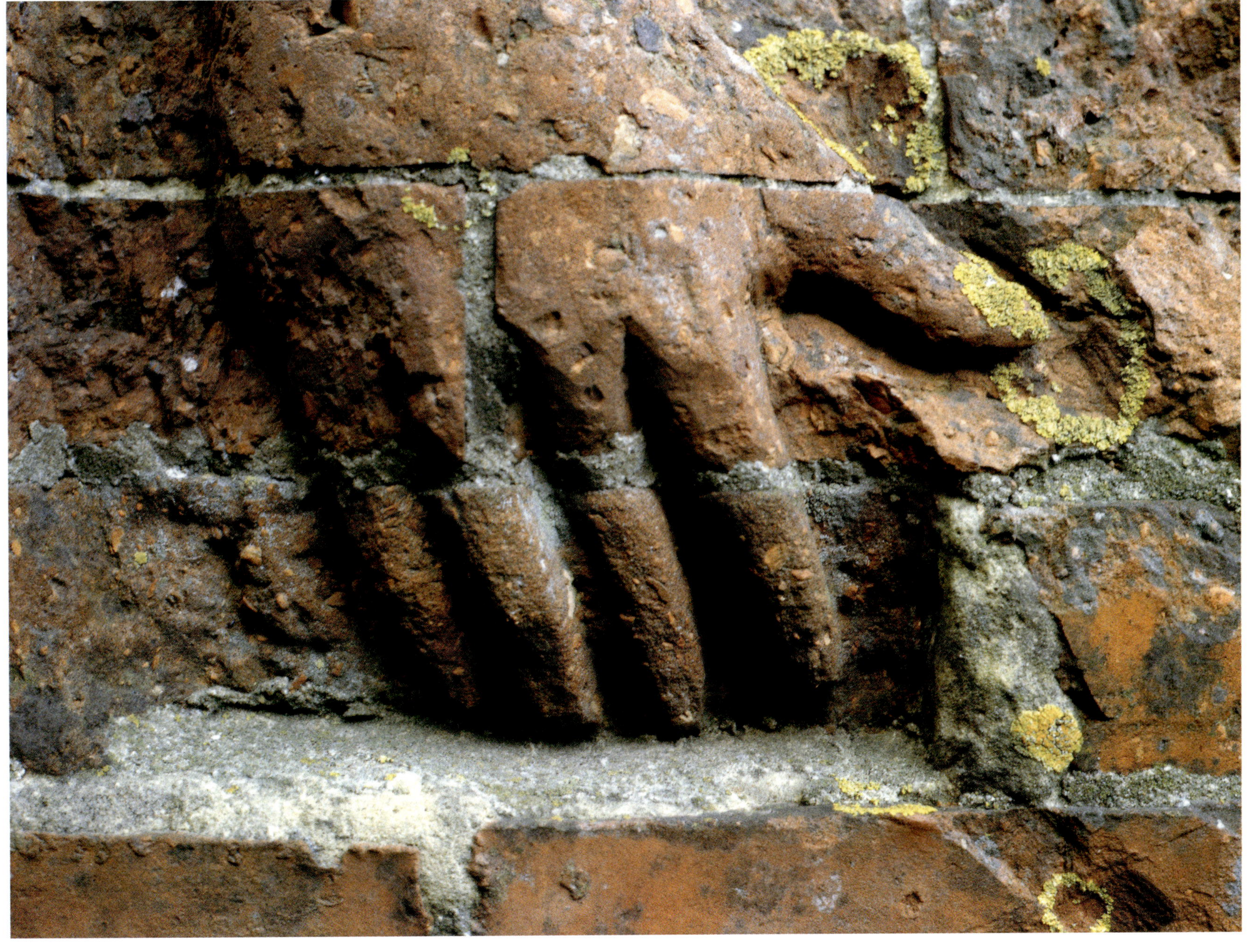

Stained glass by Quentin Bell (left) and male nude by Duncan Grant (right)

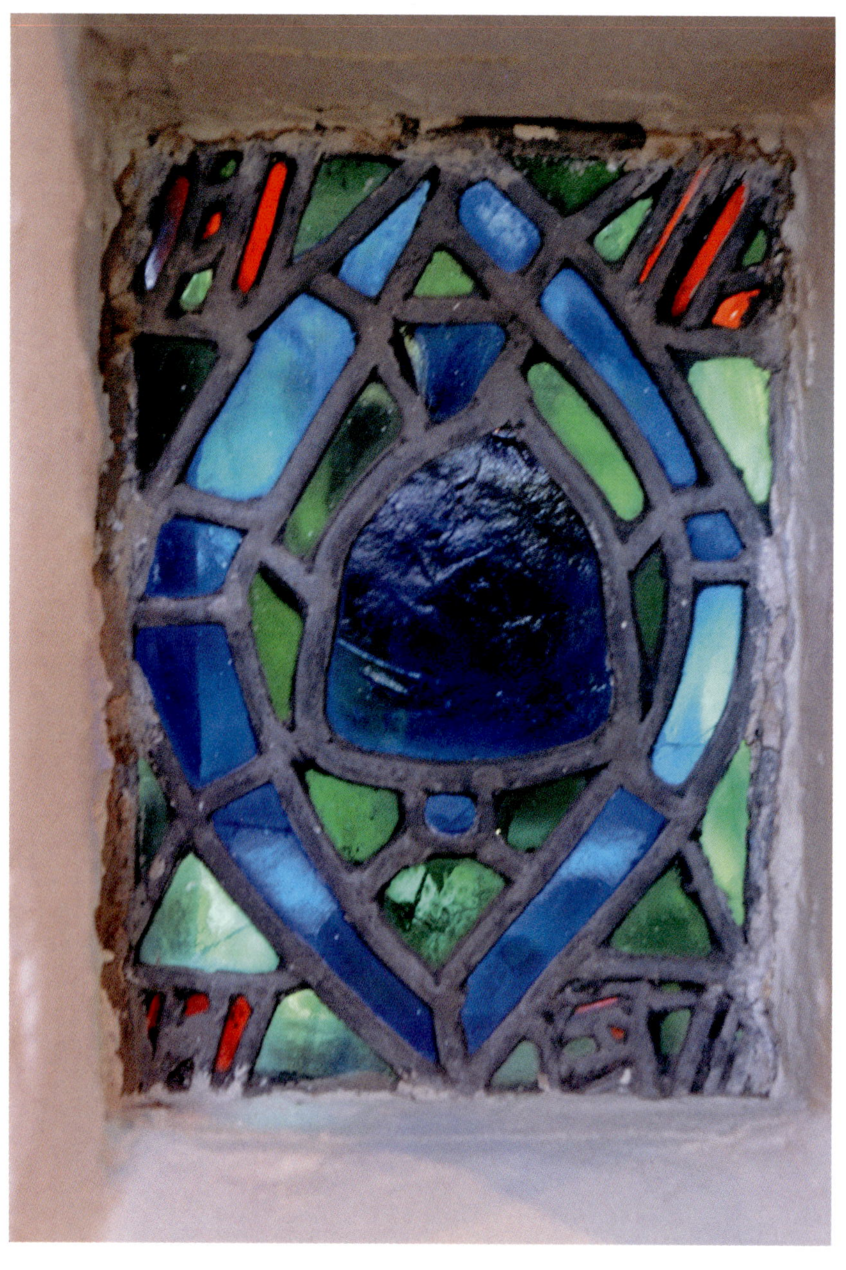

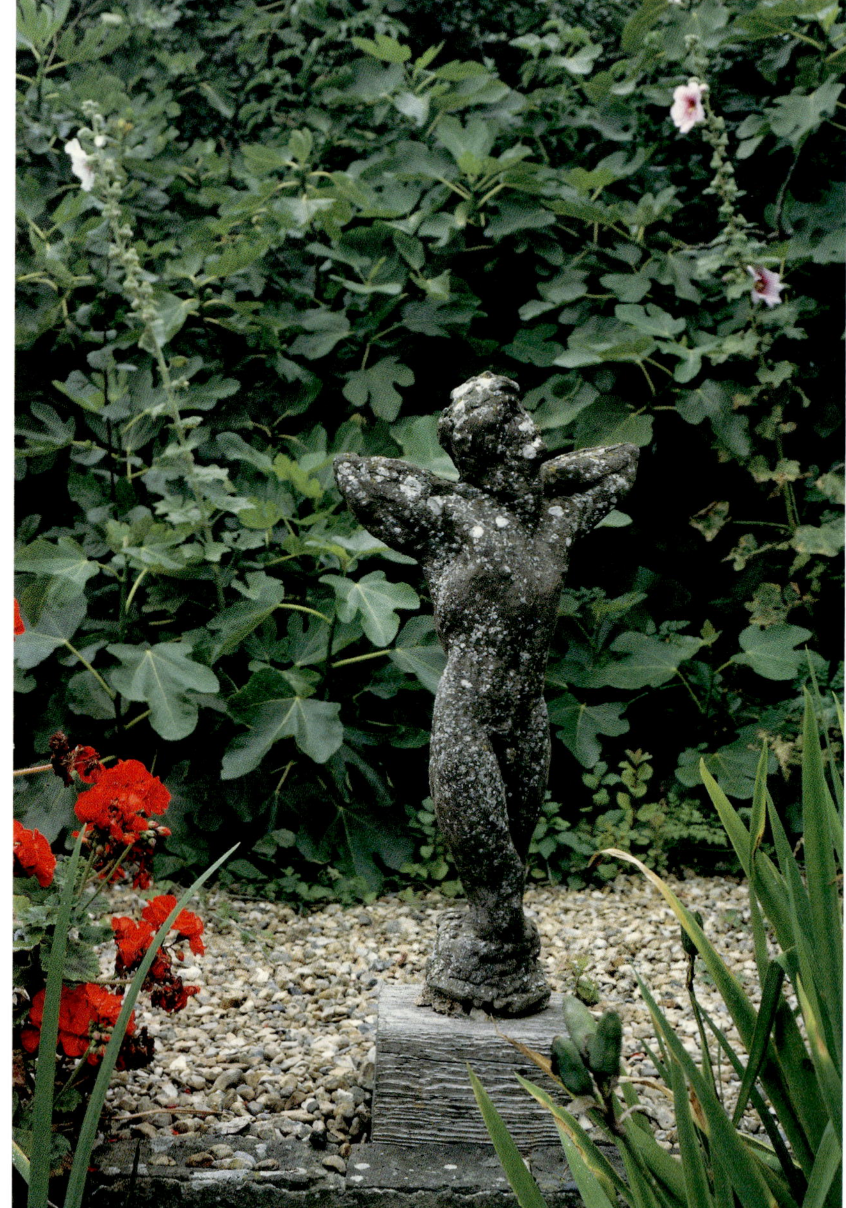

Fig

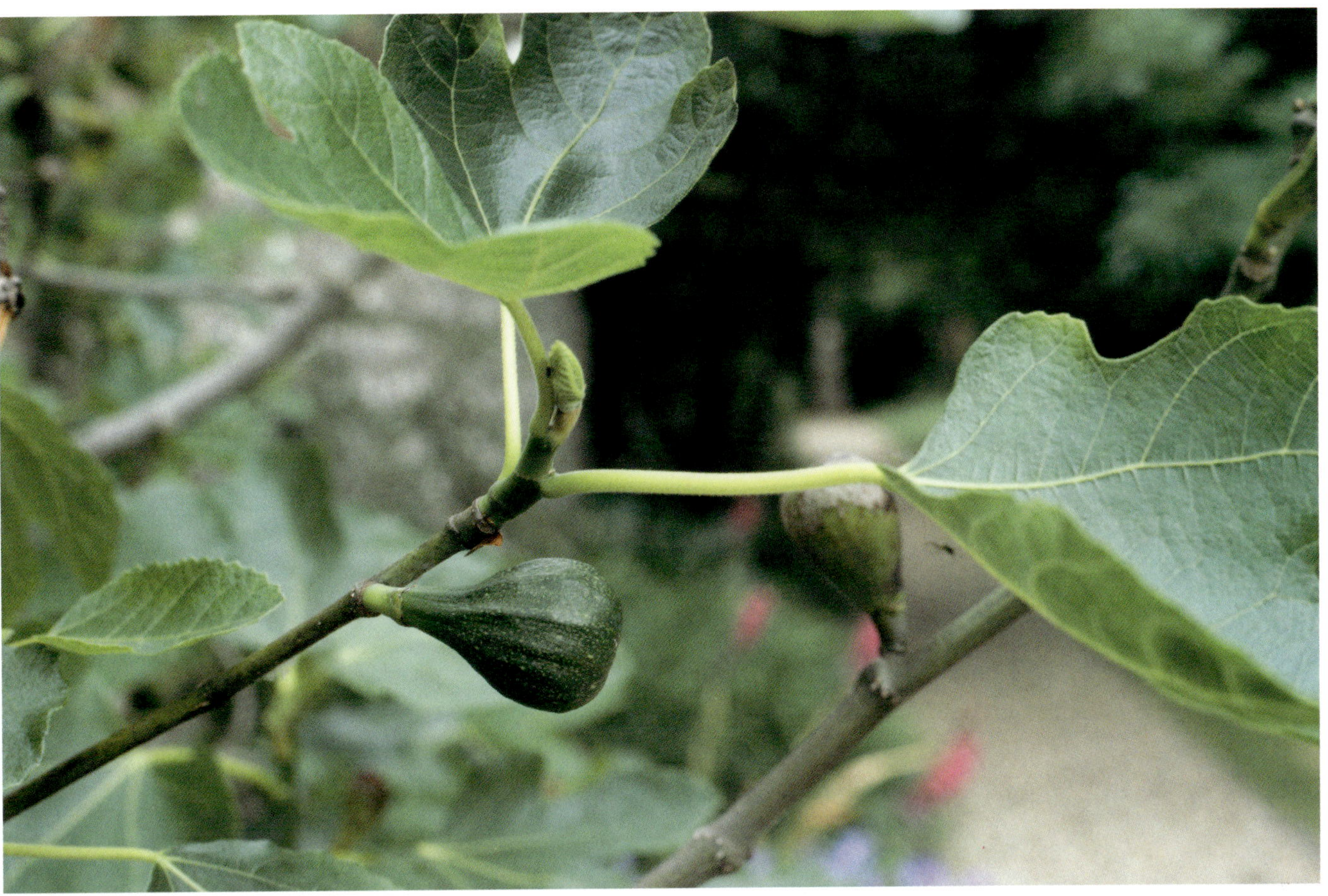

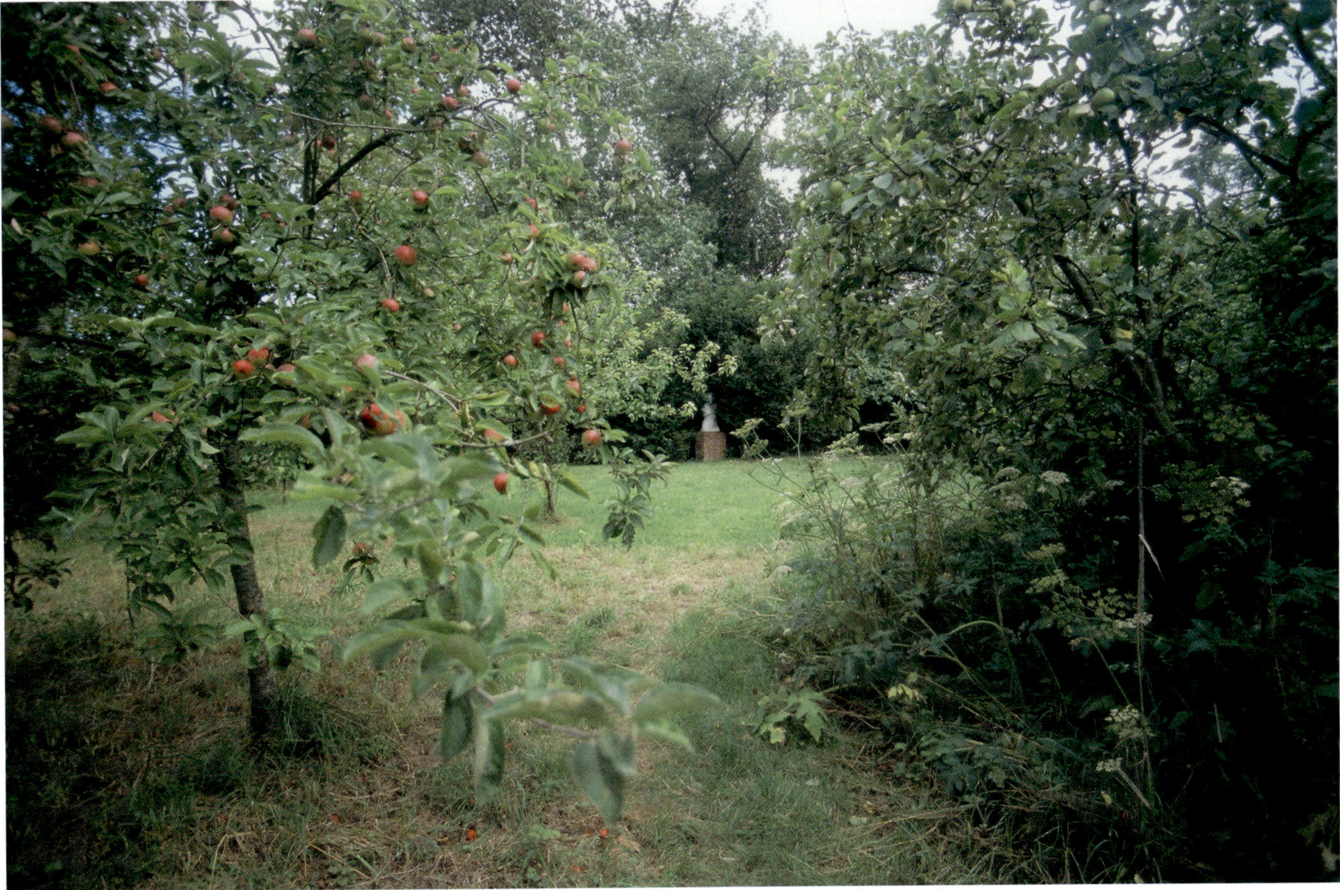

The orchard

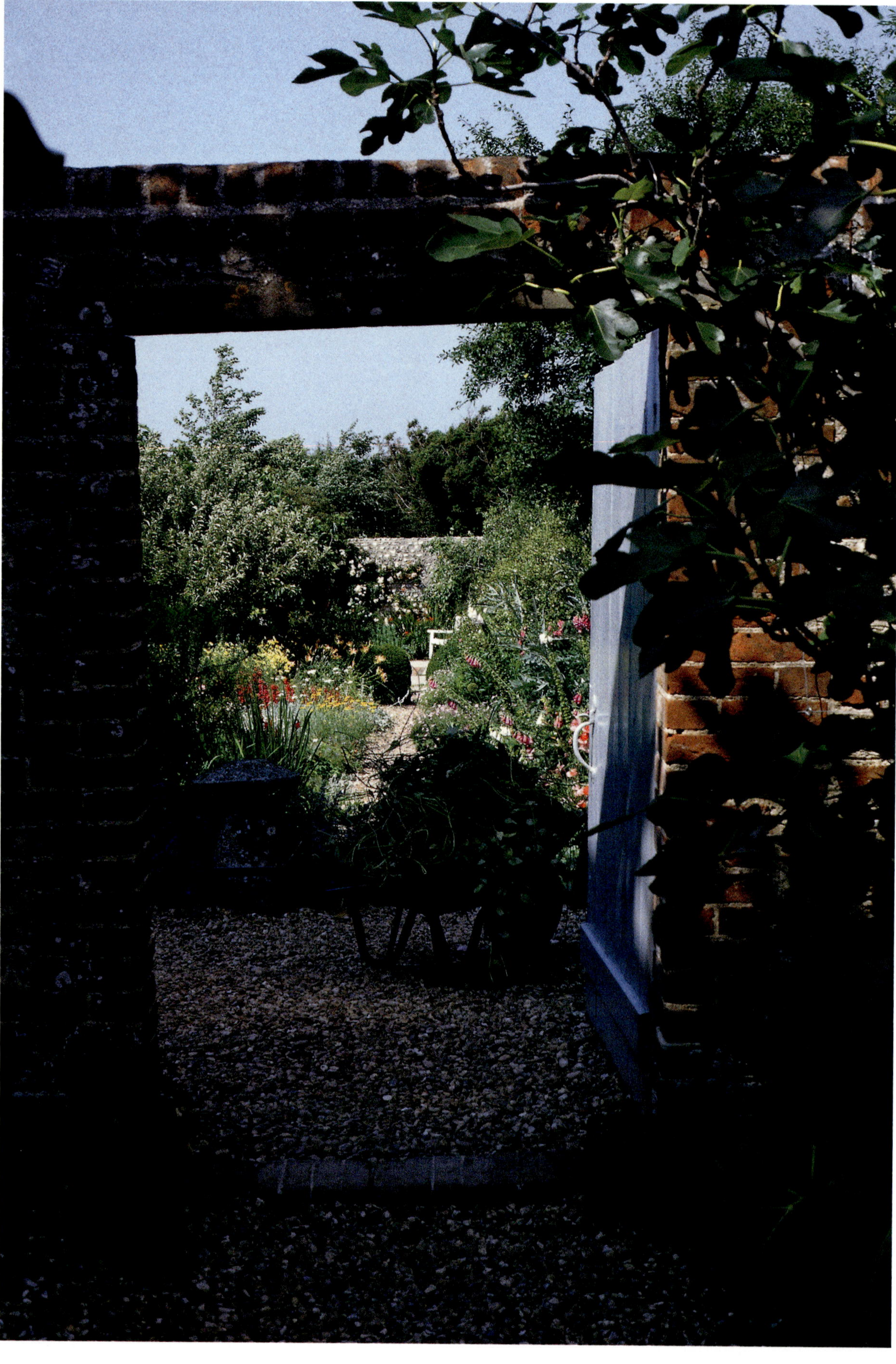

Door into the walled garden

View from the garden room

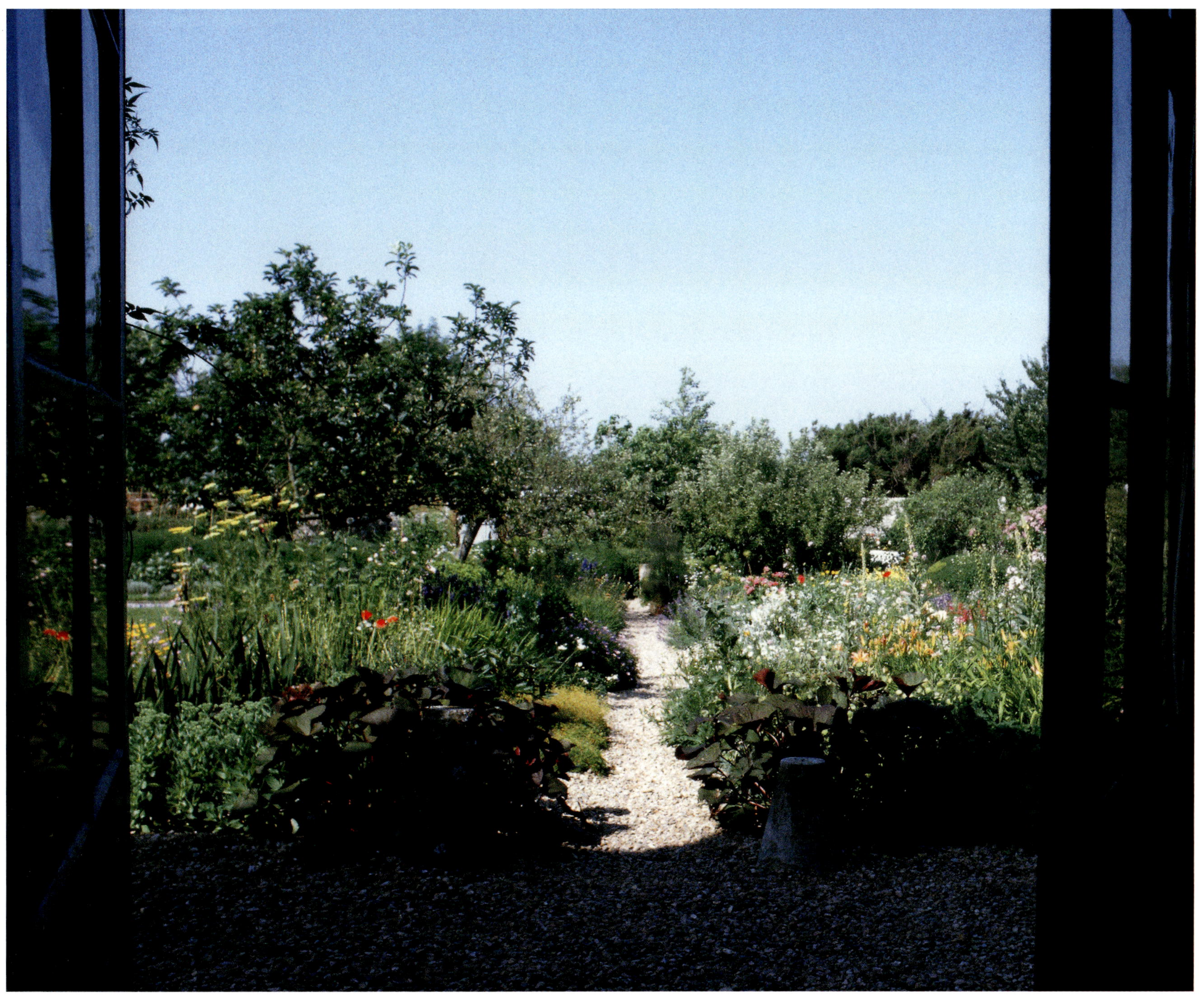

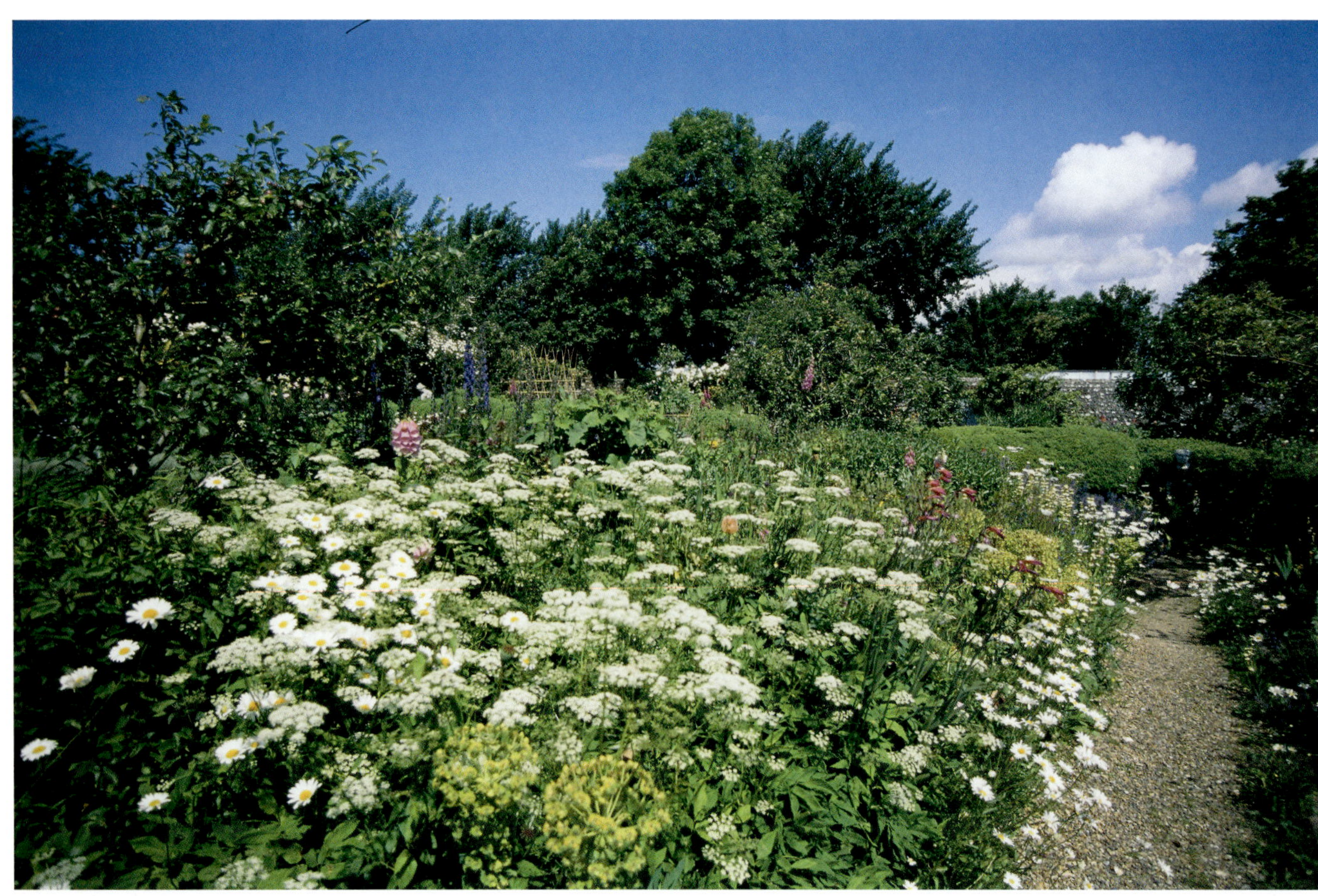

Overspilling beds

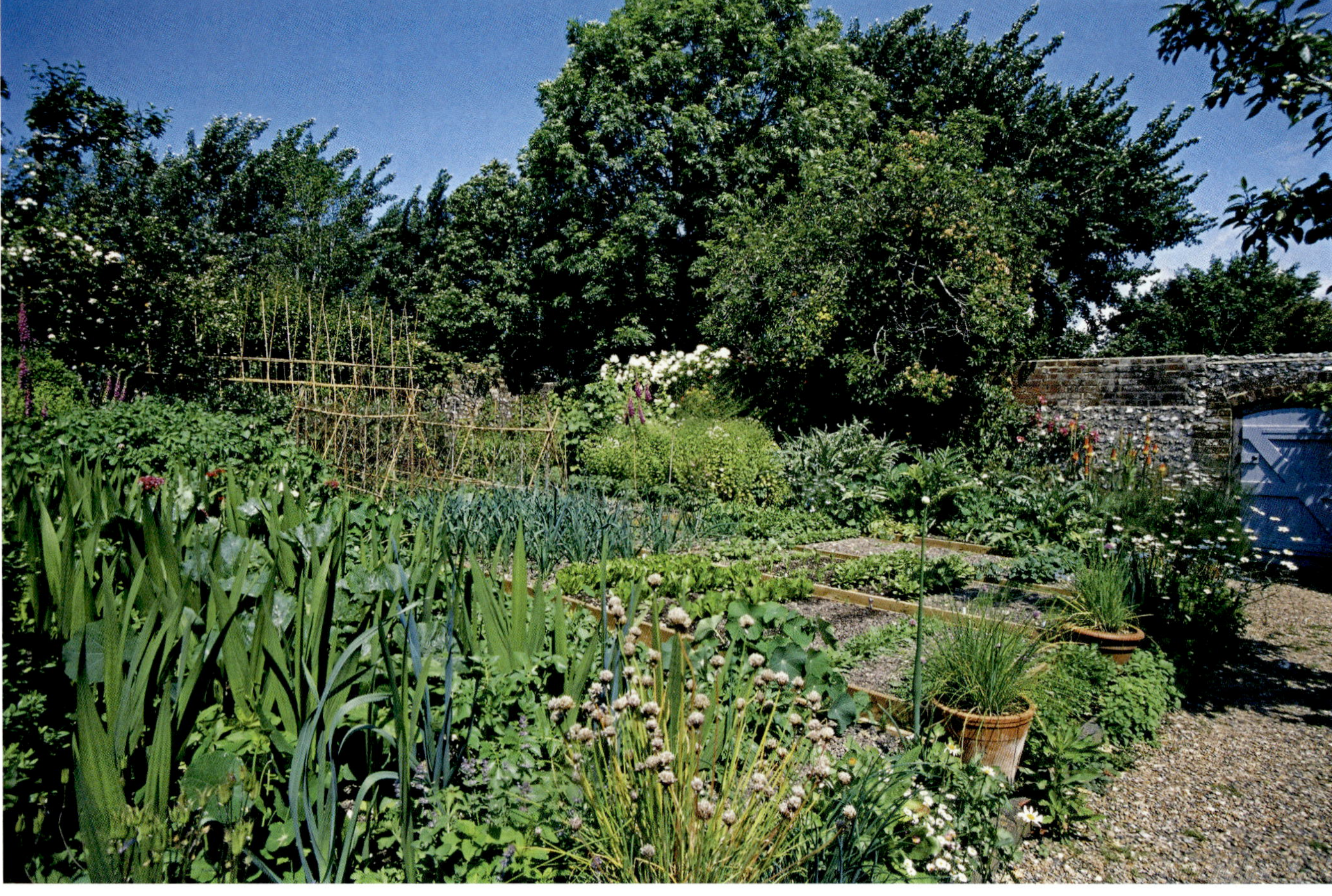

The kitchen garden

Cherries (left) and comma butterfly (right)

FOLLOWING PAGES CLOCKWISE FROM TOP LEFT
Ceramic piazza by Duncan Grant, Vanessa Bell, Angelica Garnett, Quentin Bell and Janie Bussy; cast female torso planter with hydrangea; fountain head; cast head; cast after a Venus by Giovanni da Bologna

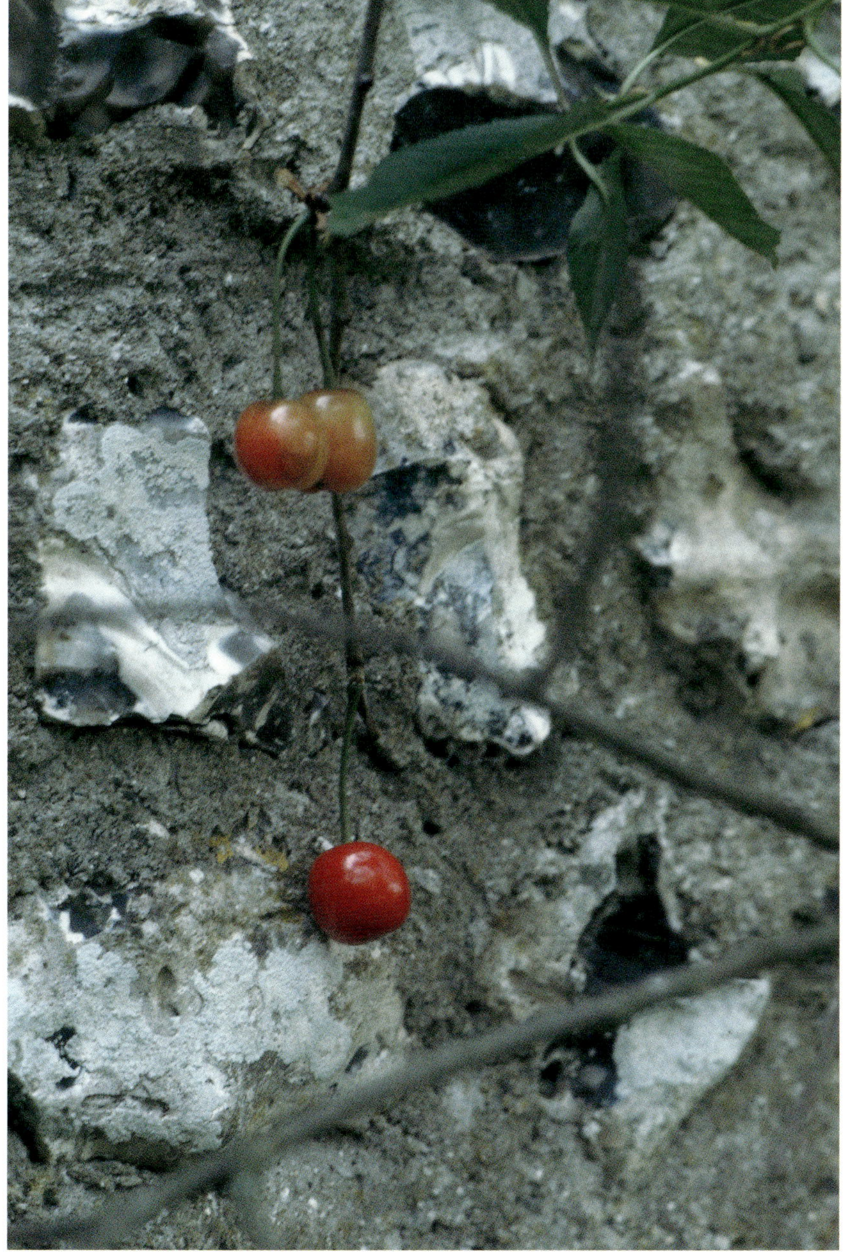

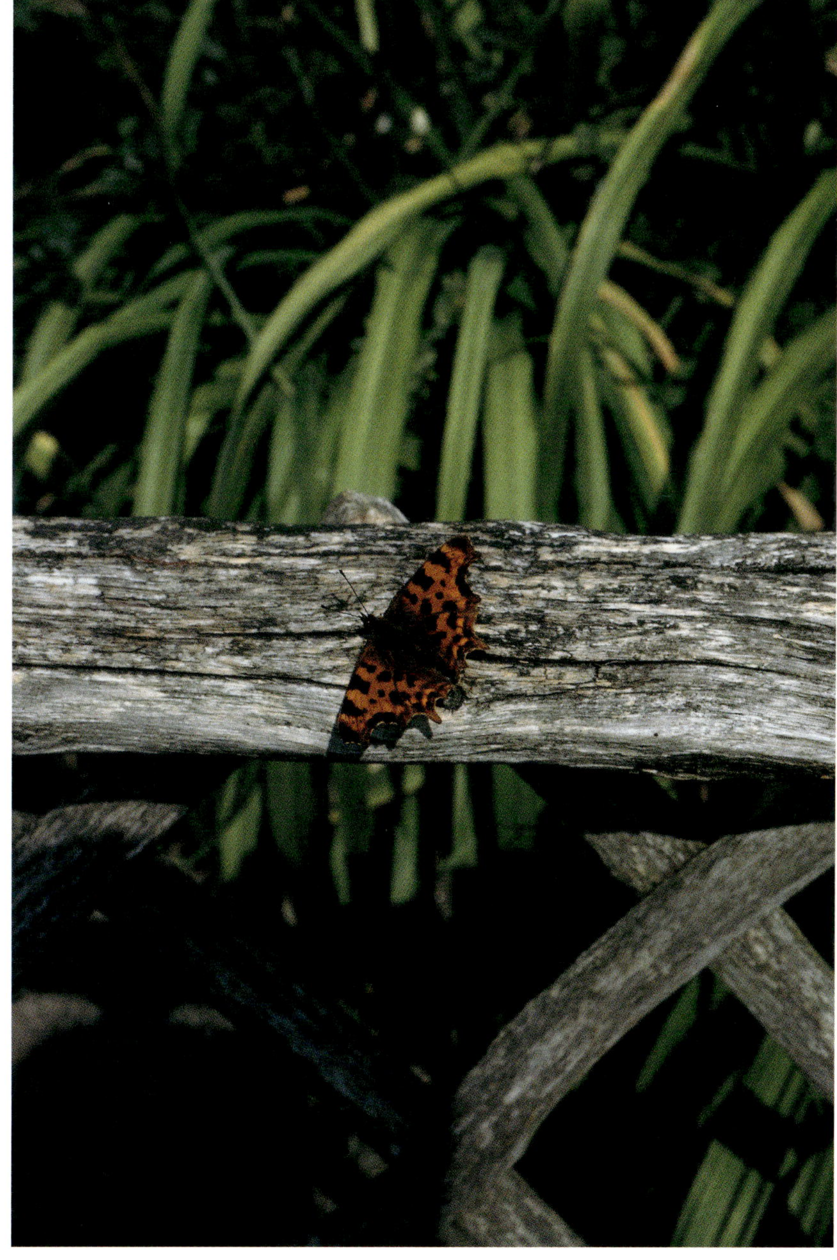

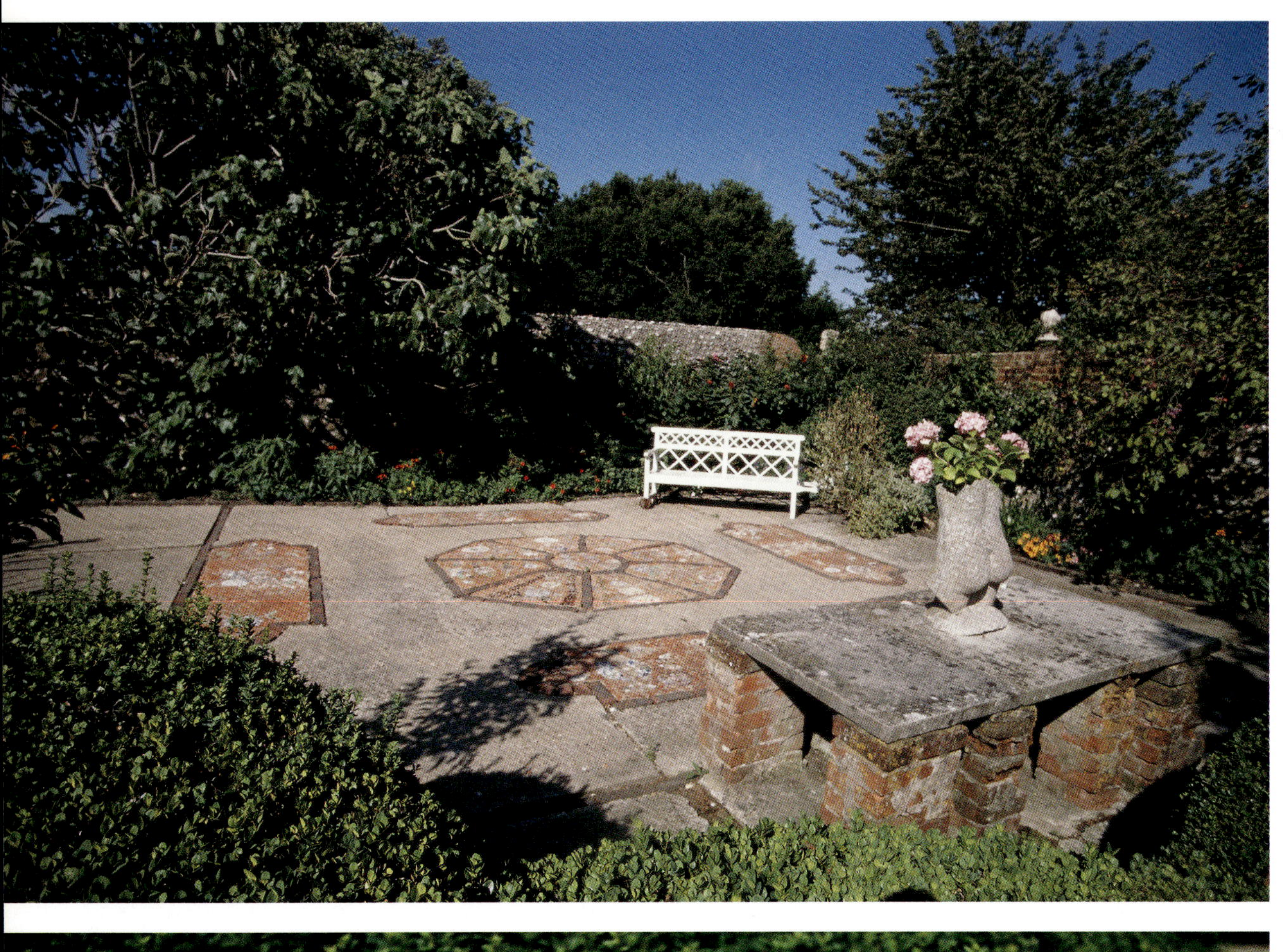
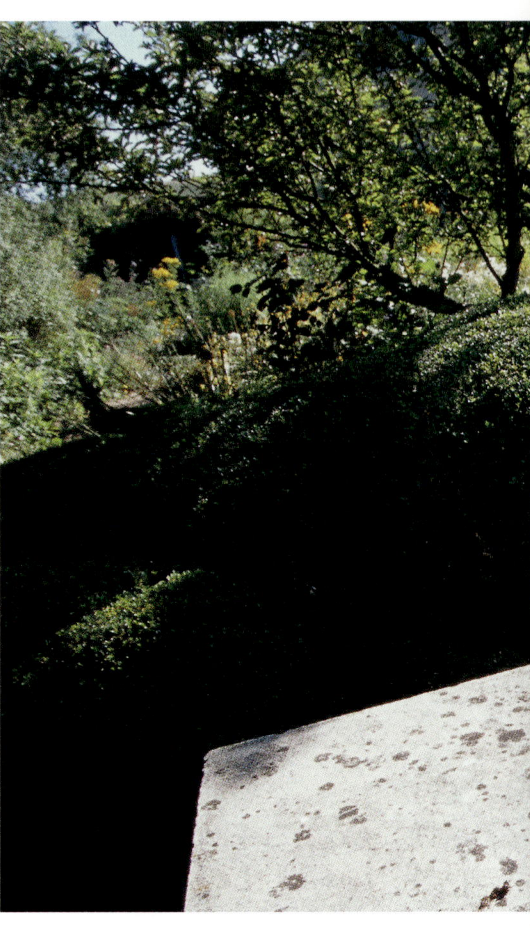
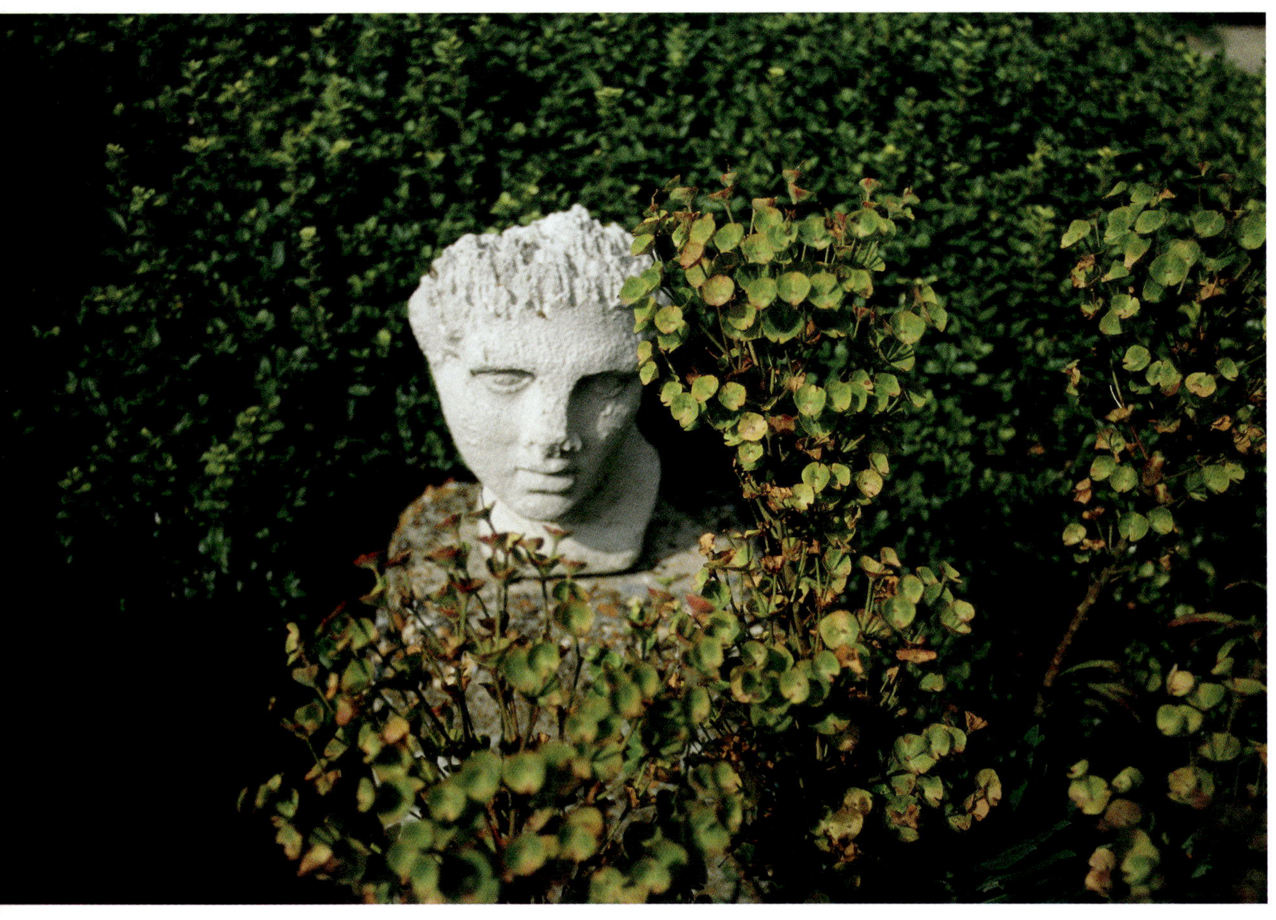
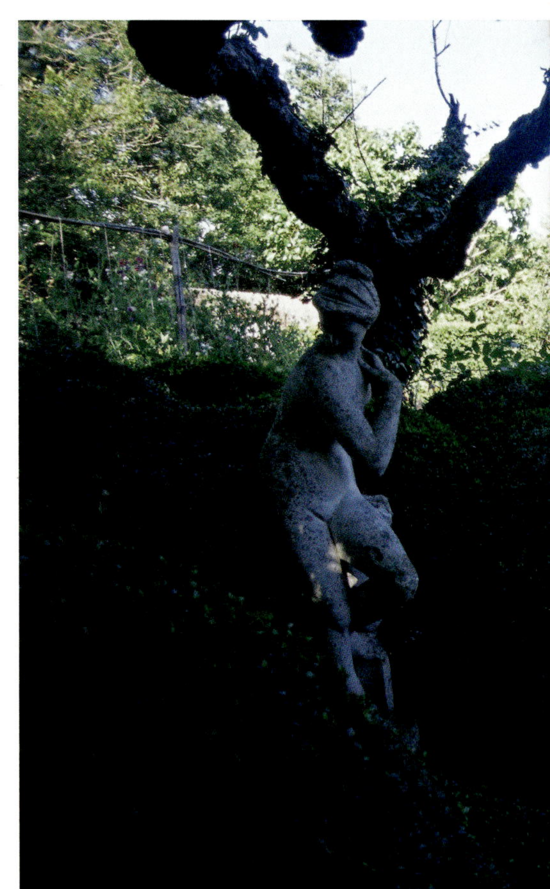

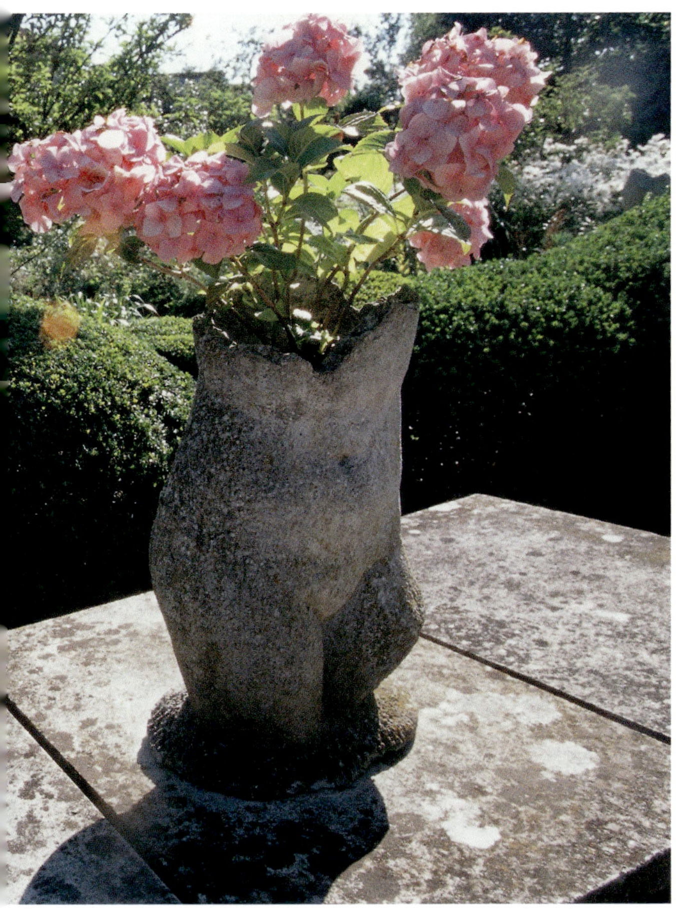

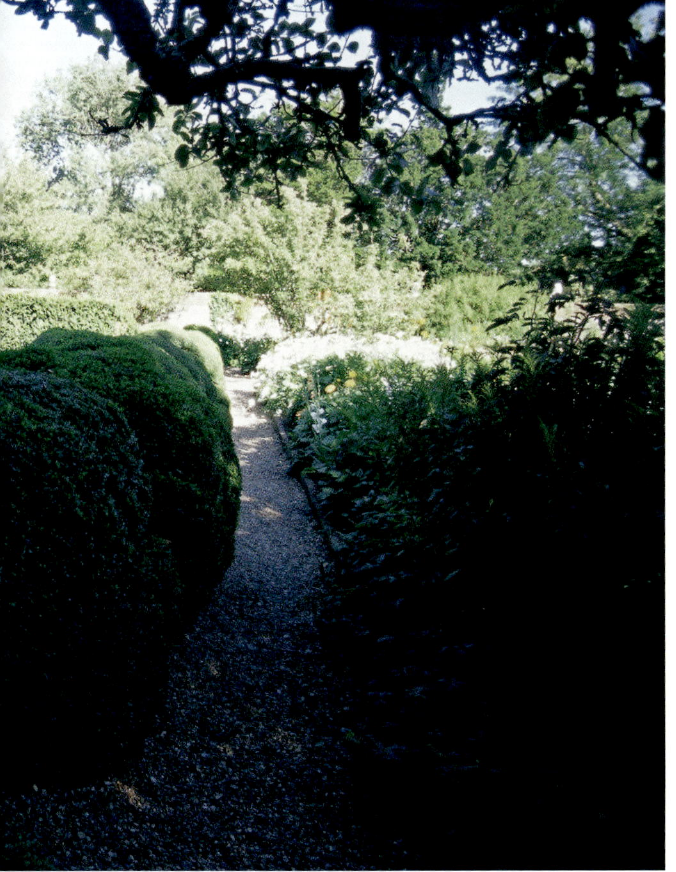

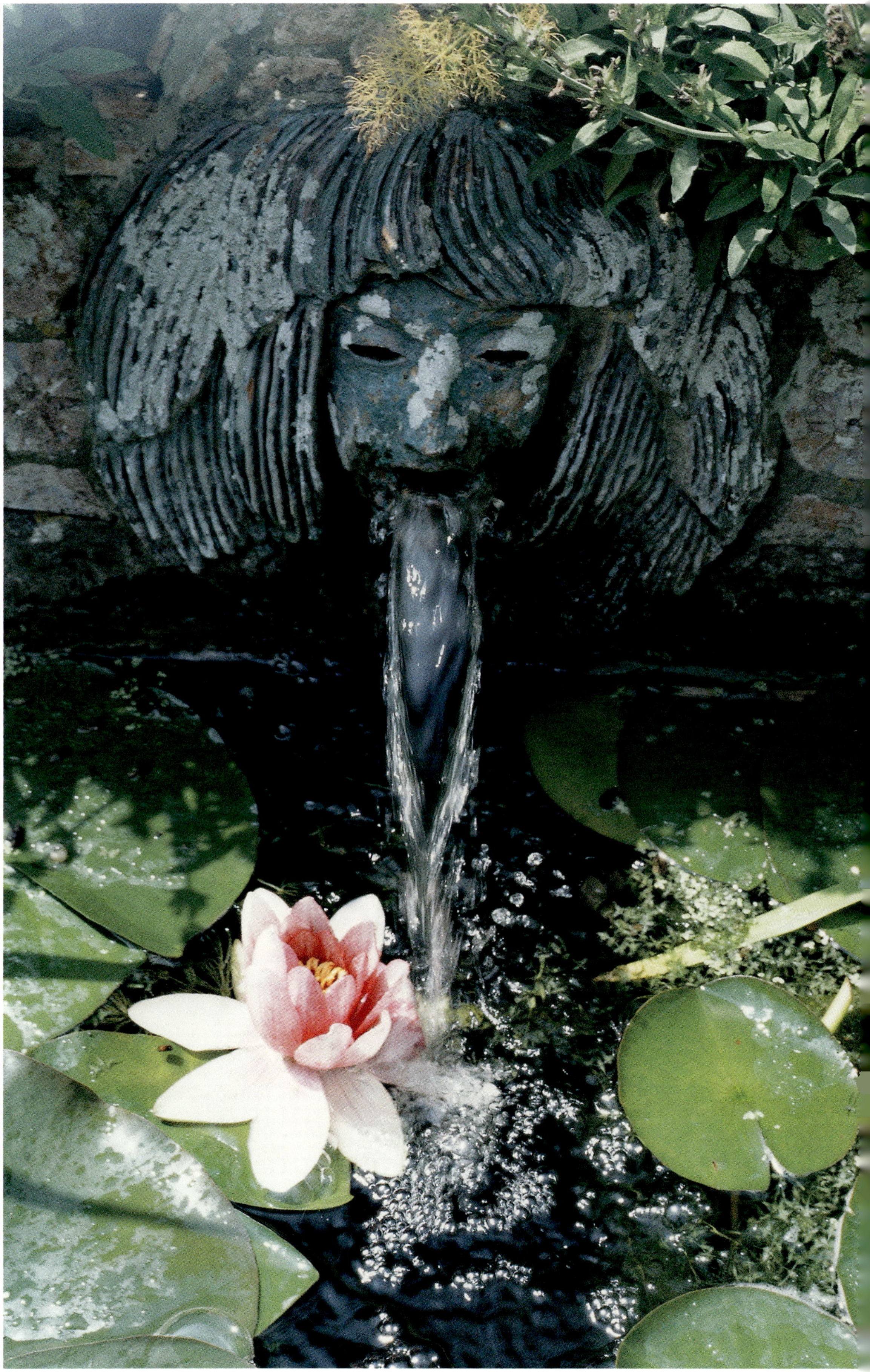

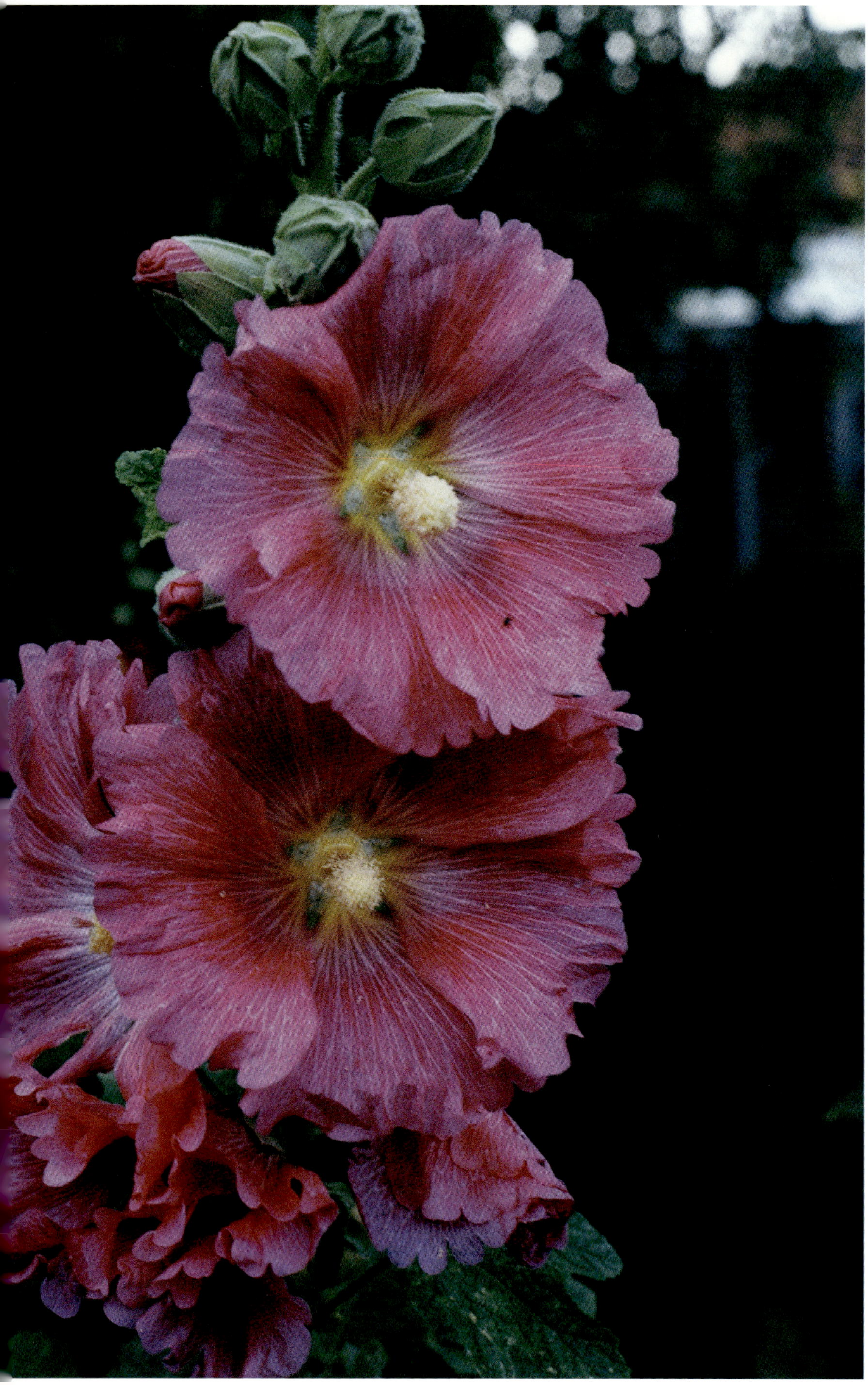

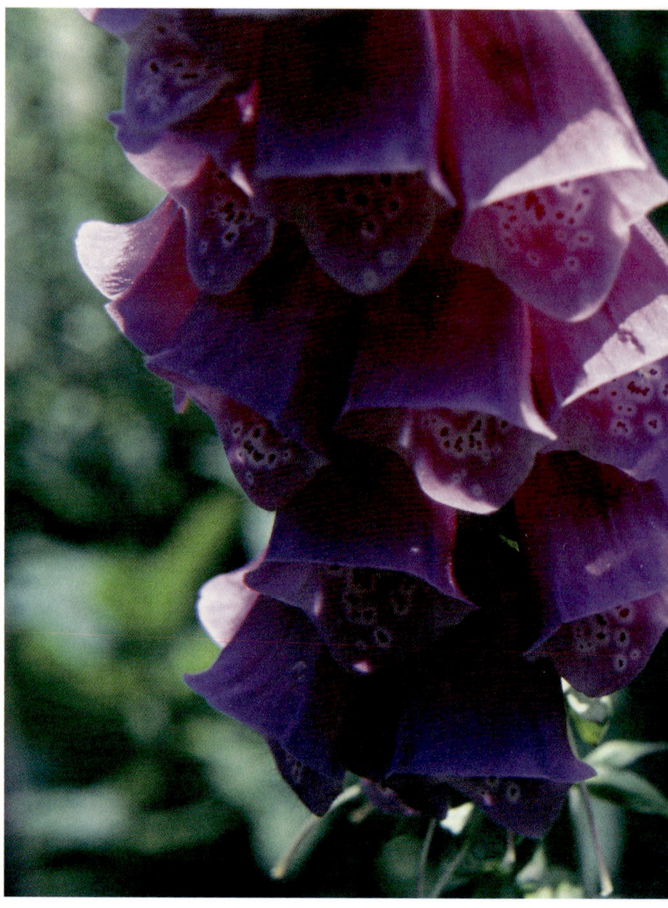

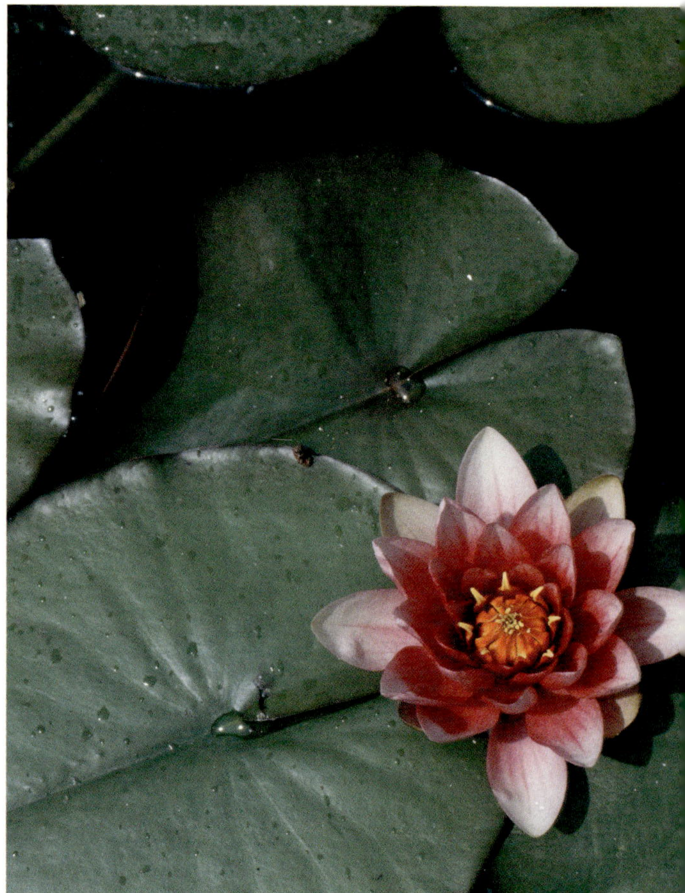

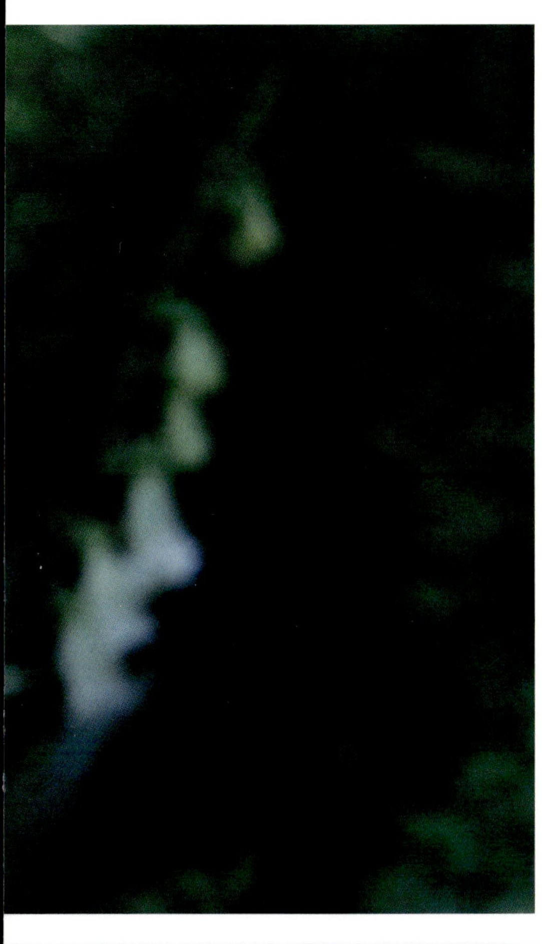
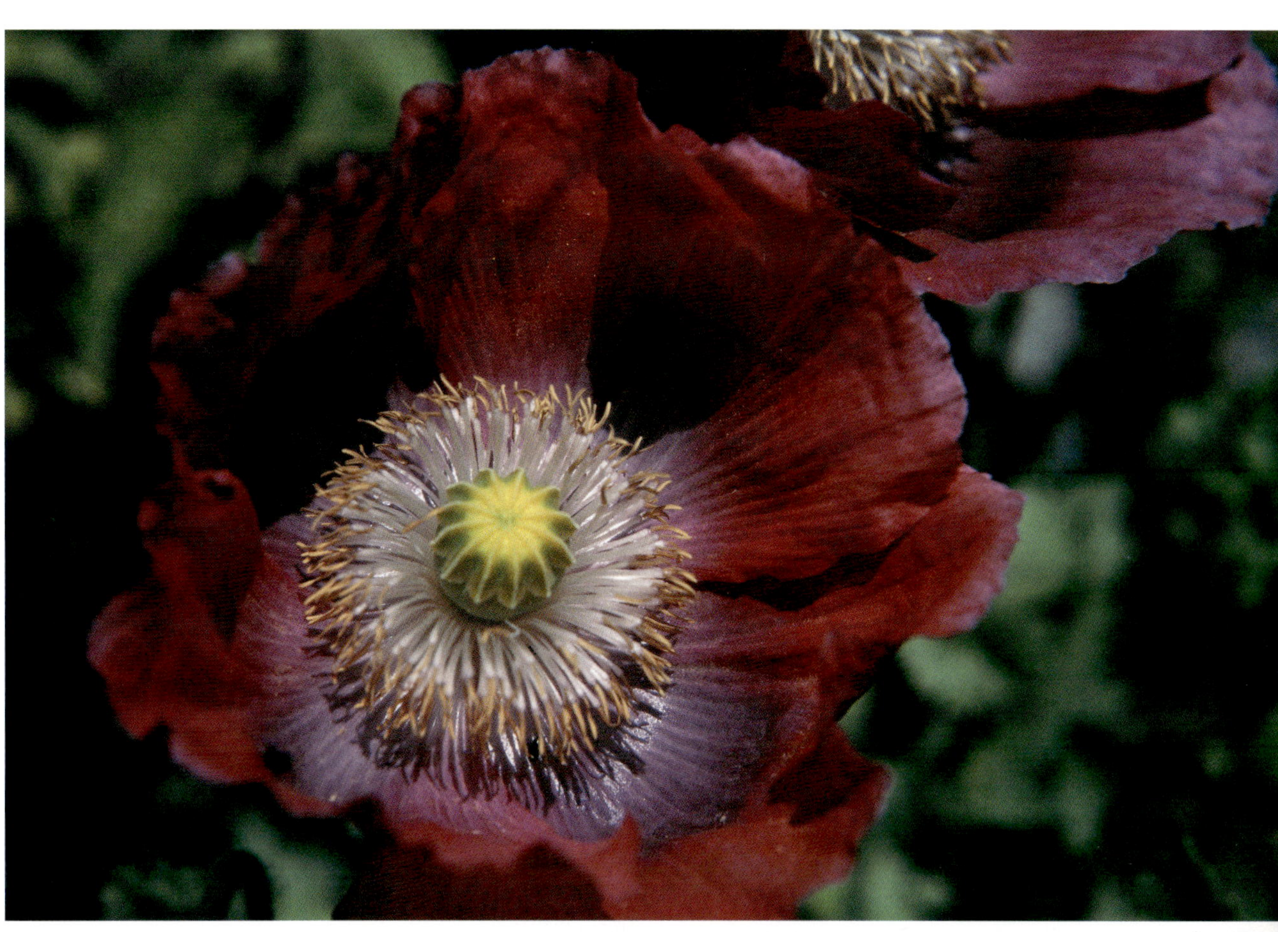
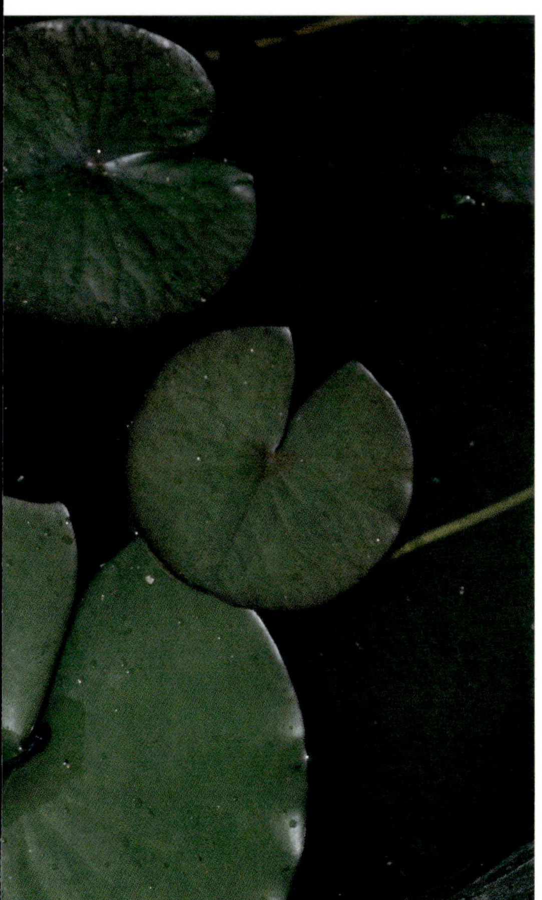
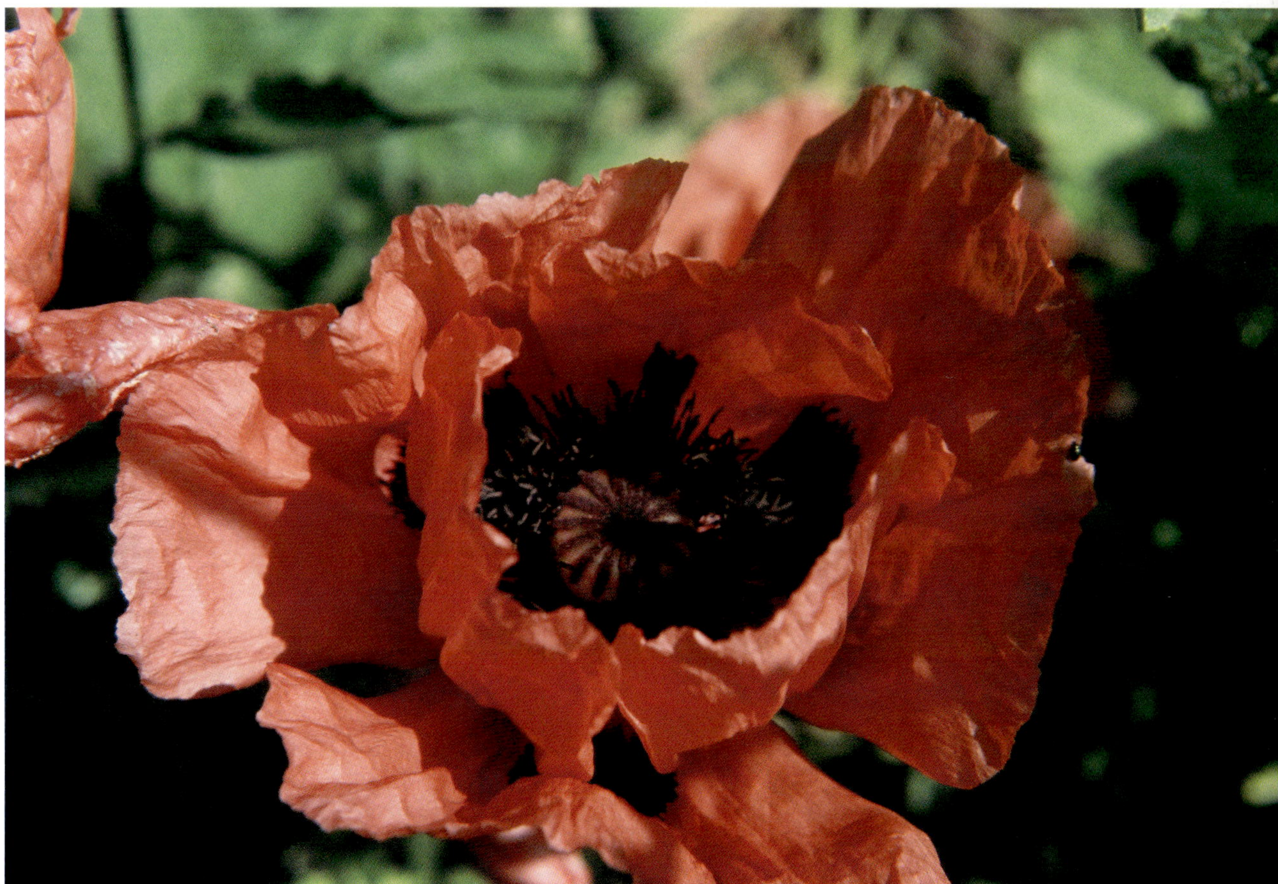

PREVIOUS PAGES CLOCKWISE FROM TOP LEFT
Hollyhock; foxglove; opium poppy; water lily; oriental poppy

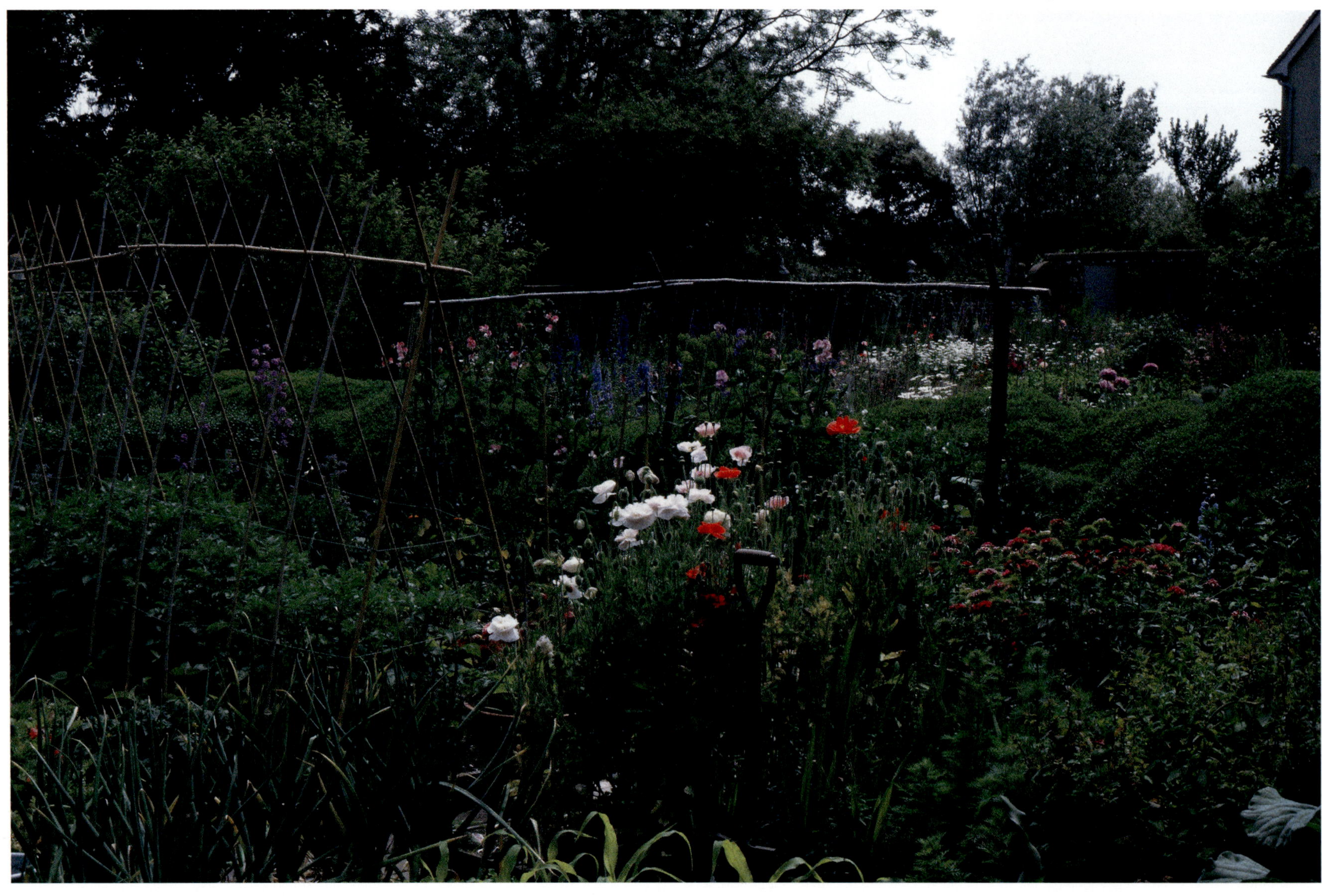

Asparagus fern

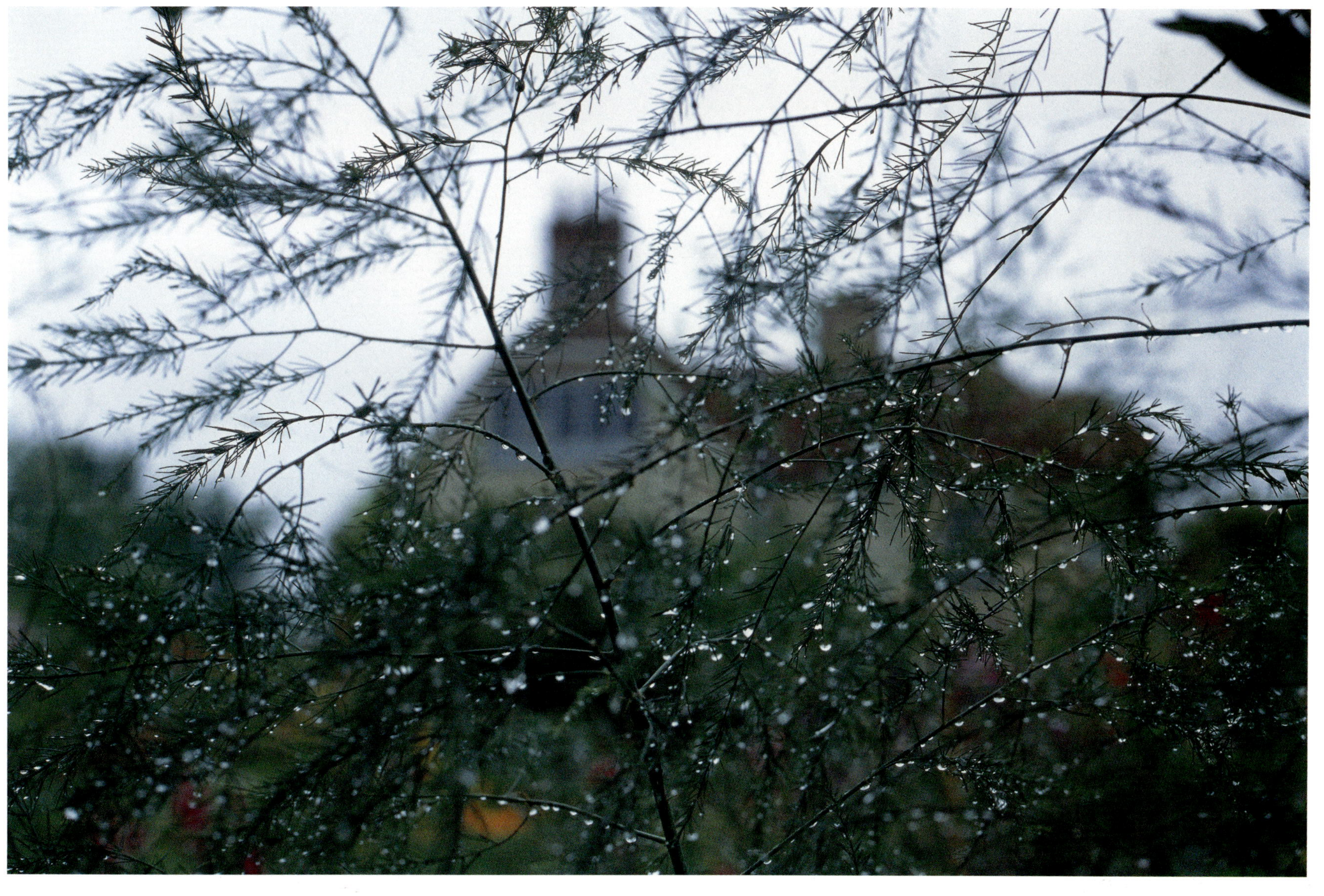

Plums (left) and apples (right)

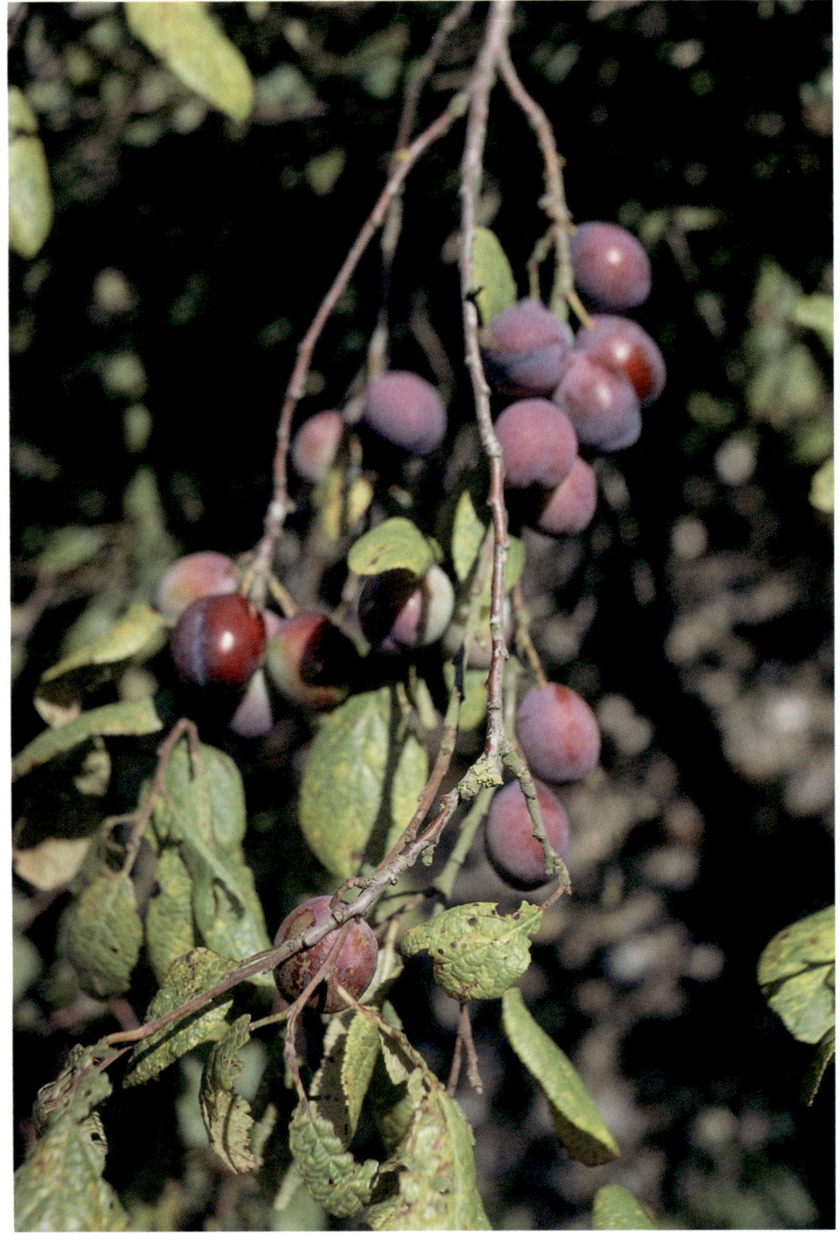

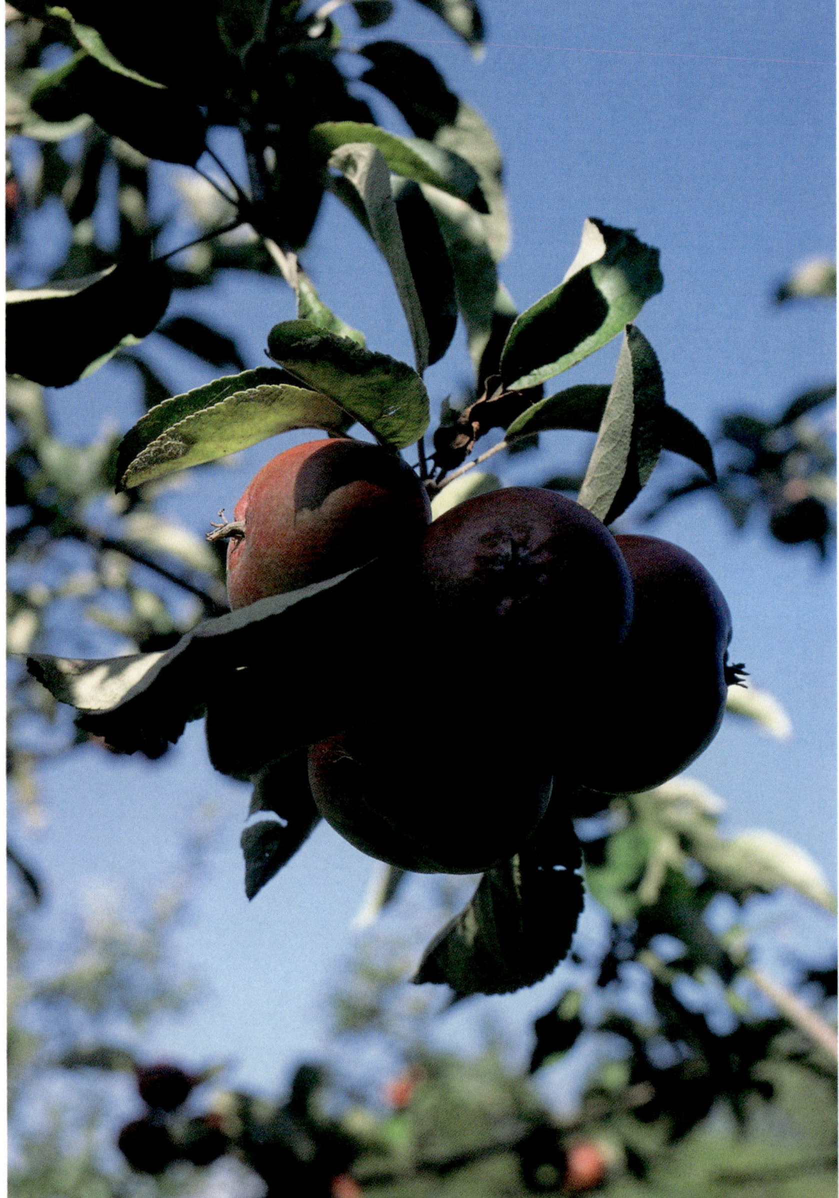

Artichoke flower head (left) and allium flower head (right)

FOLLOWING PAGES CLOCKWISE FROM LEFT
Red hot poker; *Ligularia dentata* 'Desdemona'; tiger lily; oriental poppy and *Iris sibirica*; roses

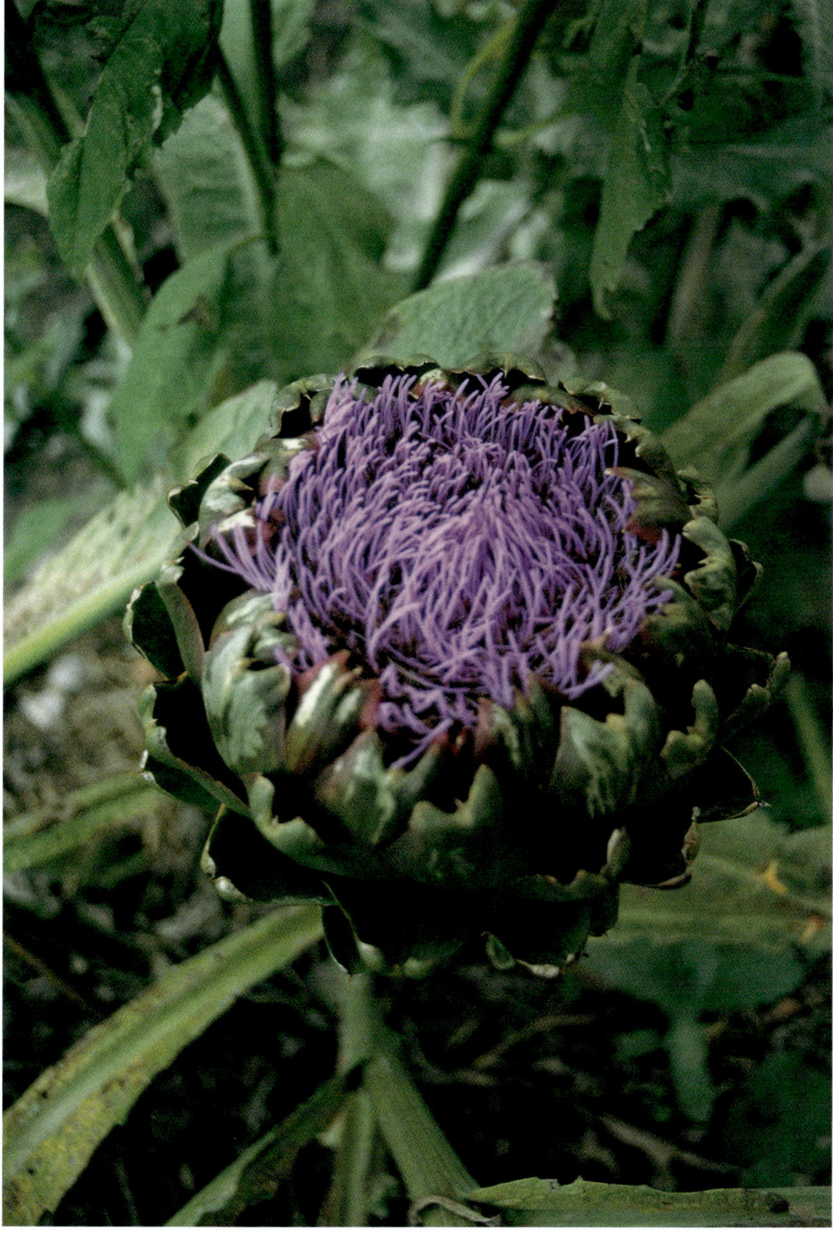

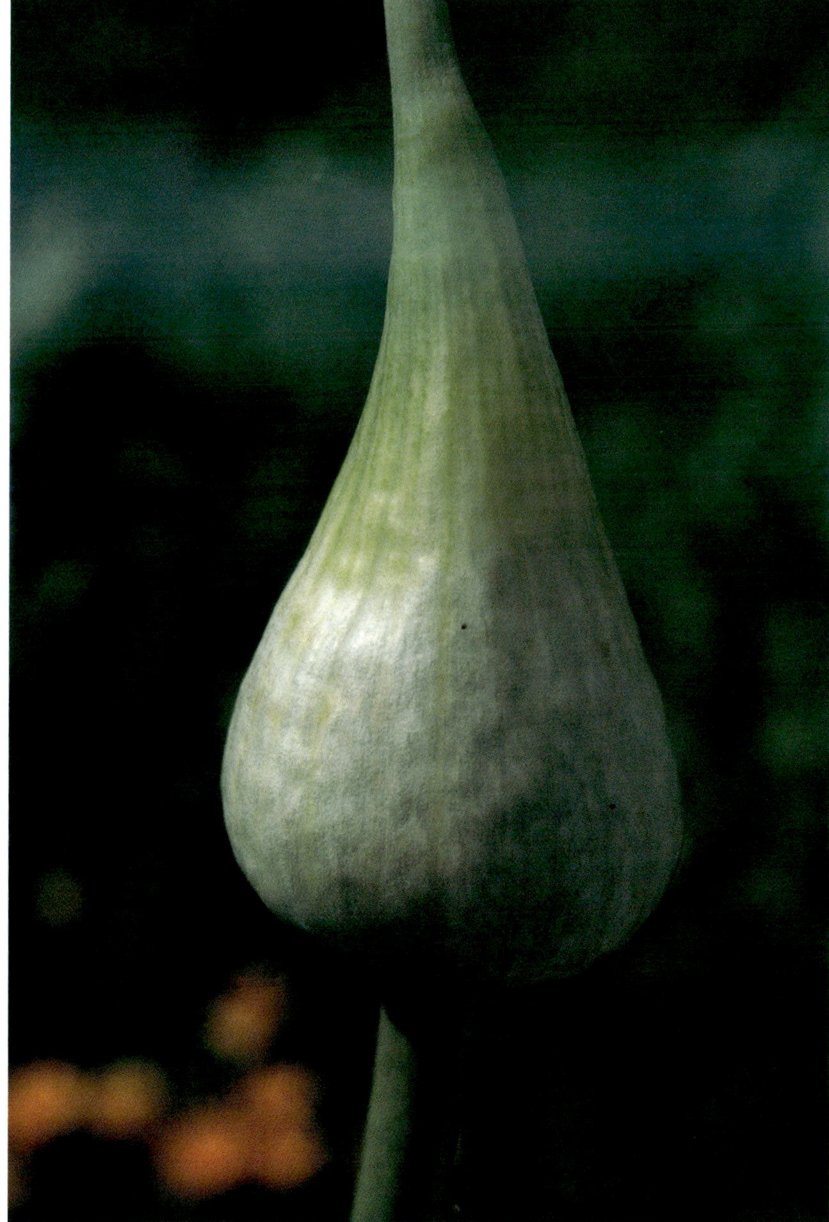

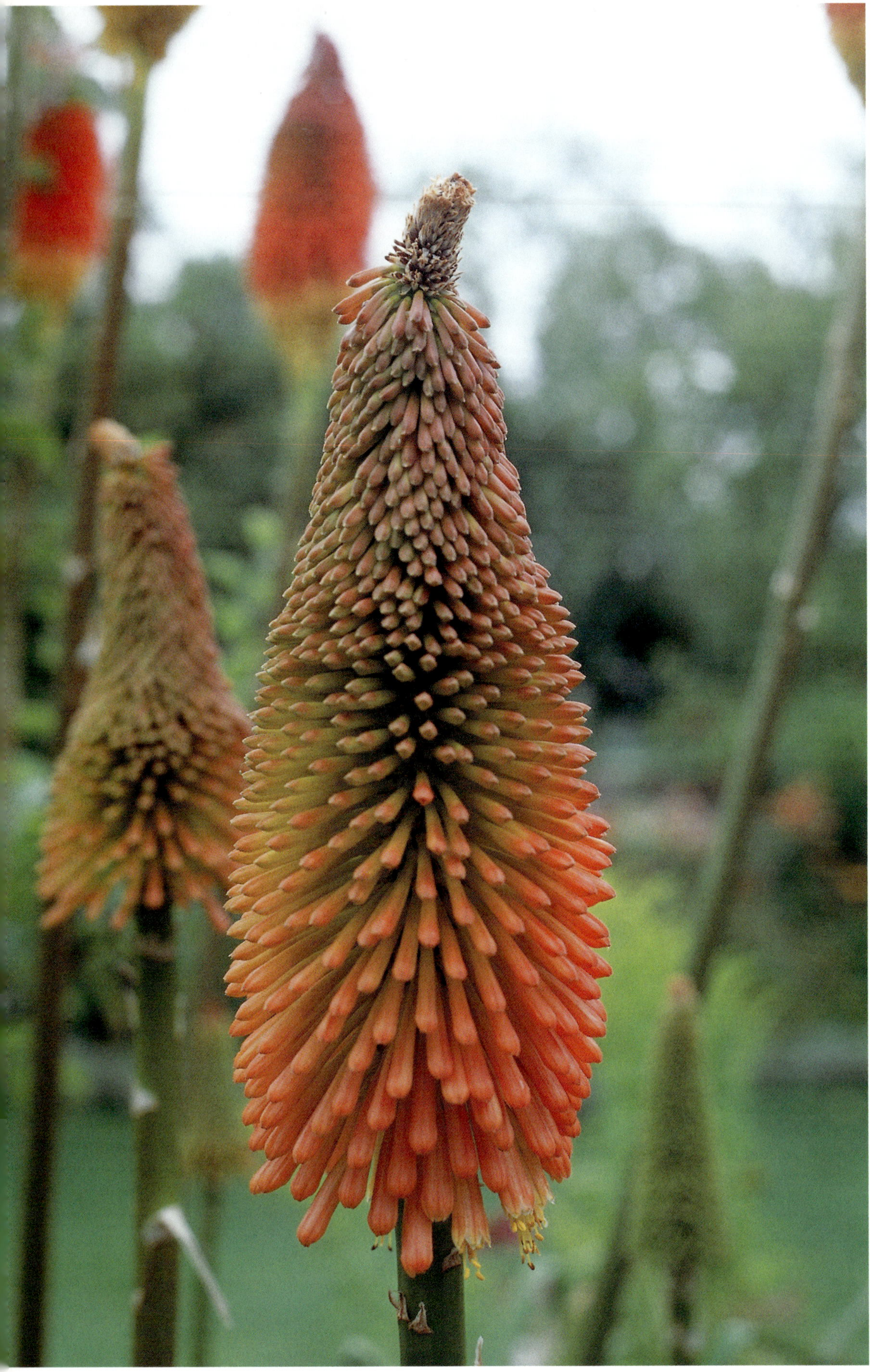

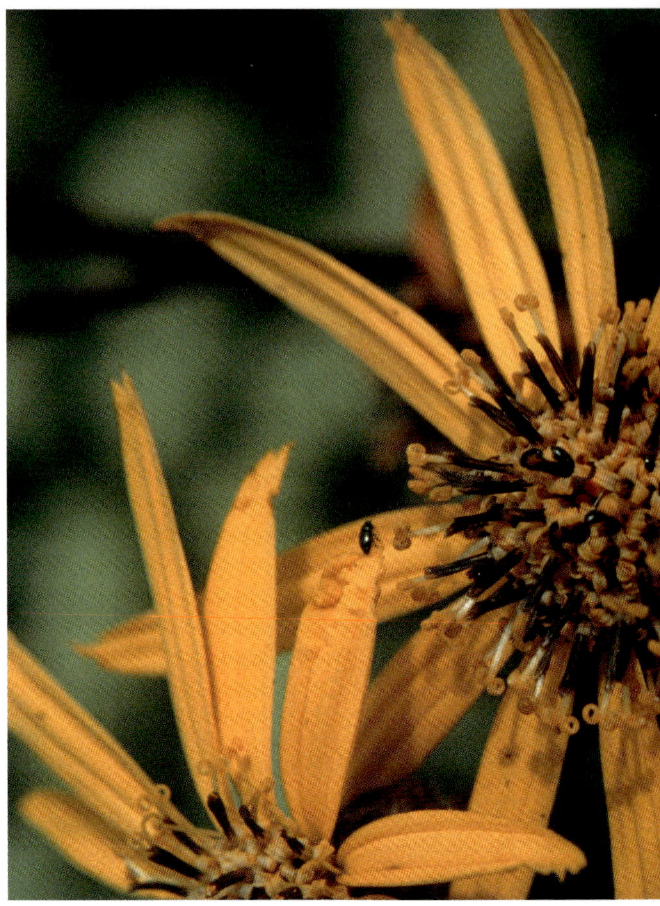

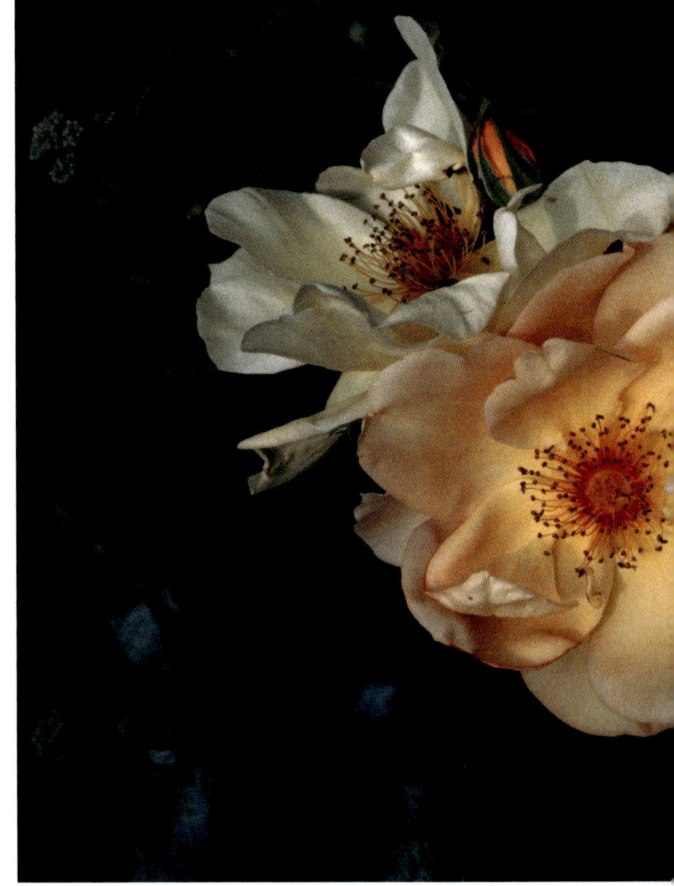

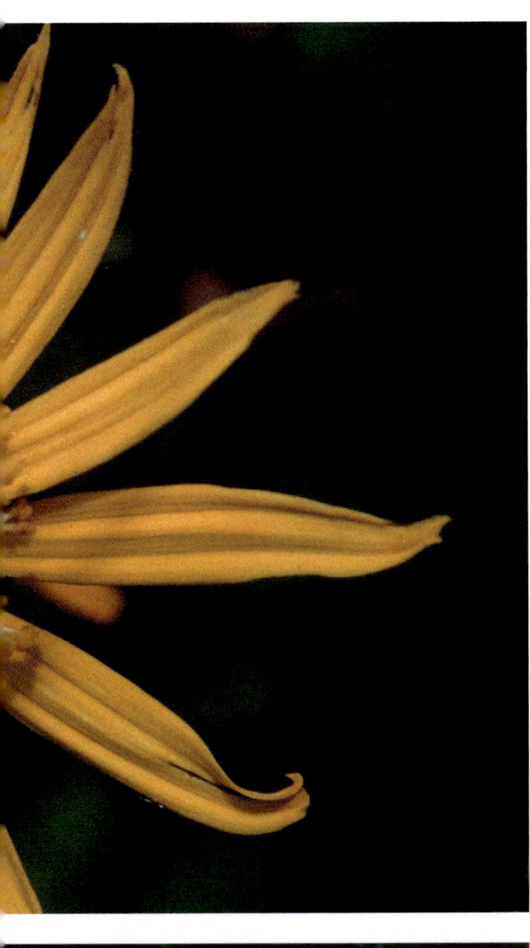
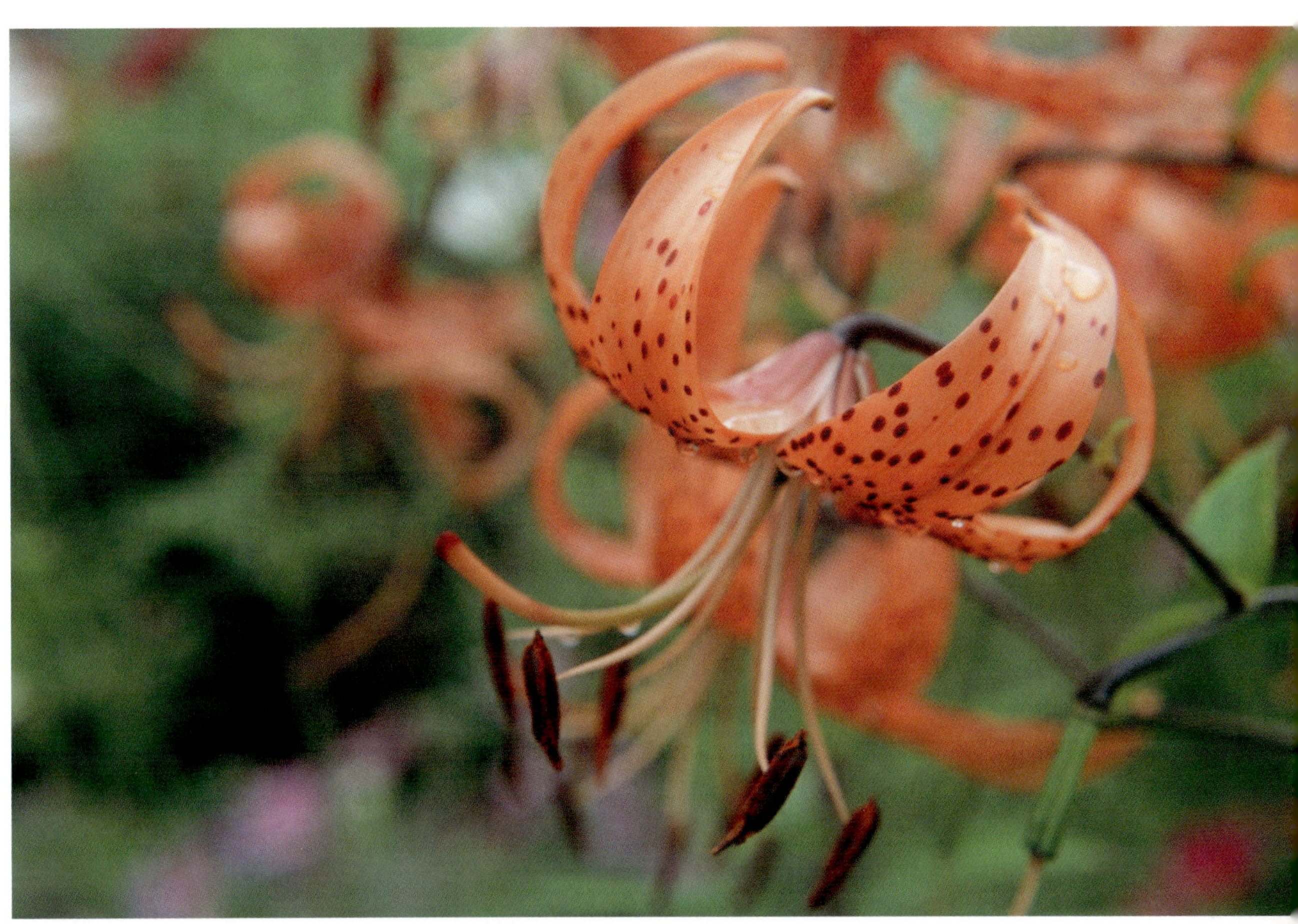
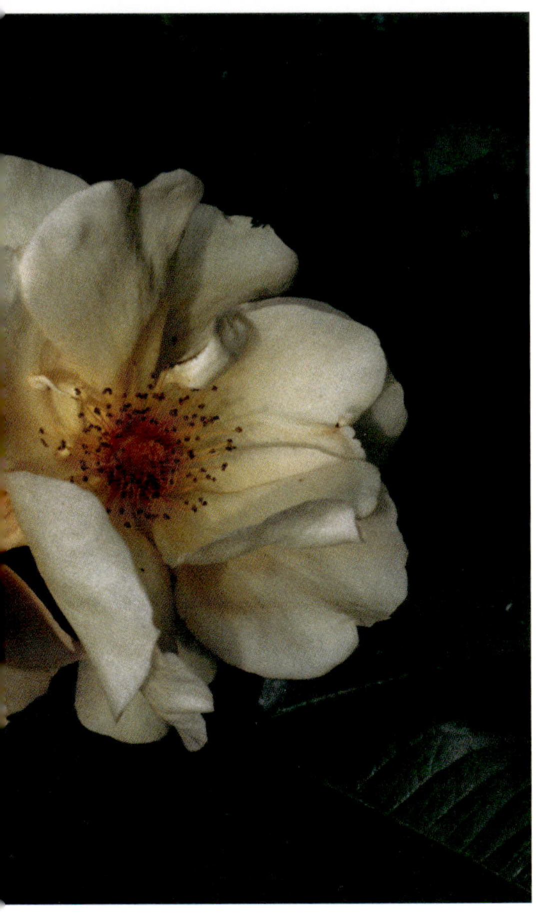
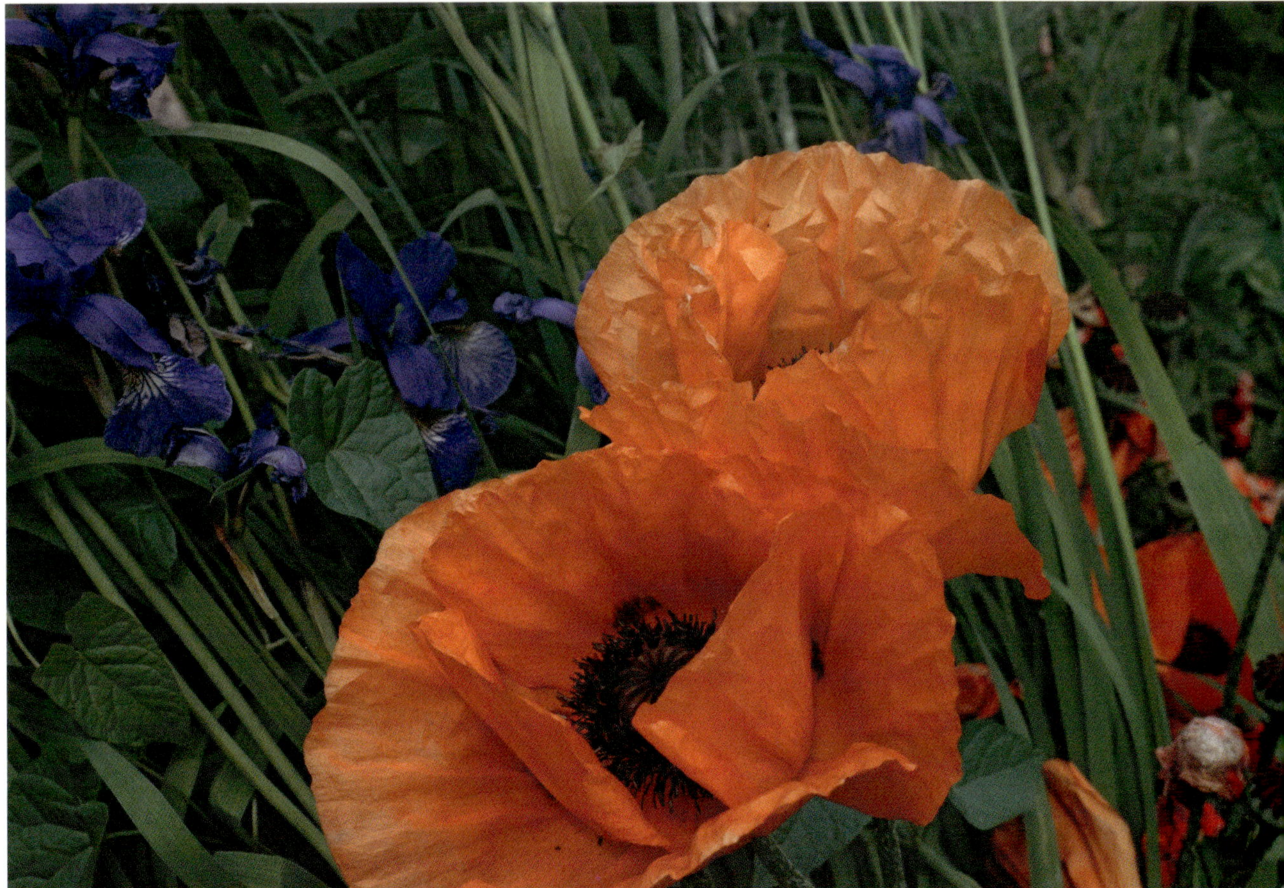

autumn

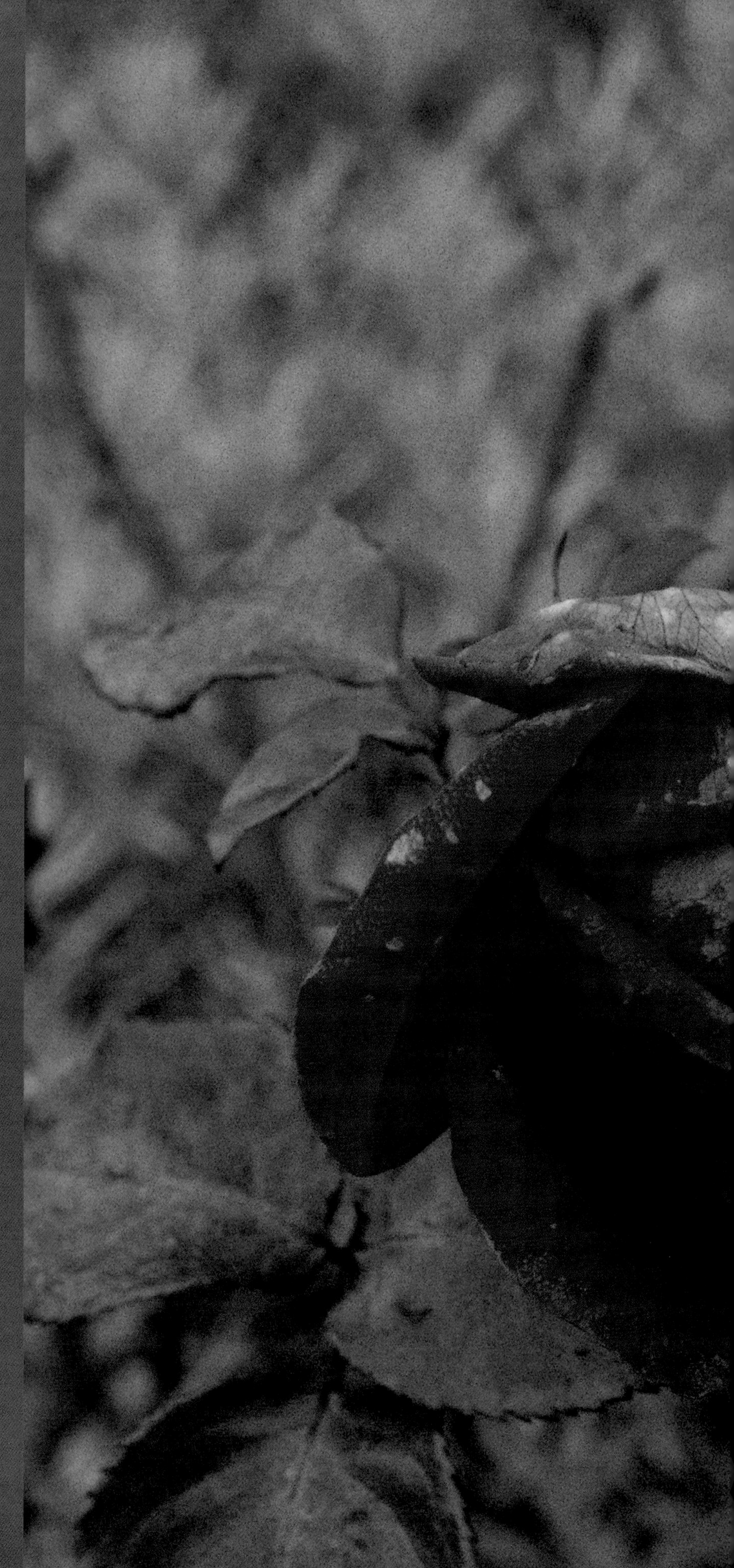

Fading roses

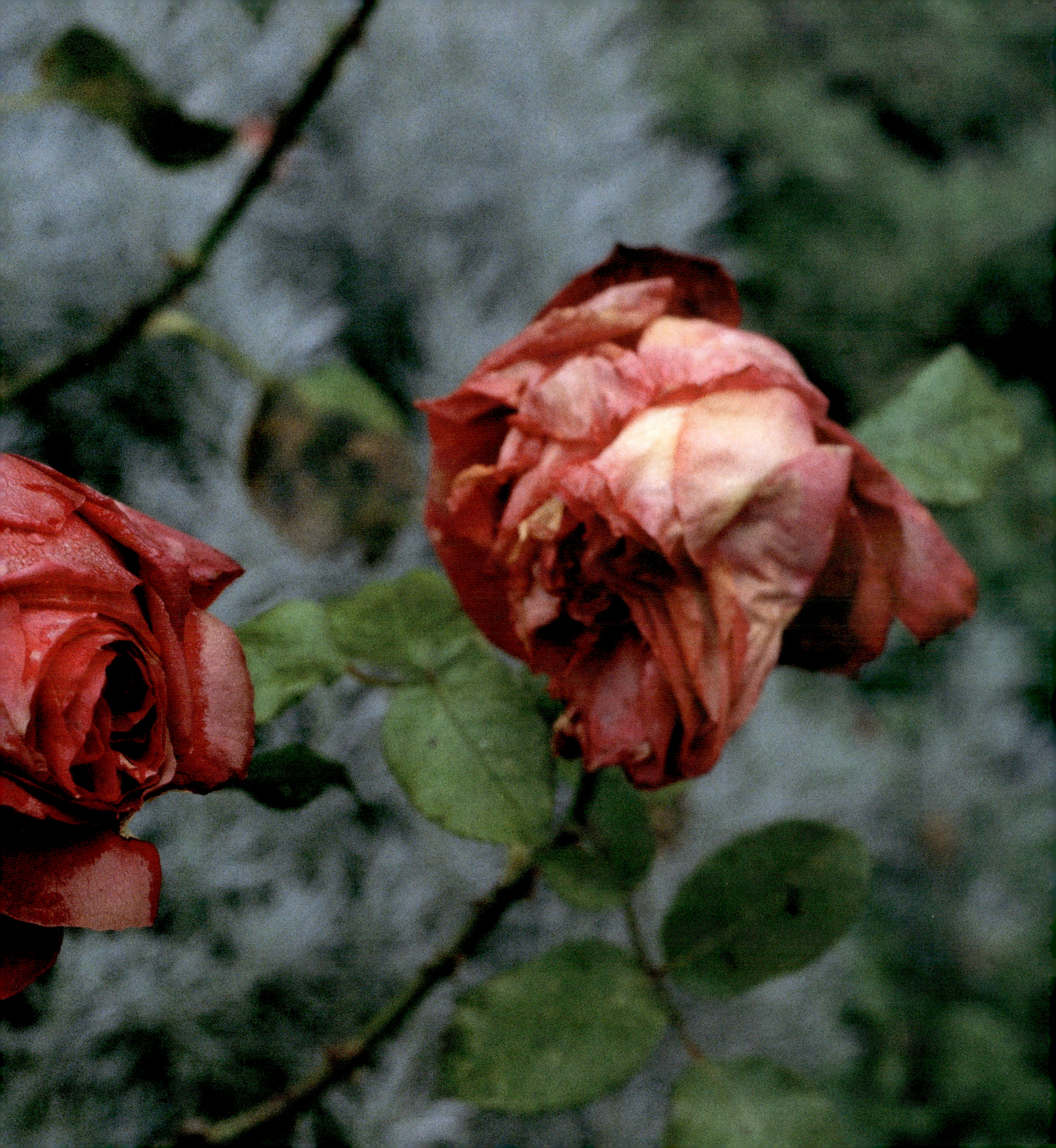

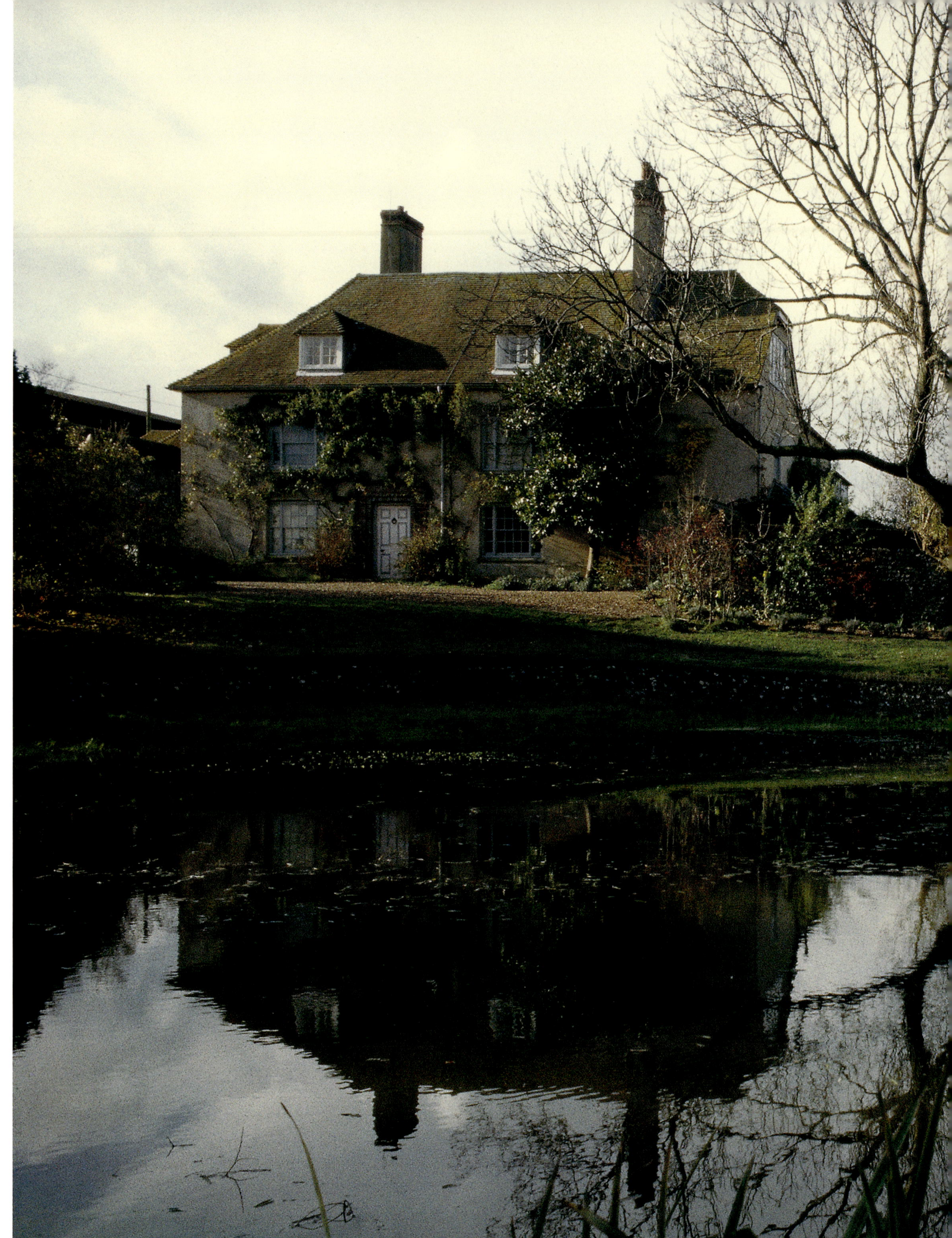

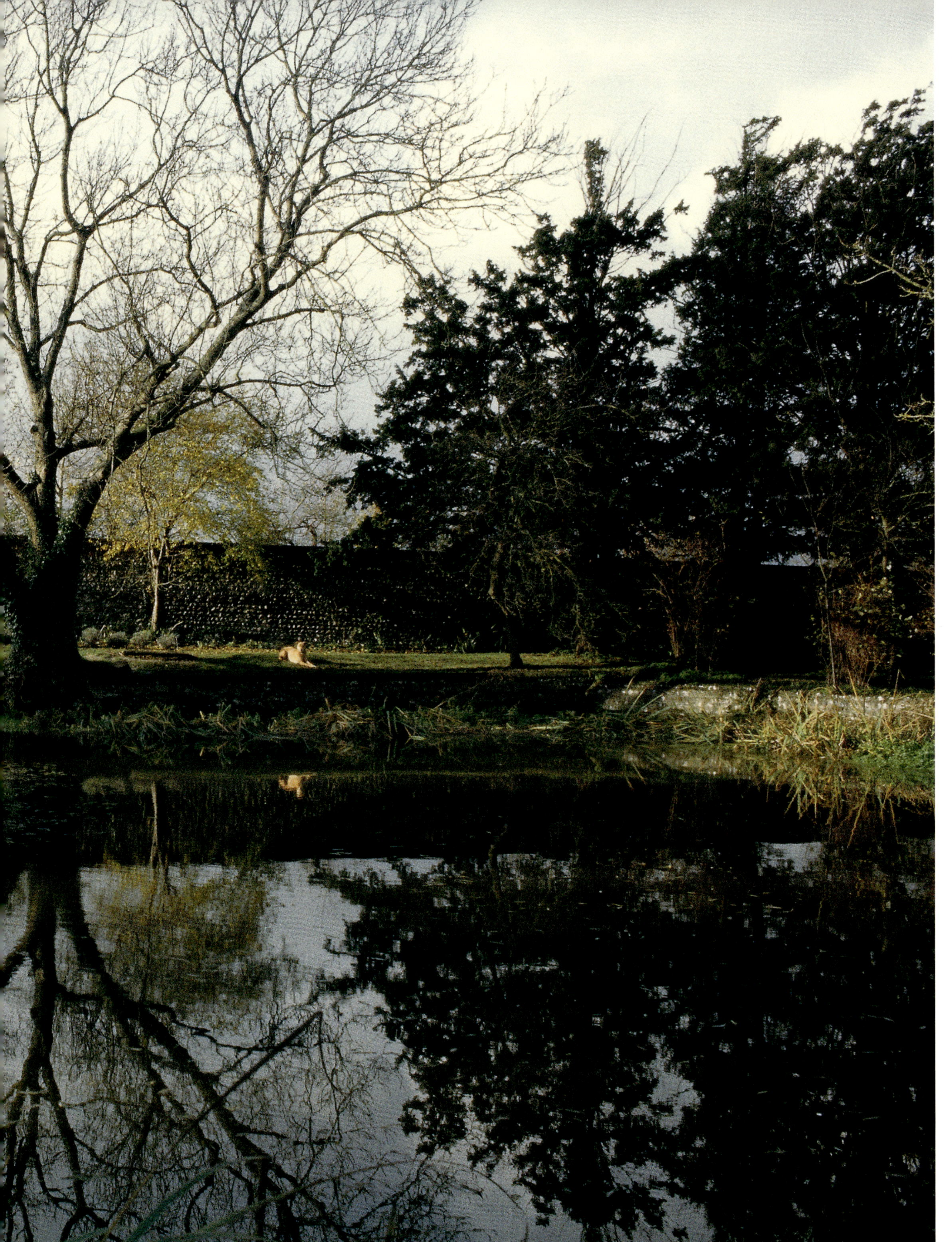

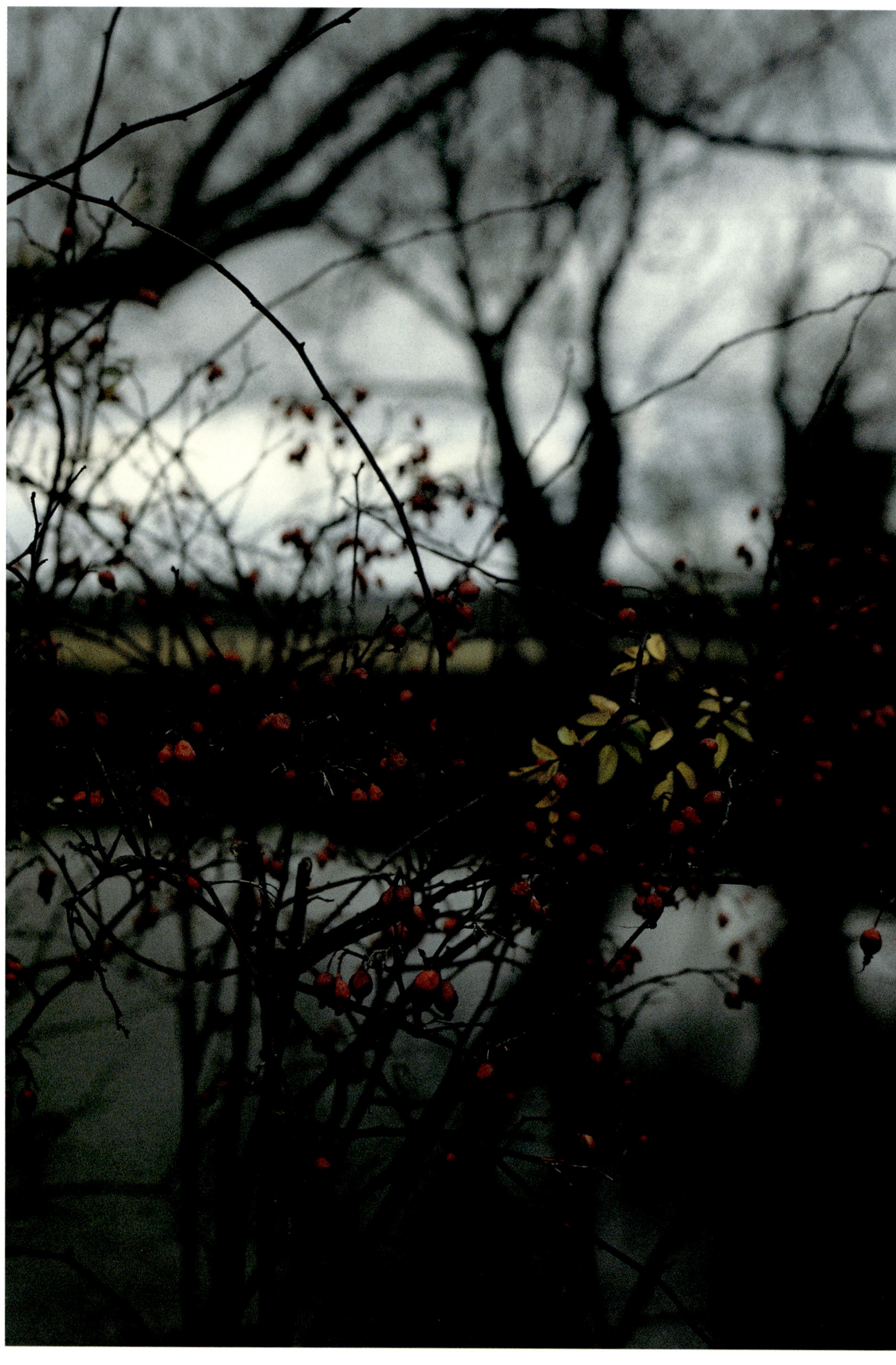

Rosehips

Willows and fields

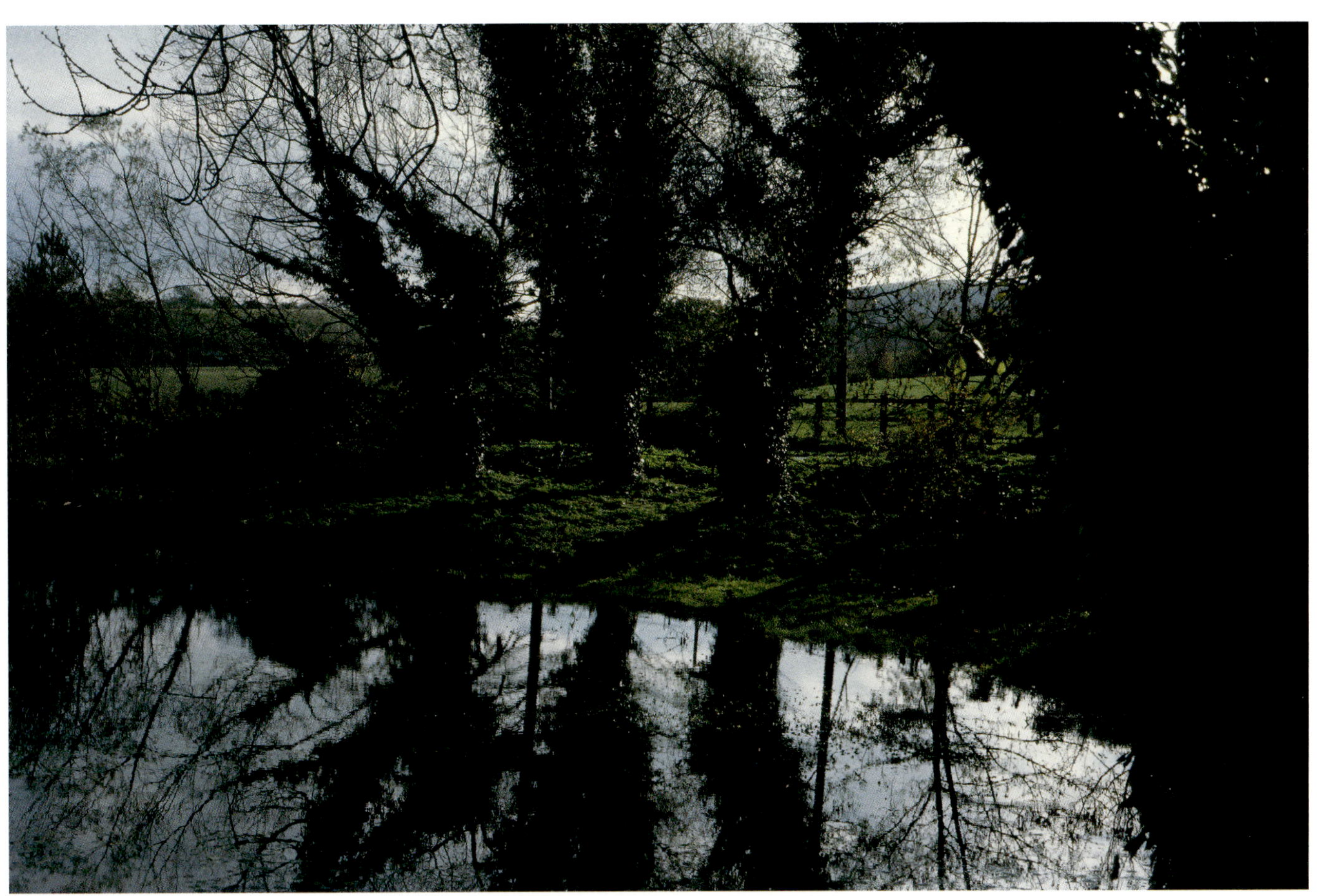

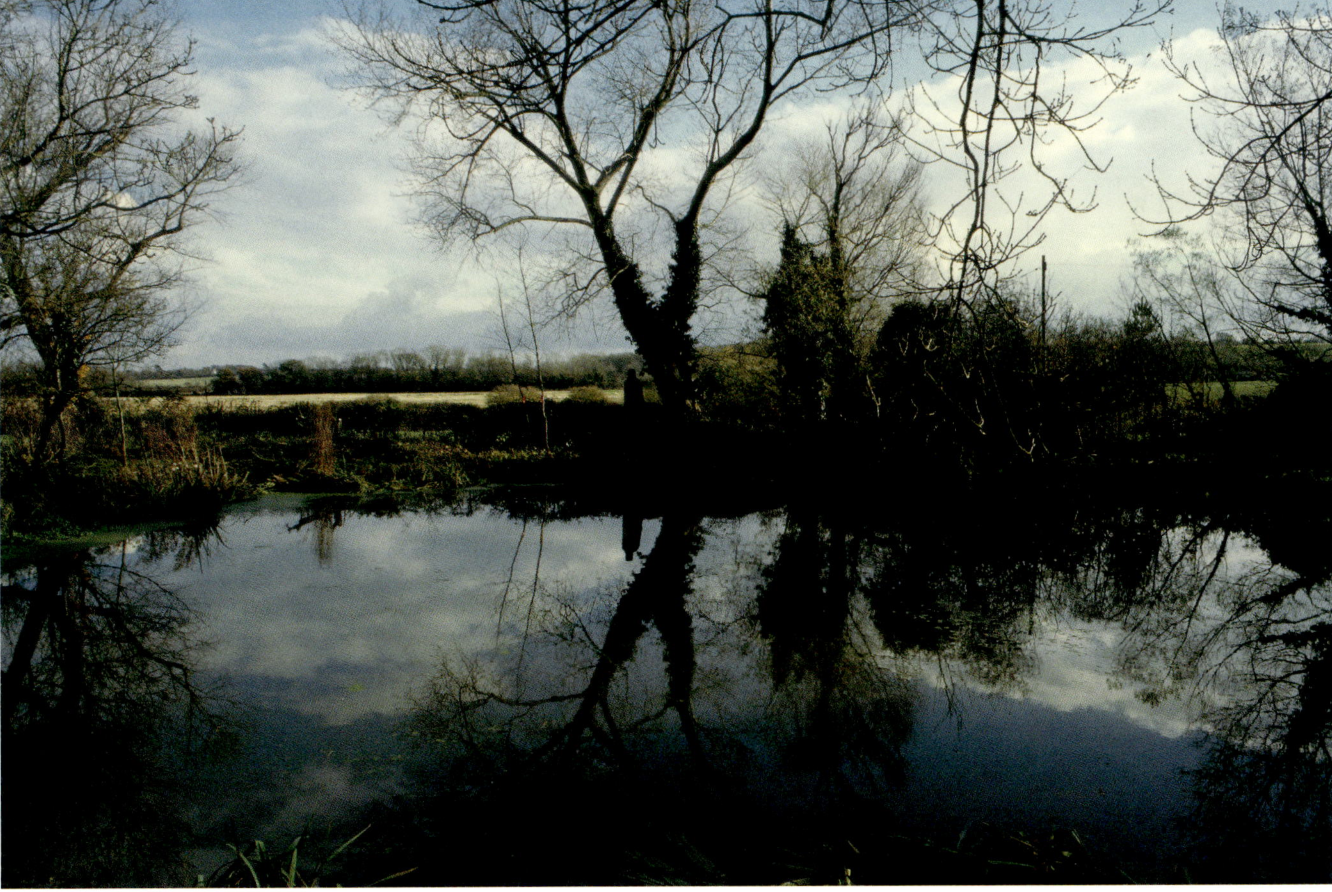

Leaning Female Figure by Quentin Bell

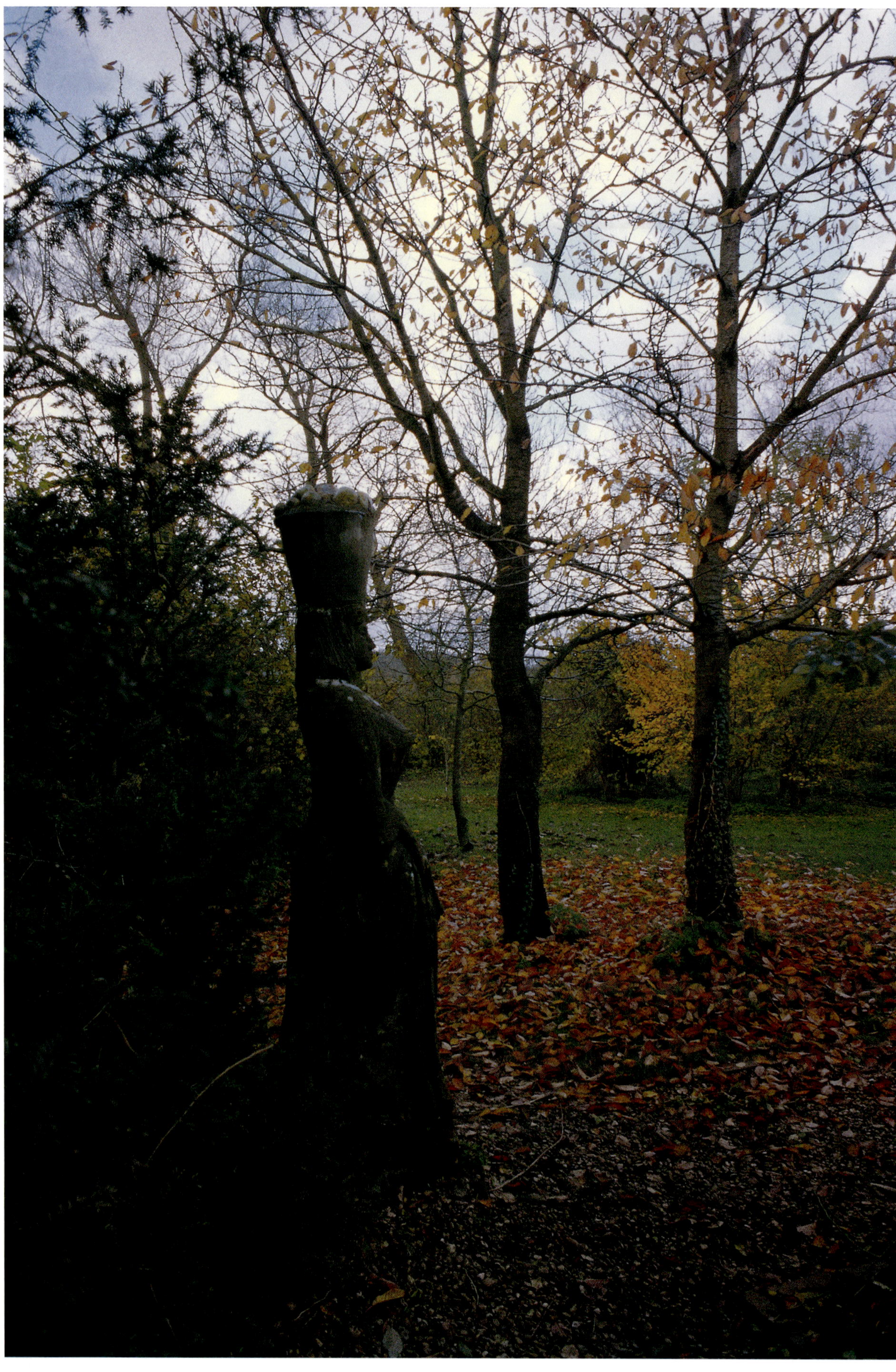

Pomona by Quentin Bell

Cast head

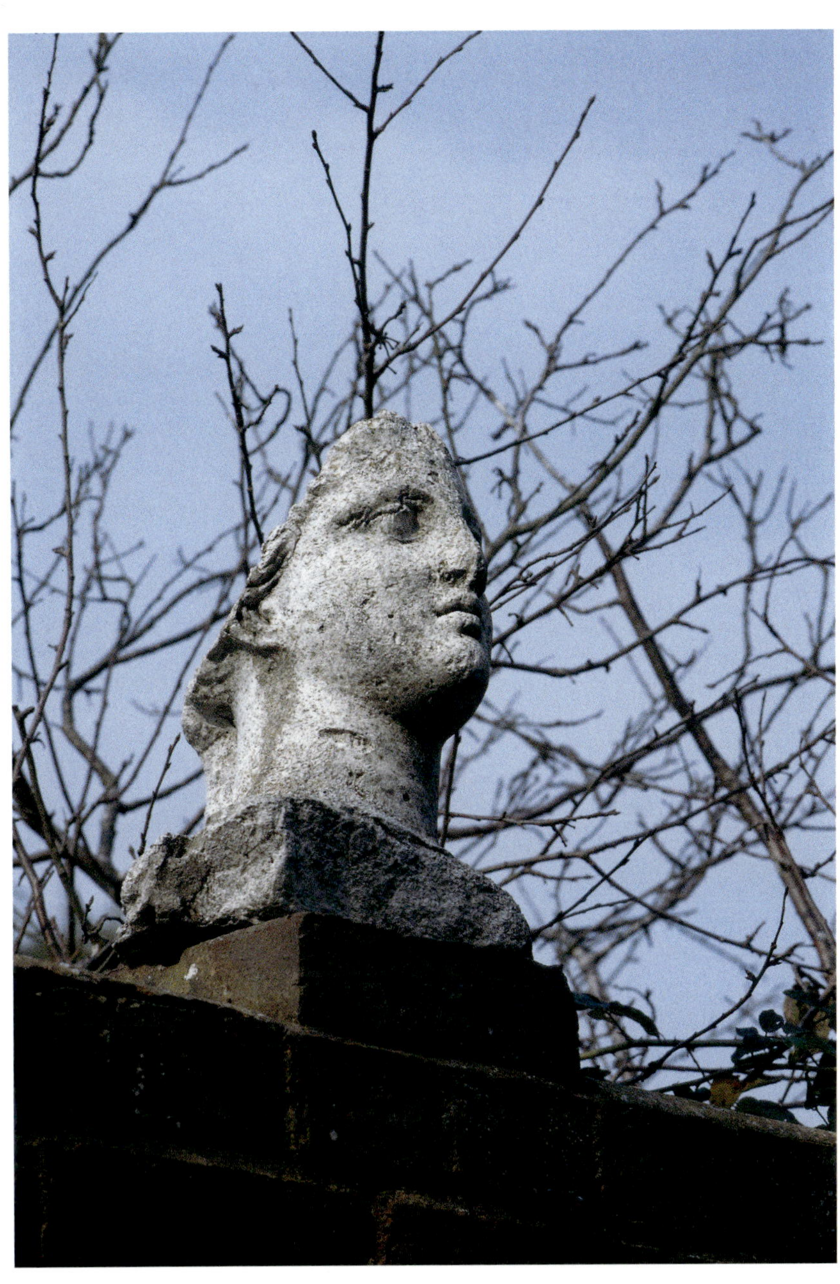

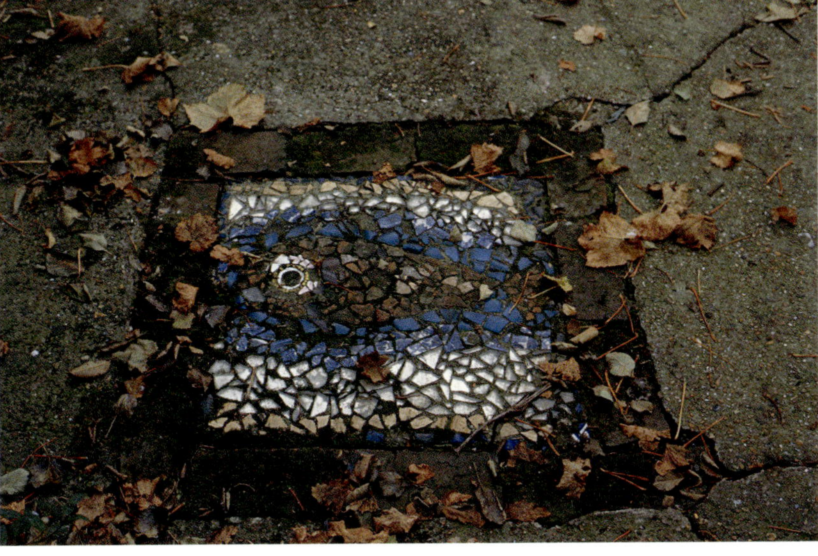

Mosaic fish by Vanessa Bell and Duncan Grant

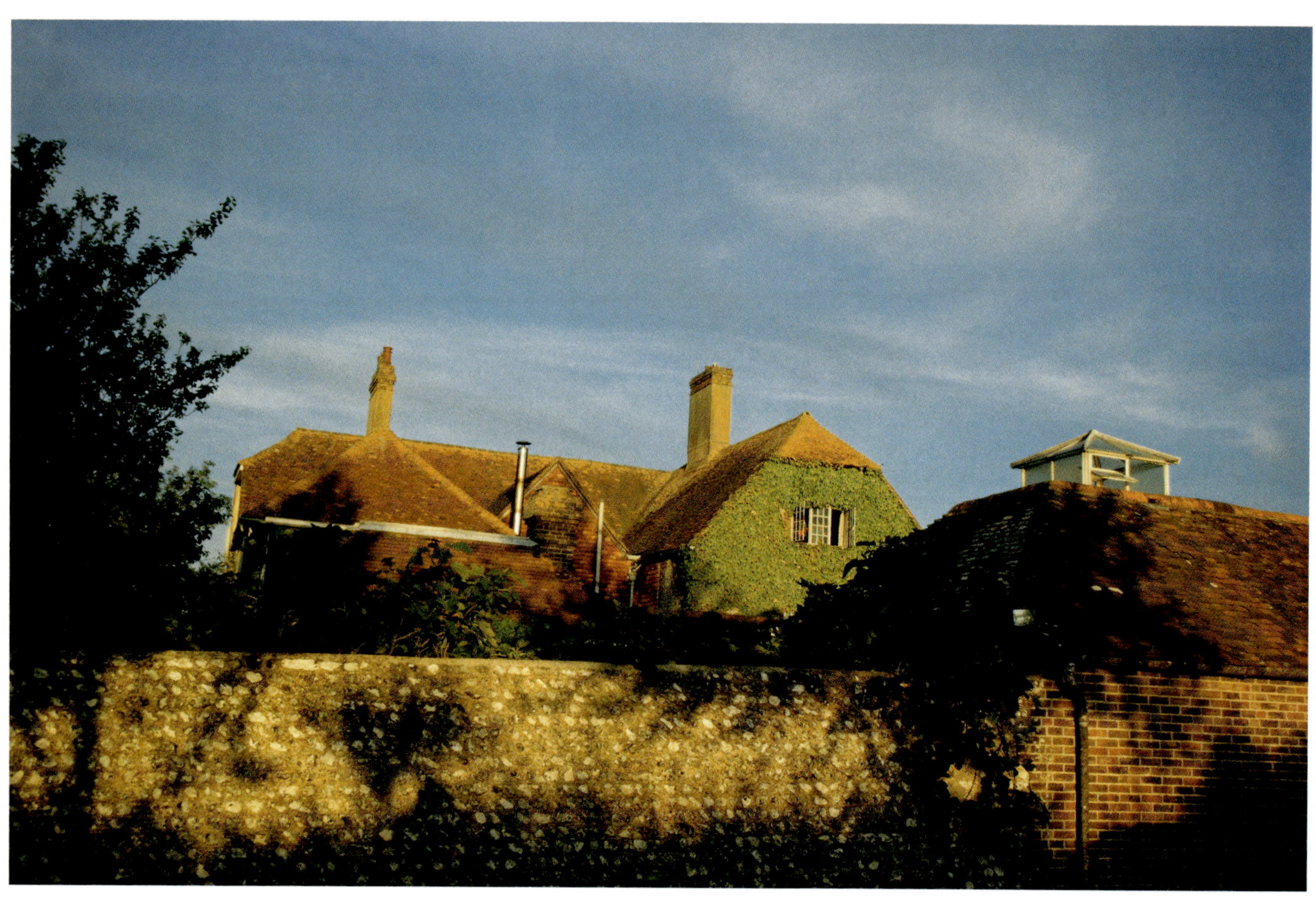

The house with Virginia creeper

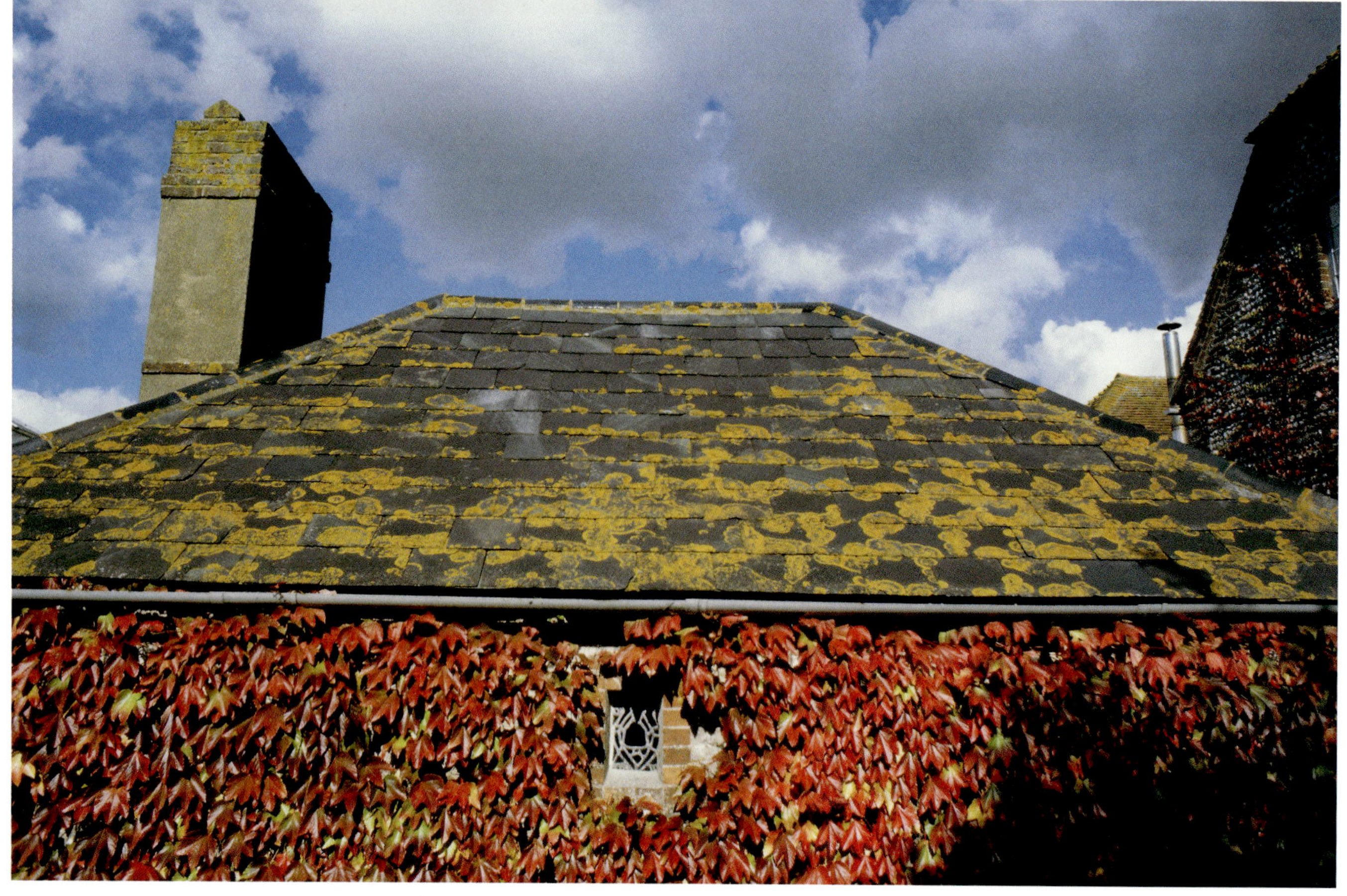

Stained-glass window by Quentin Bell

Hand-painted sign

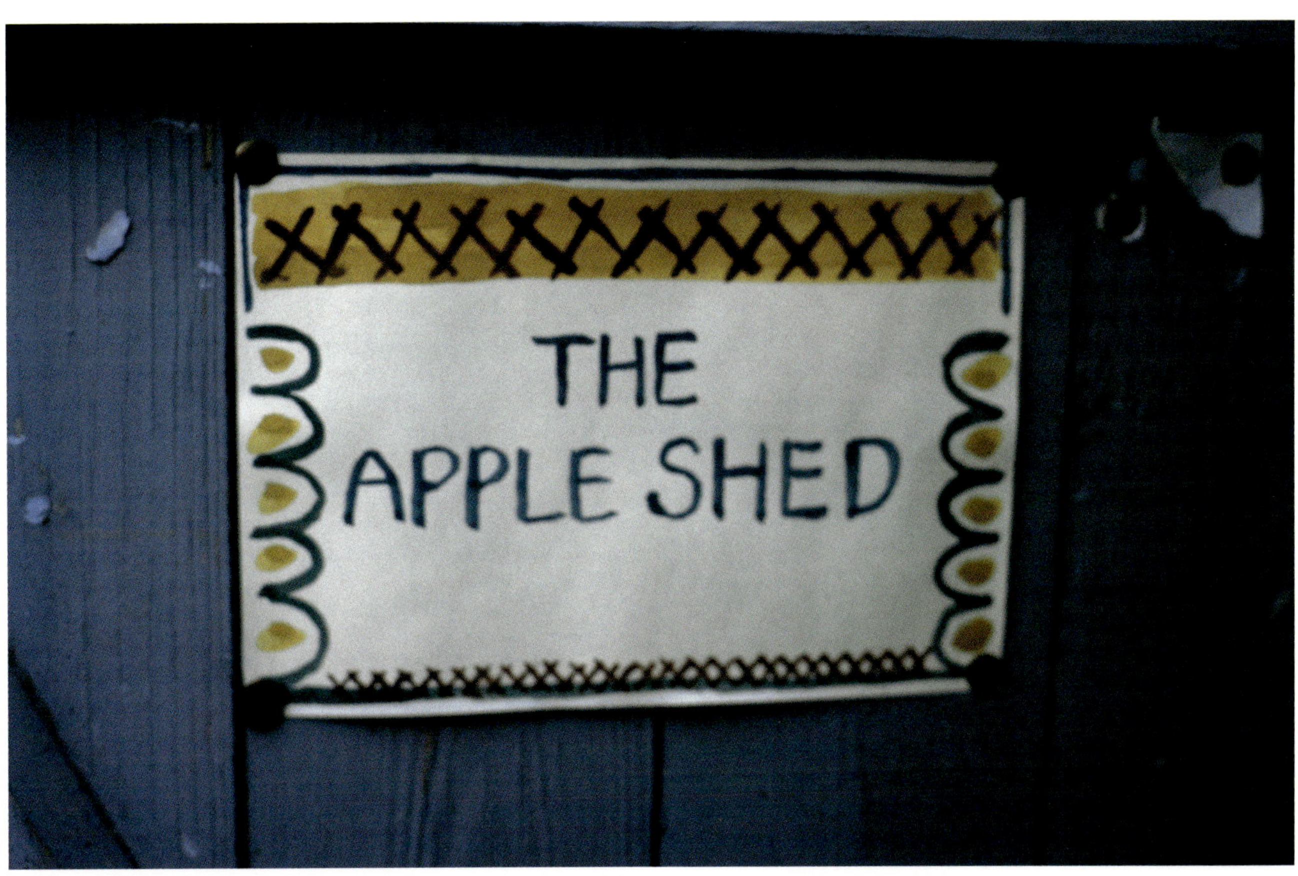

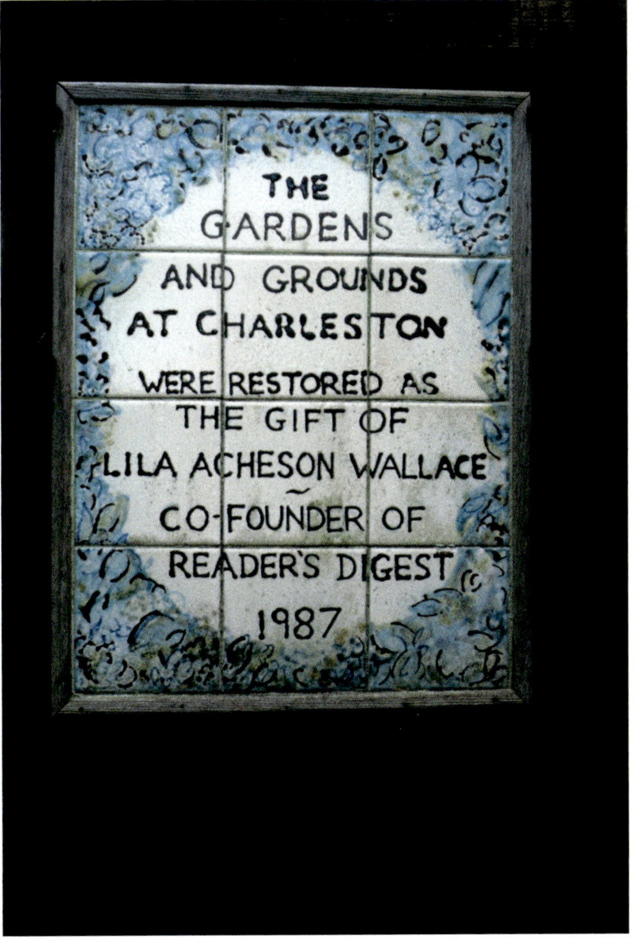

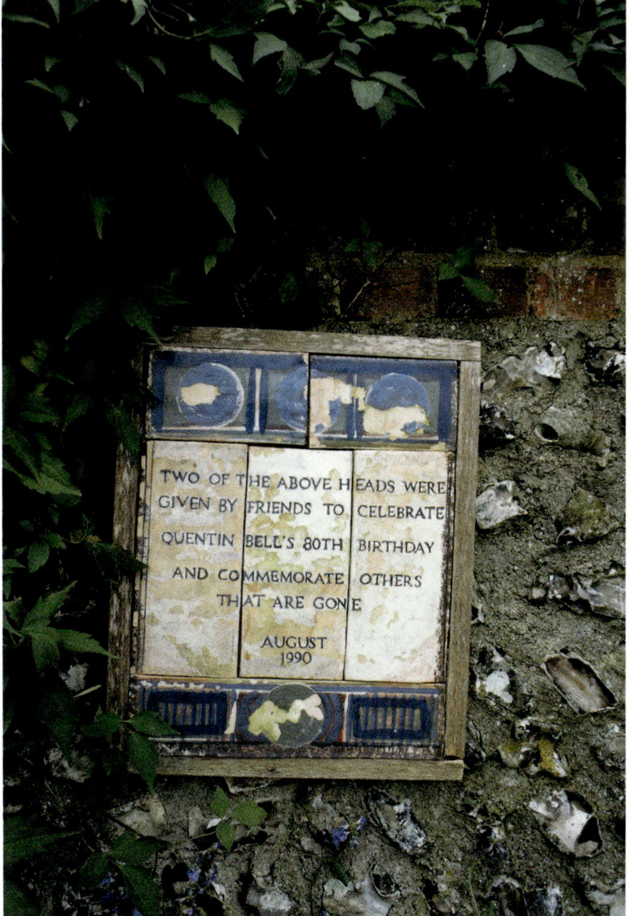

Ceramic plaque by Quentin Bell (left) and plaque to Quentin Bell by Vicki Walton (right)

Front door knocker (left) and postcard of Virginia Woolf by George Charles Beresford in the potting shed (right)

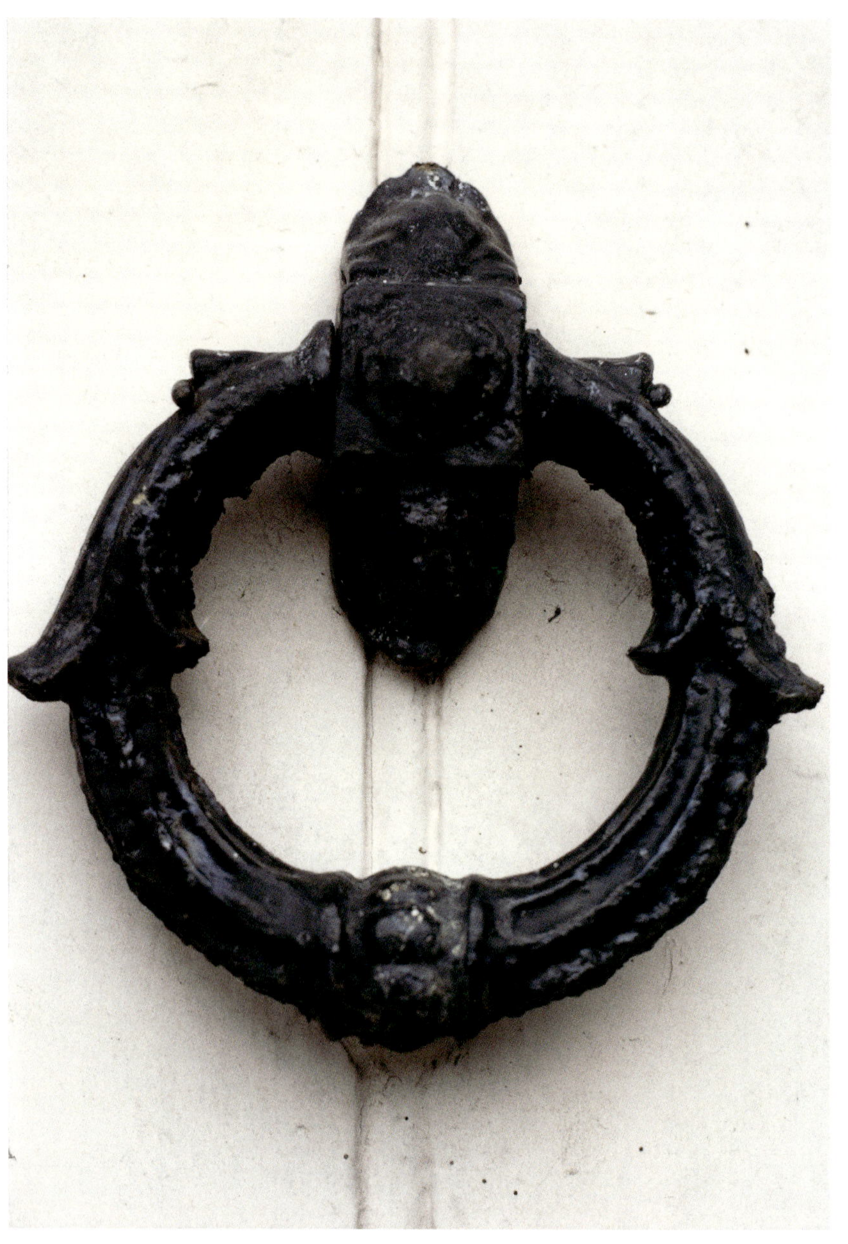

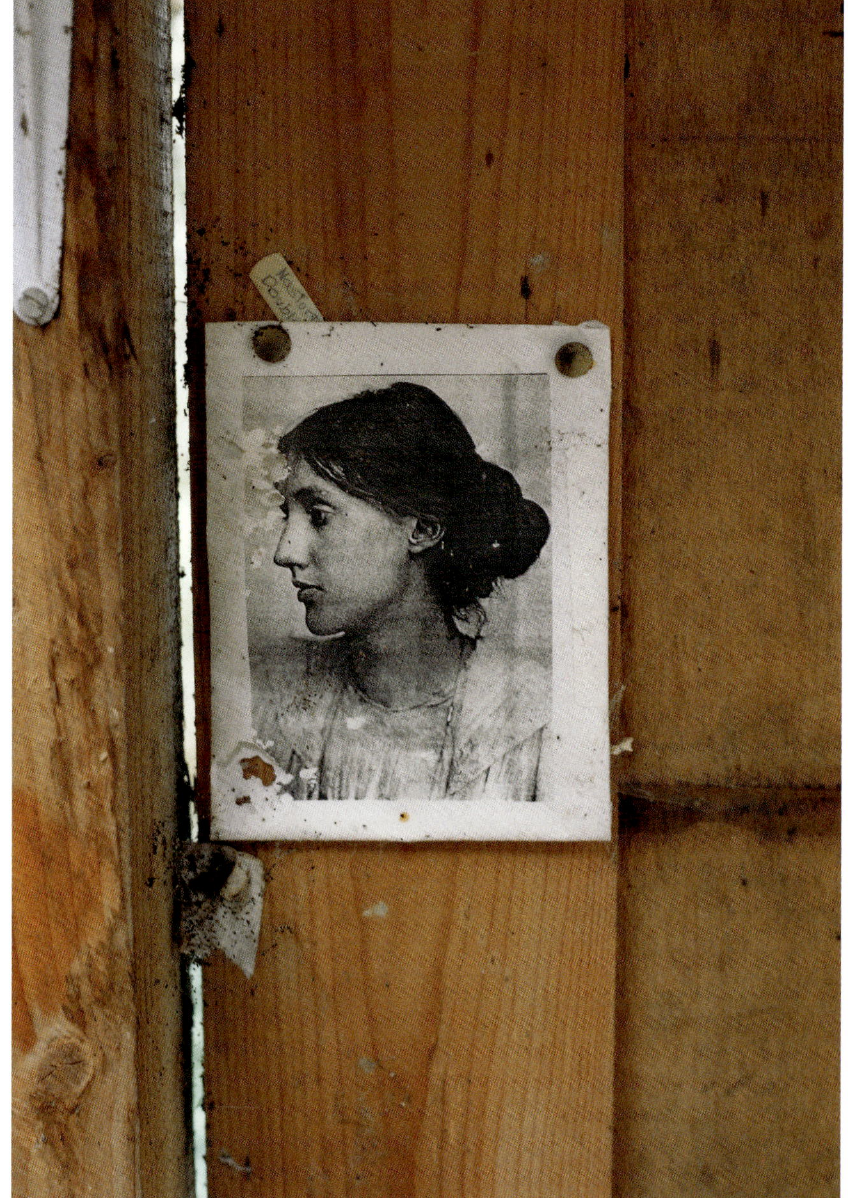

Allium seedheads (left) and faded hydrangeas in the female torso planter (right)

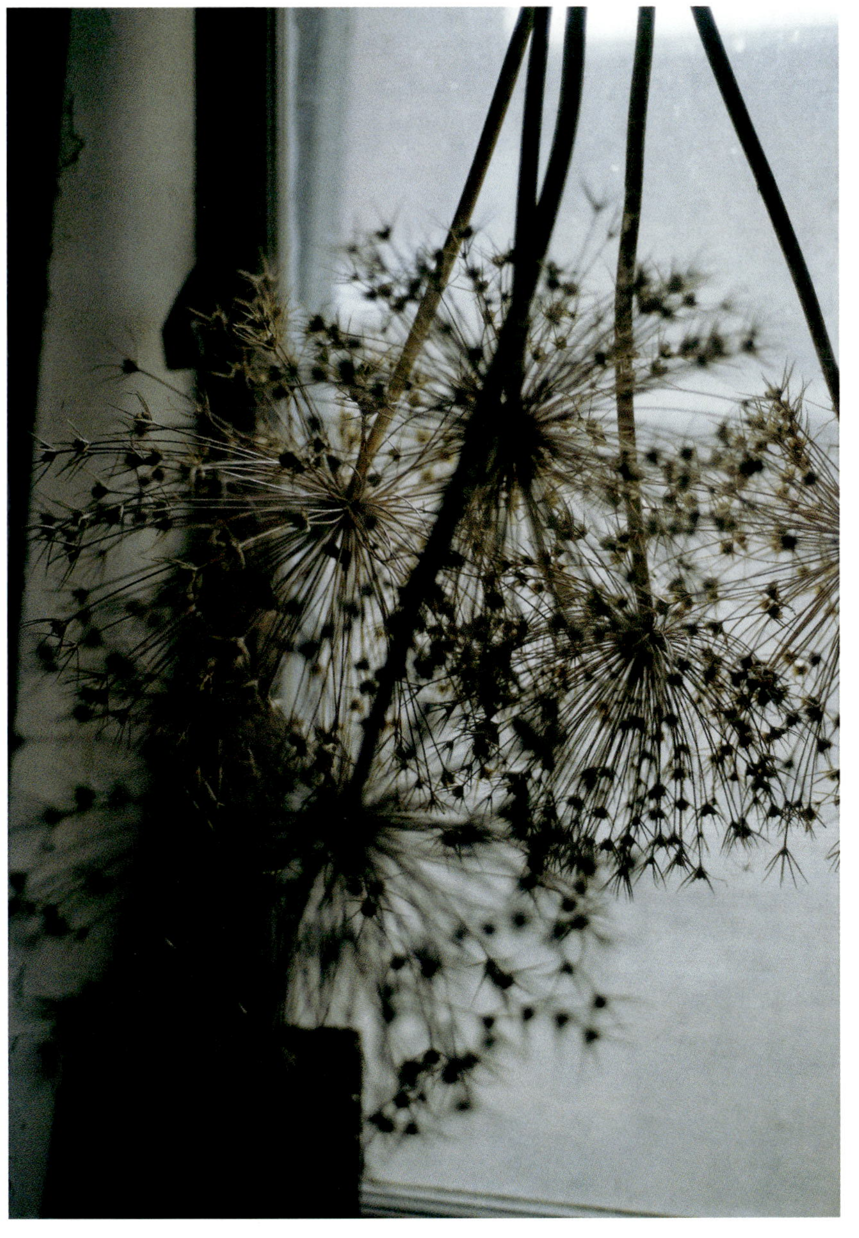

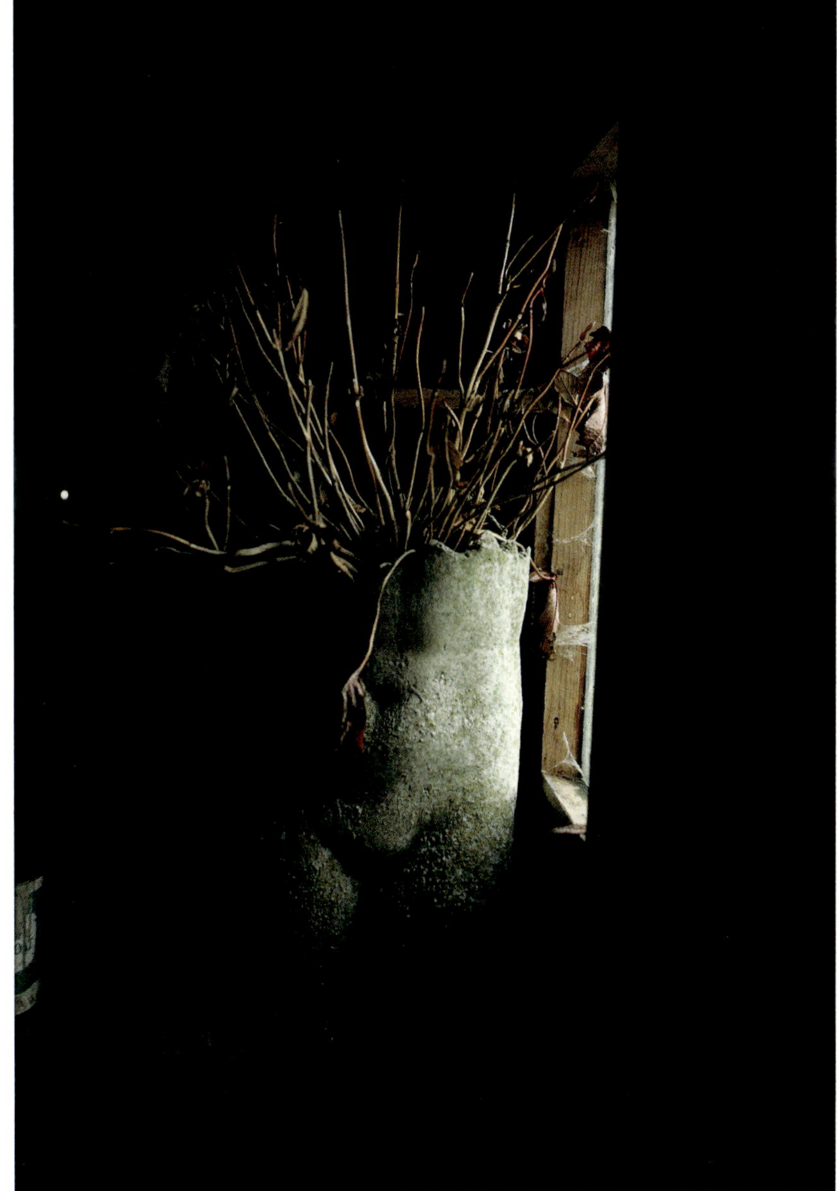

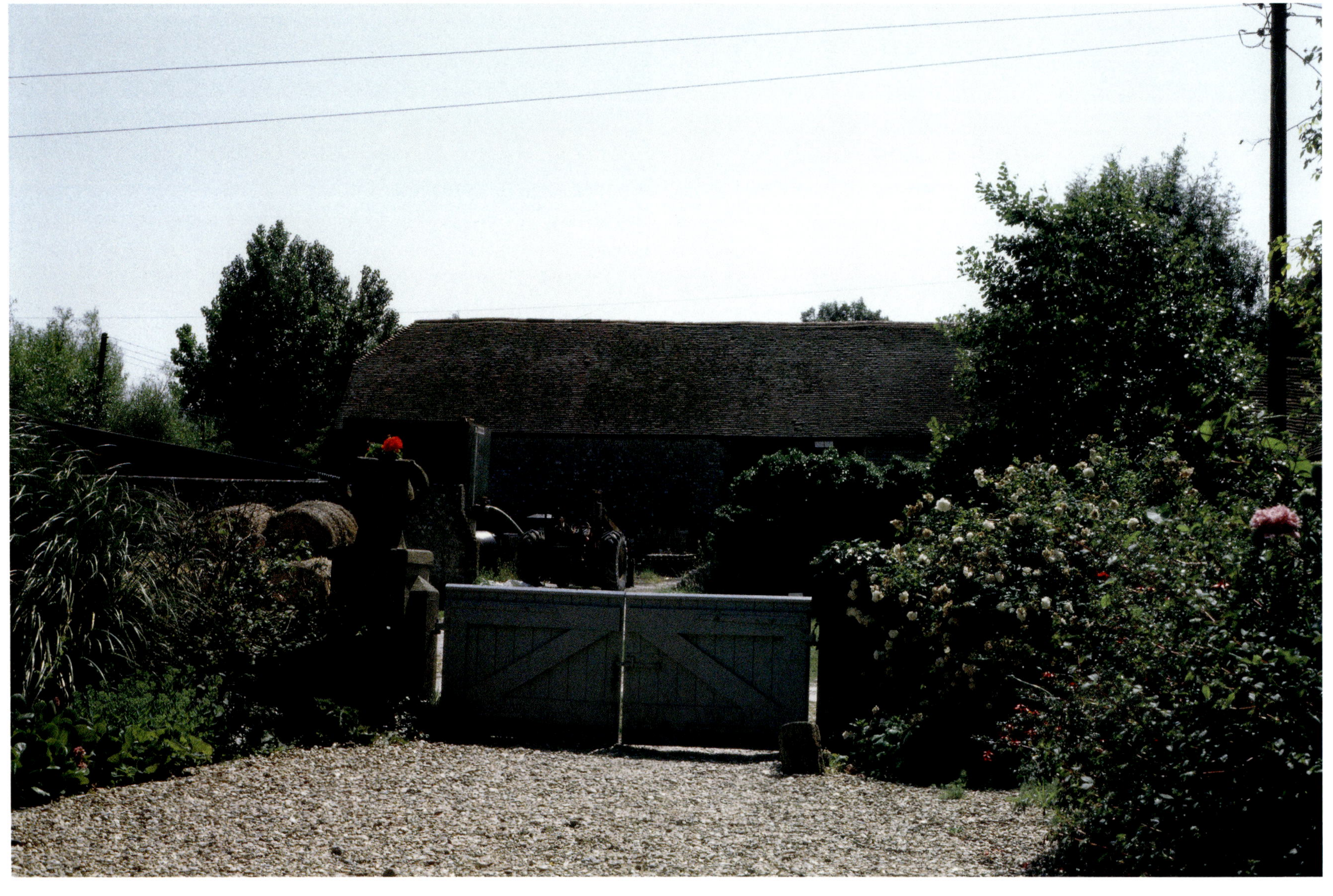

The garden begins to fade

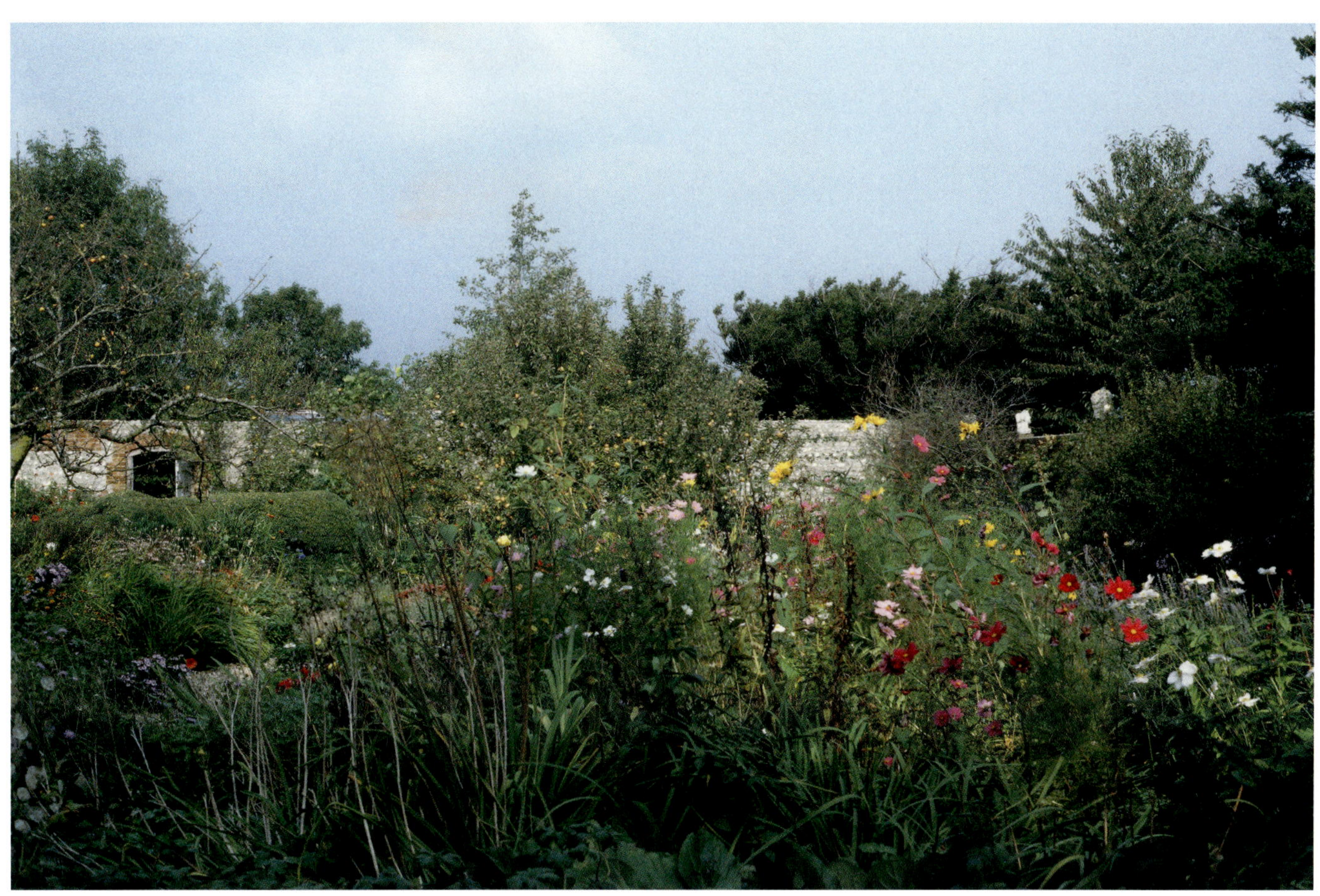

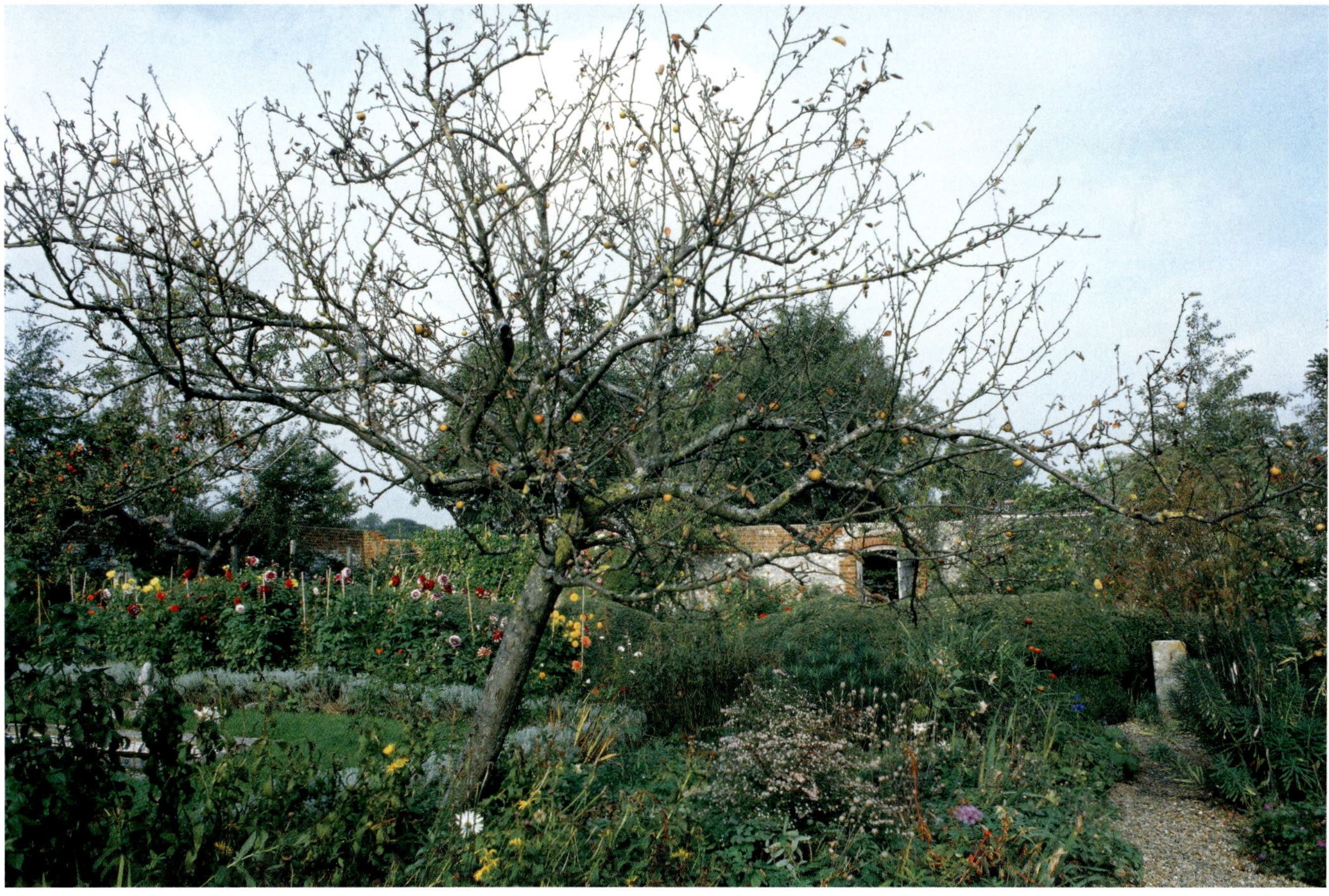

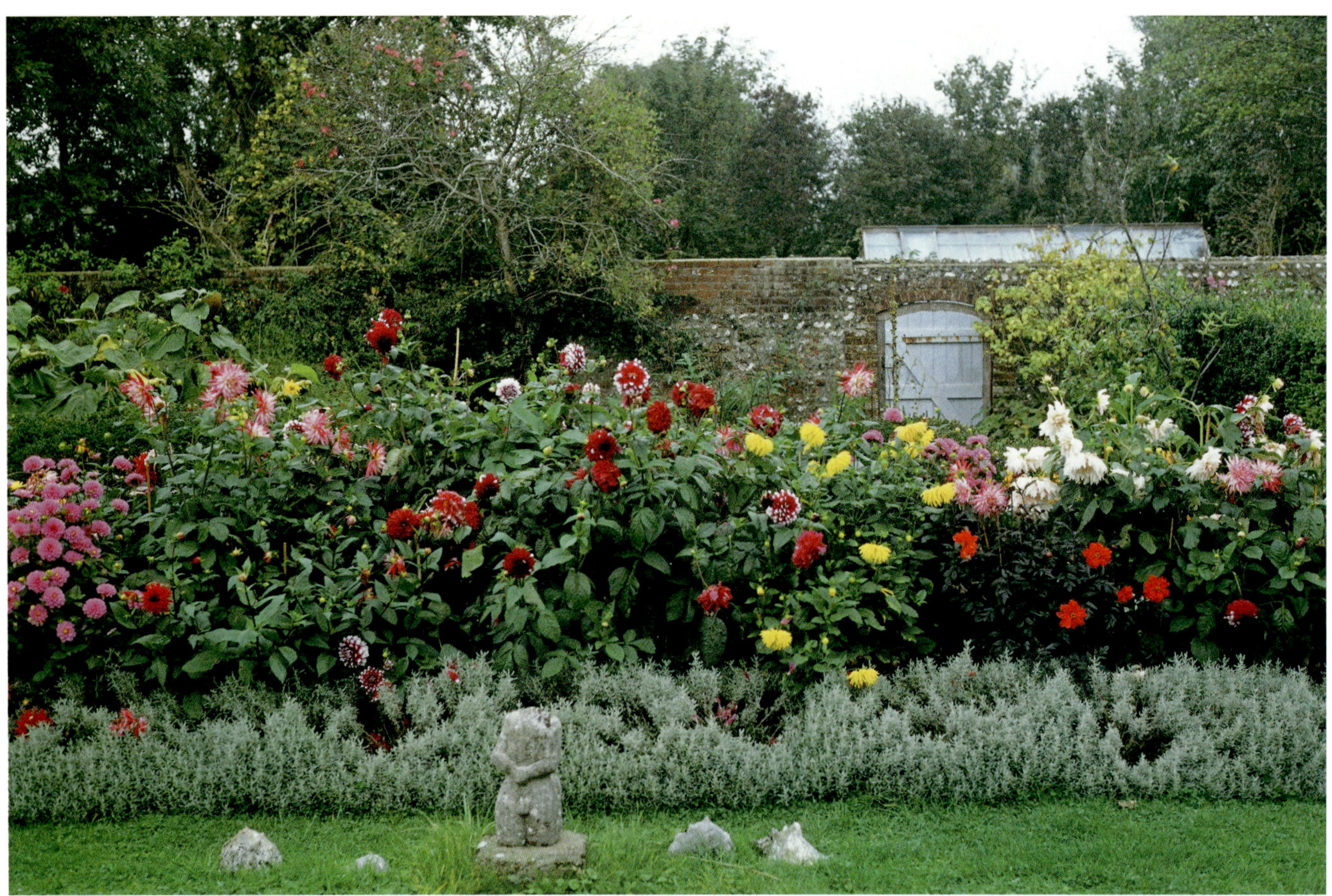

Male nude by John Skeaping with dahlias

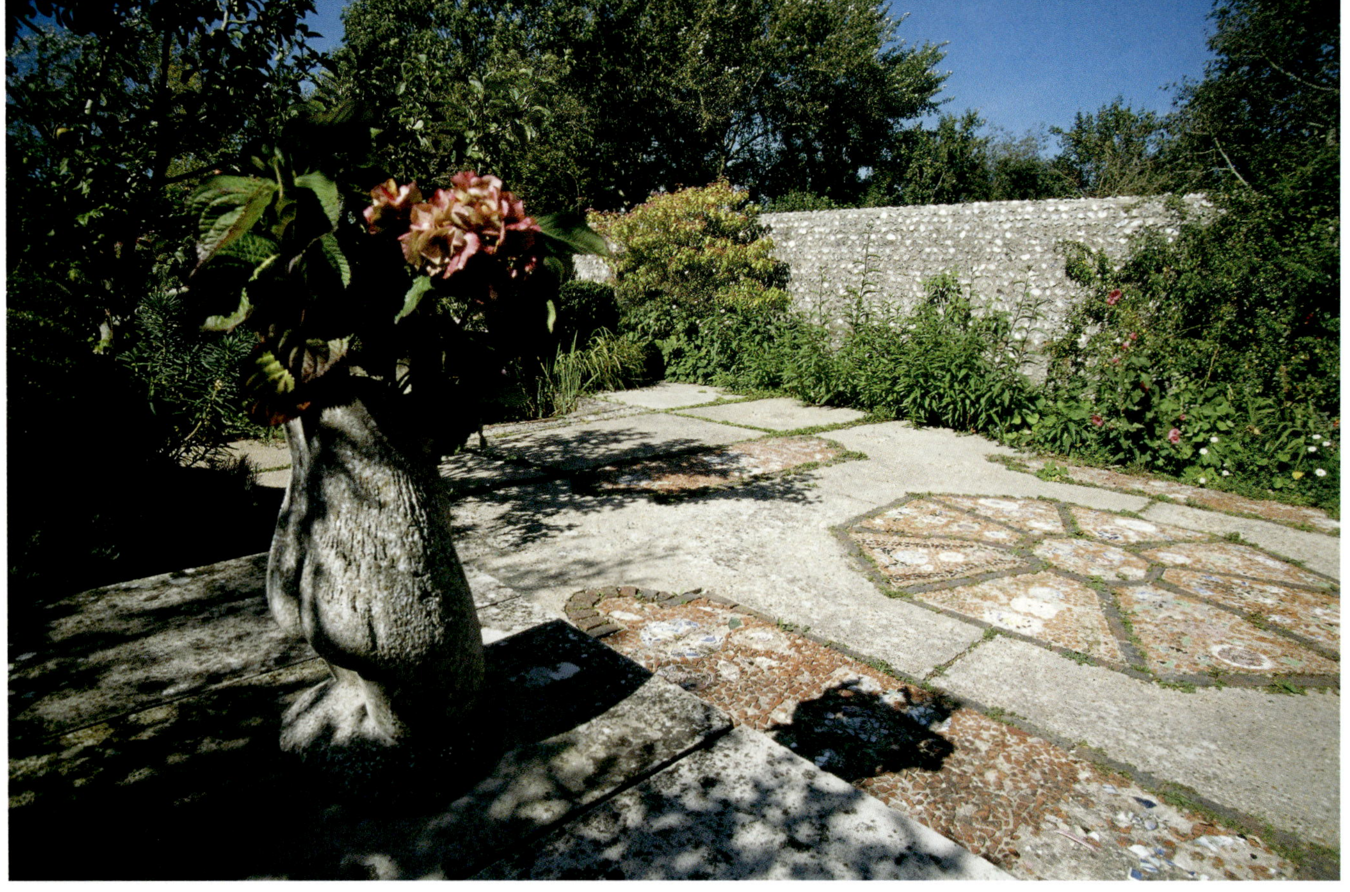

Cast female torso planter and the ceramic piazza

Cast after a Venus by Giovanni da Bologna and 'Bismarck' apples

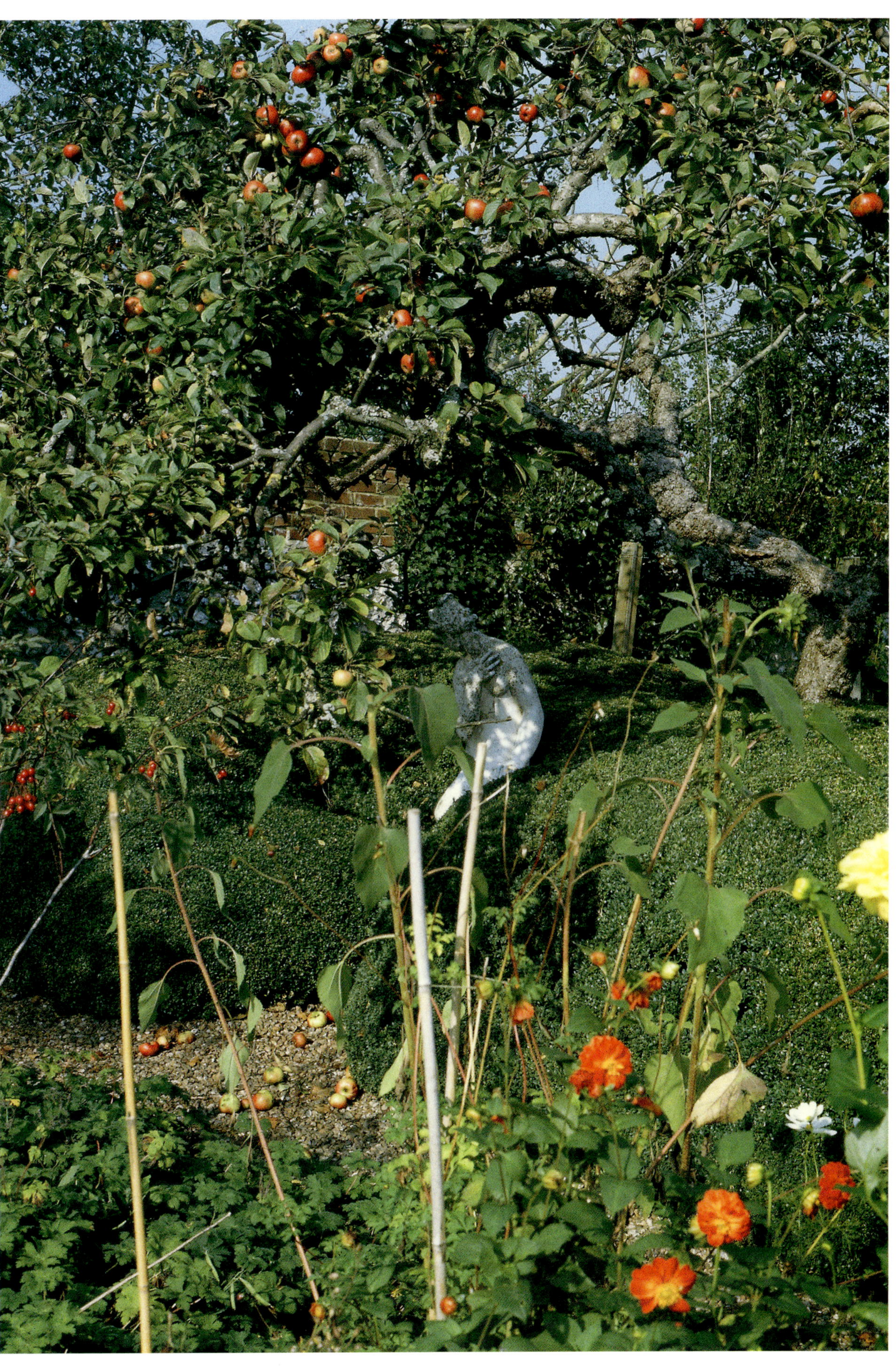

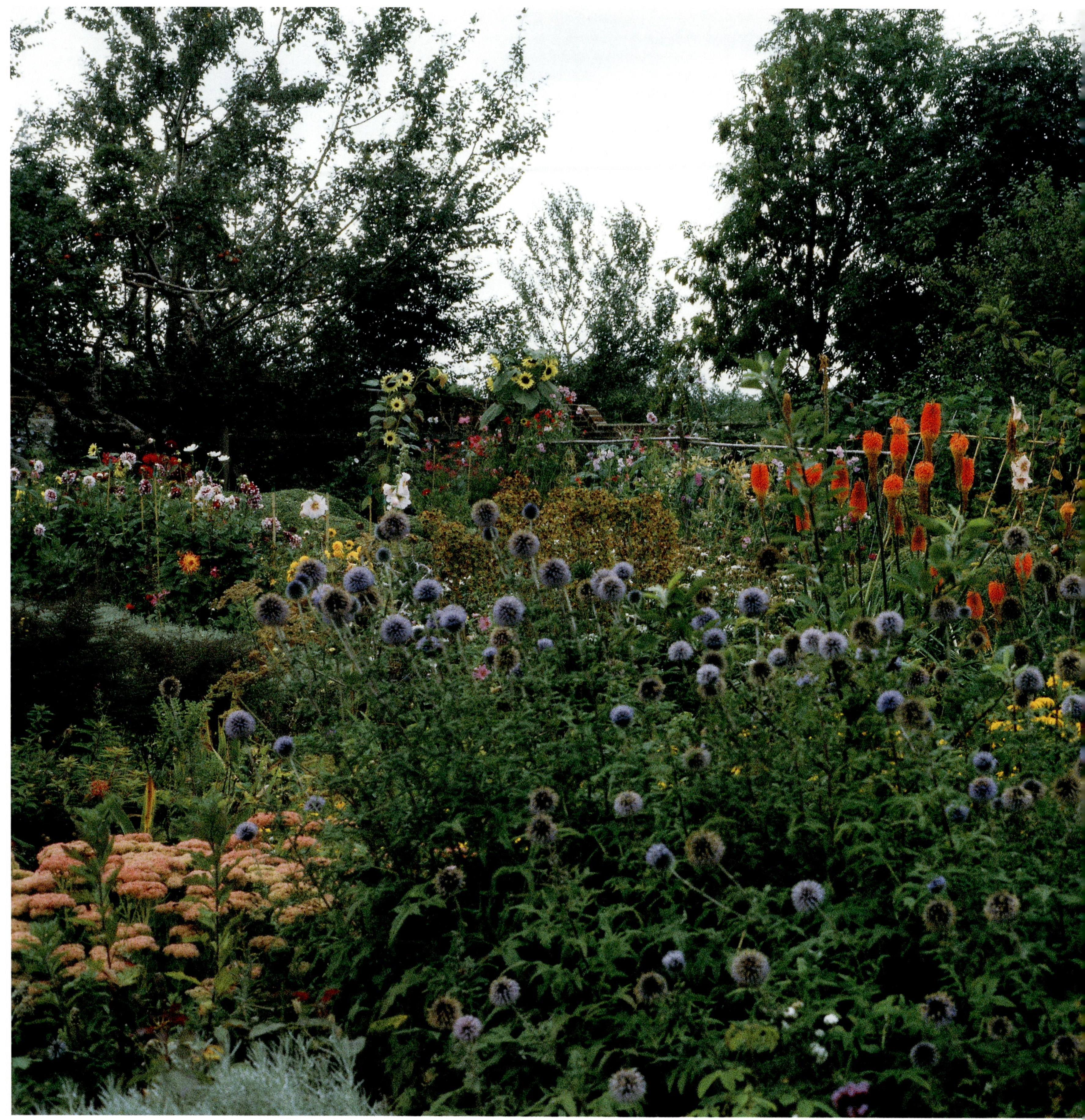

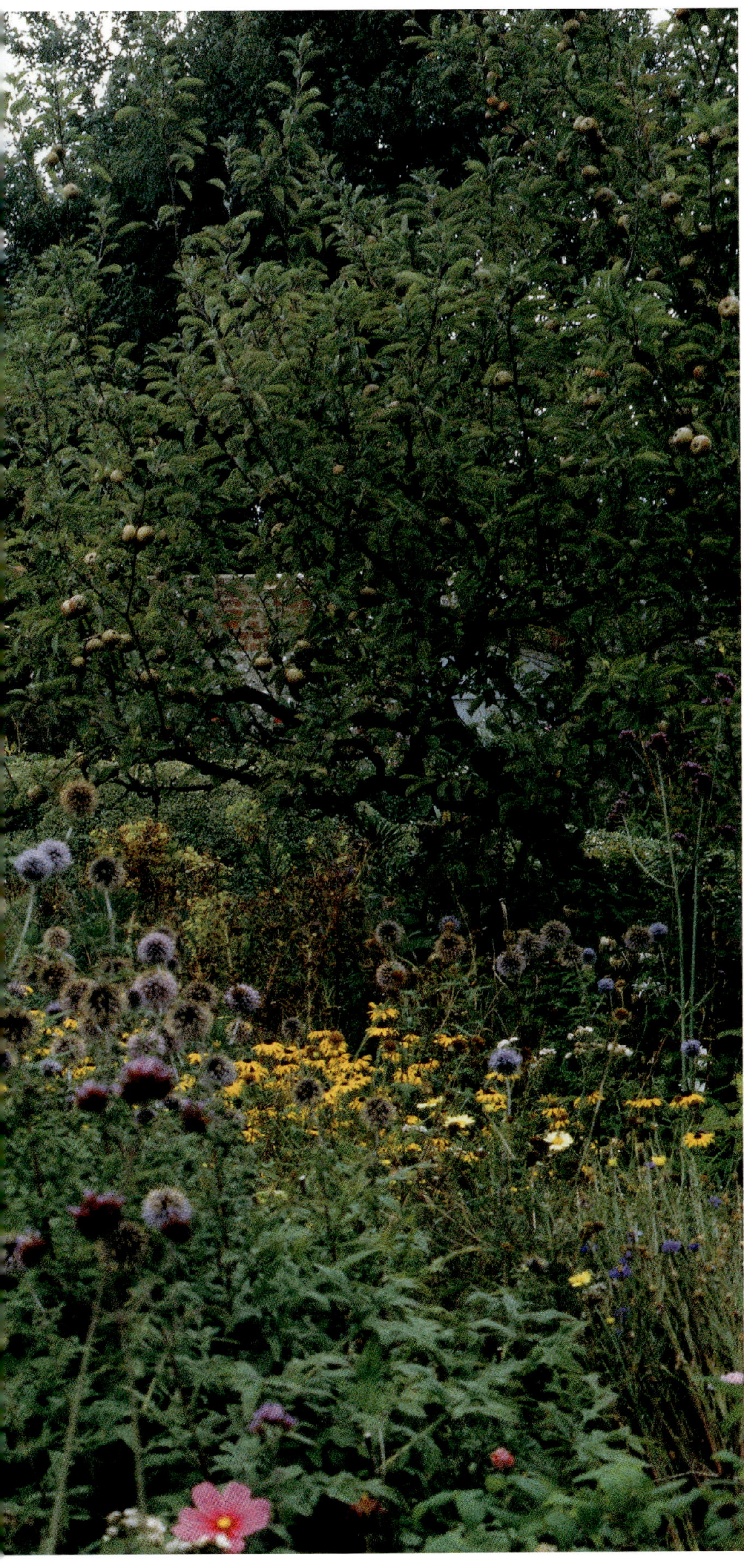

Late flowers

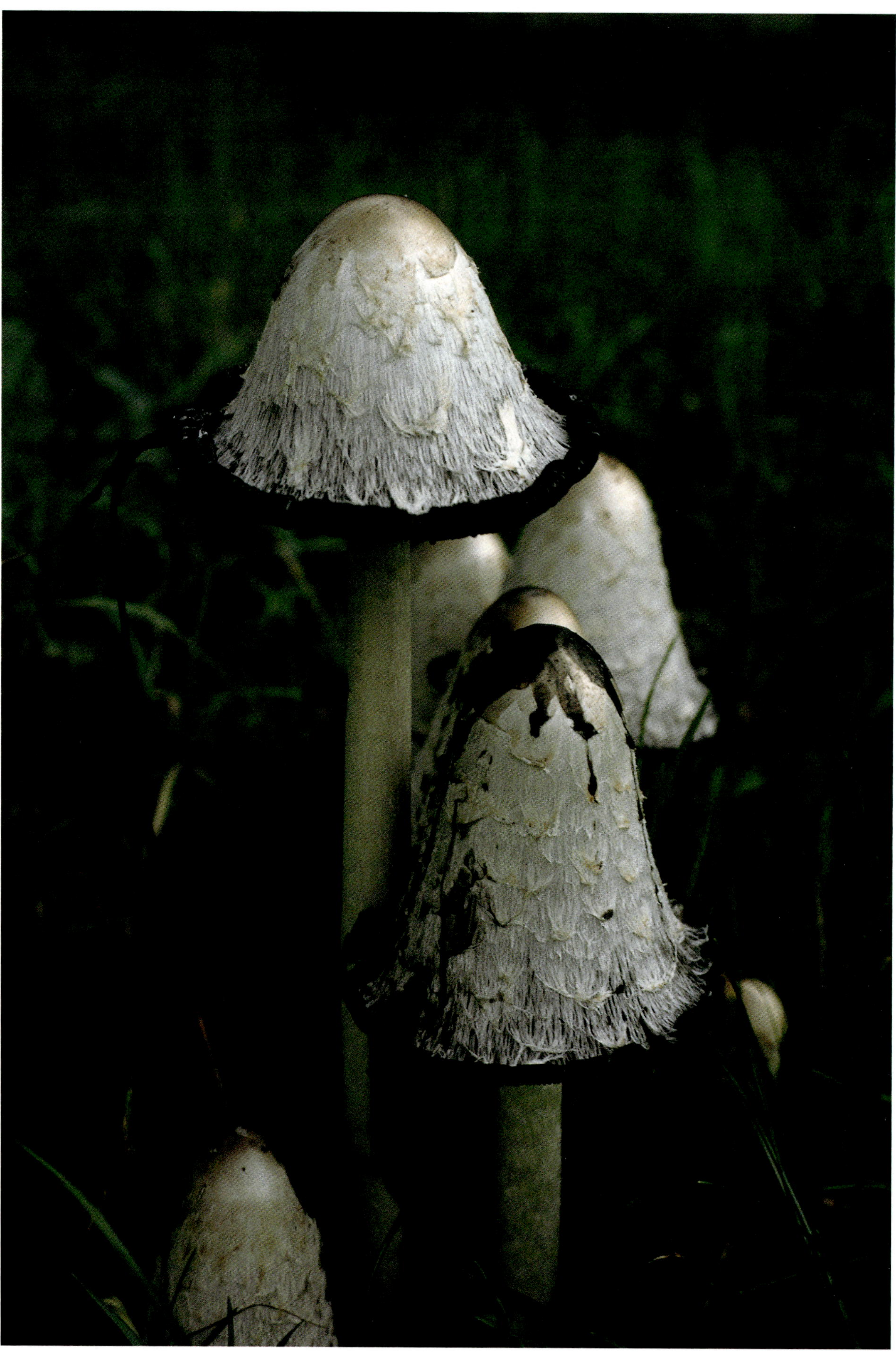

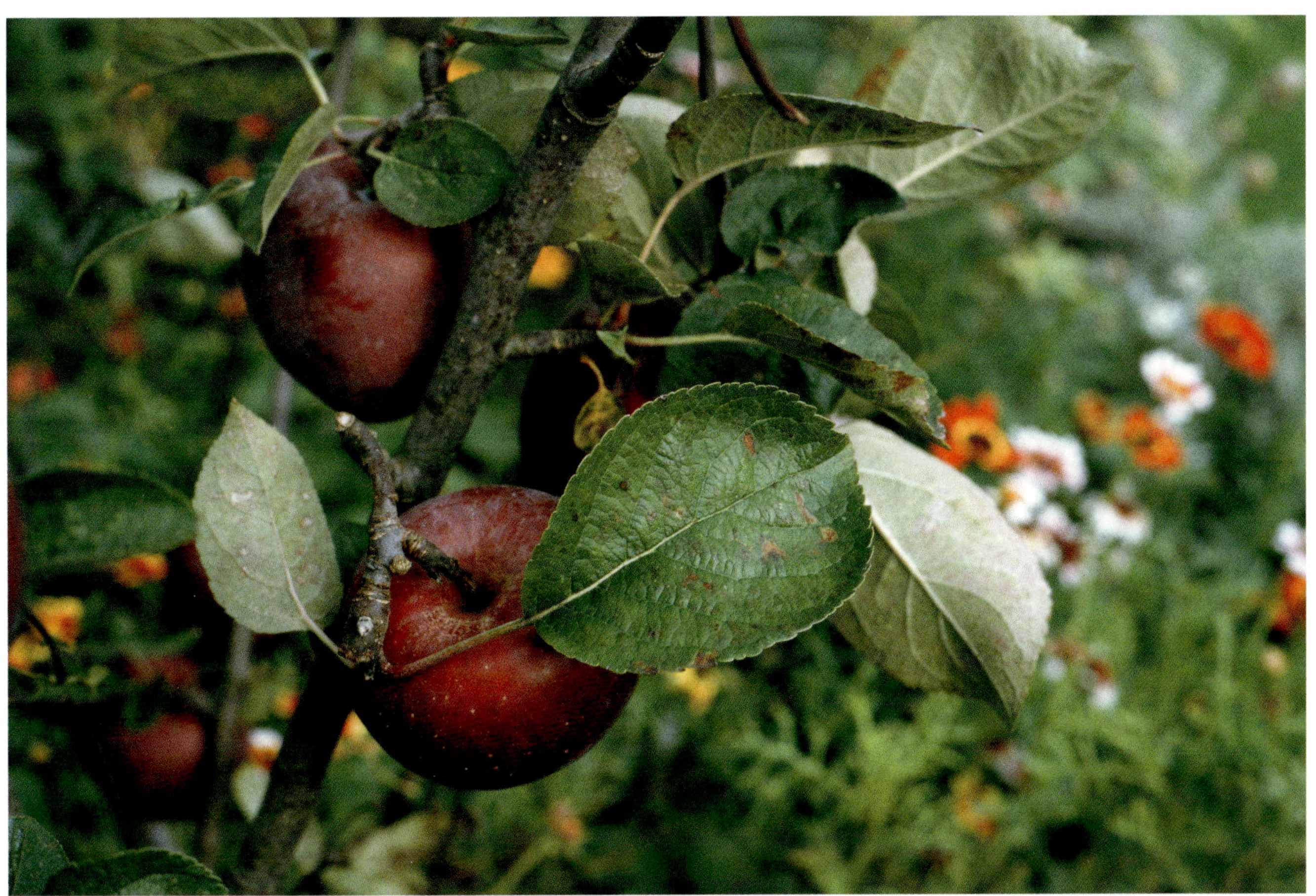

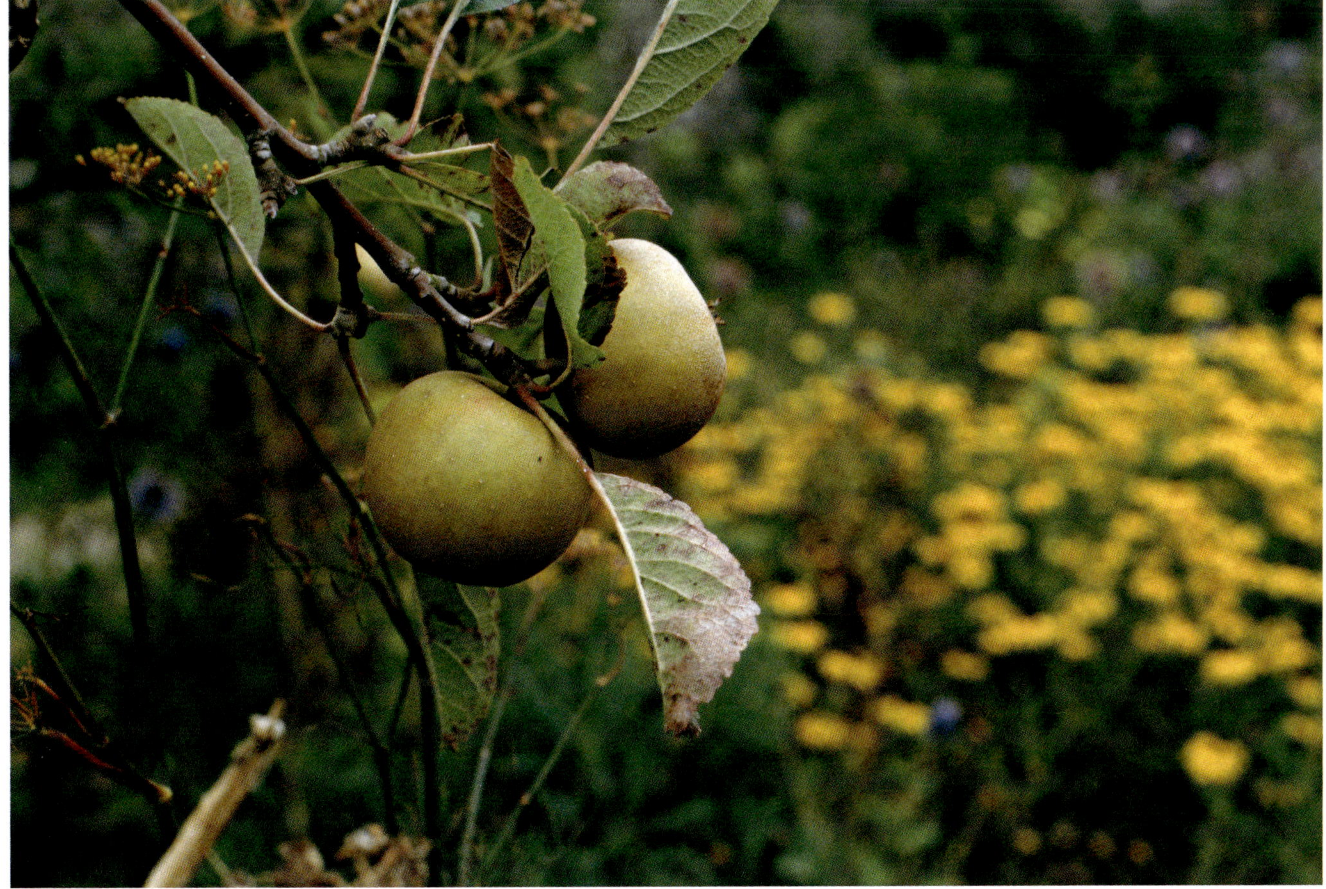

'Spartan' apples (above) and 'Egremont Russet' apples (below)

FOLLOWING PAGES
Dahlias with (centre) hollyhock (above) and zinnia (below)

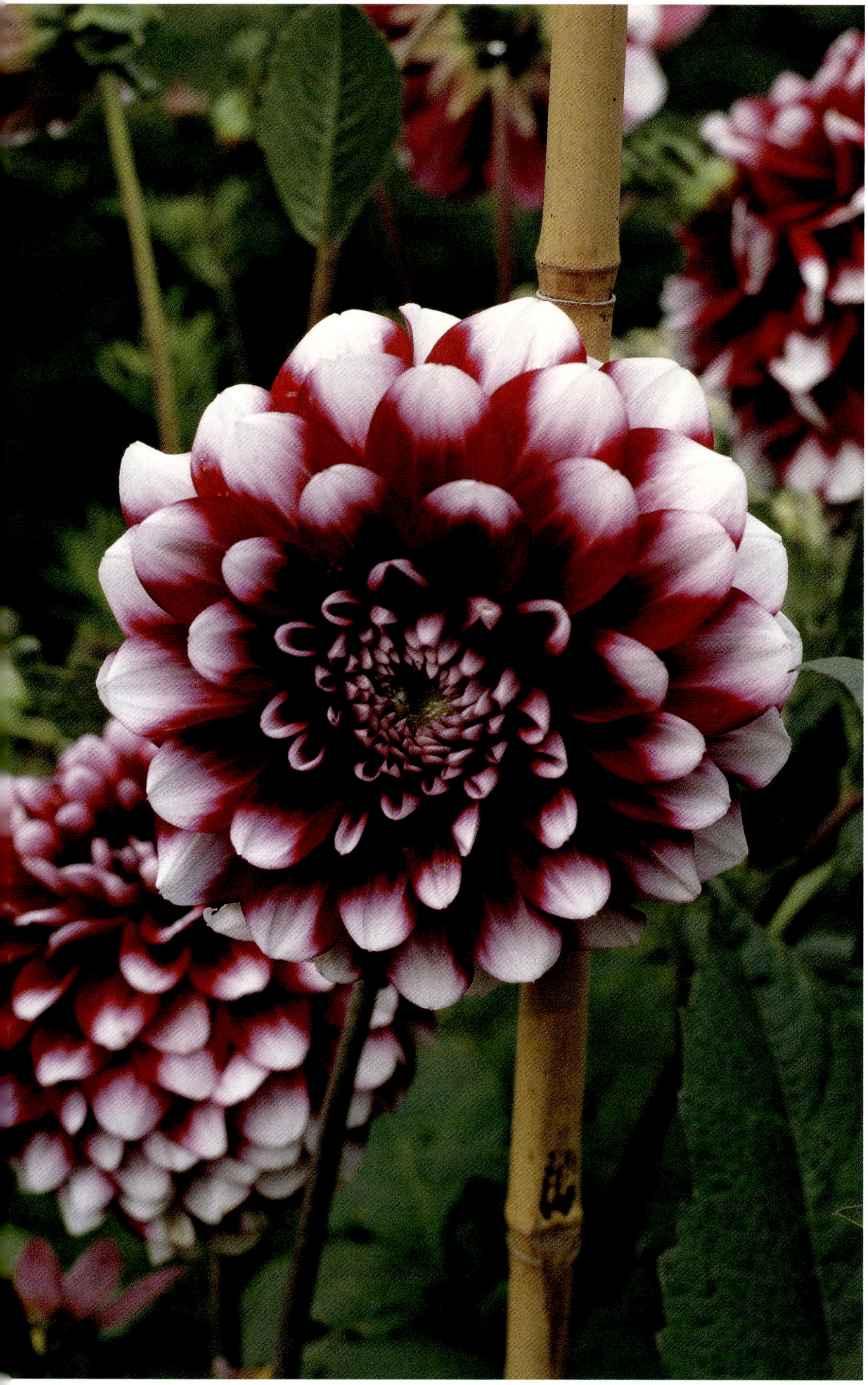

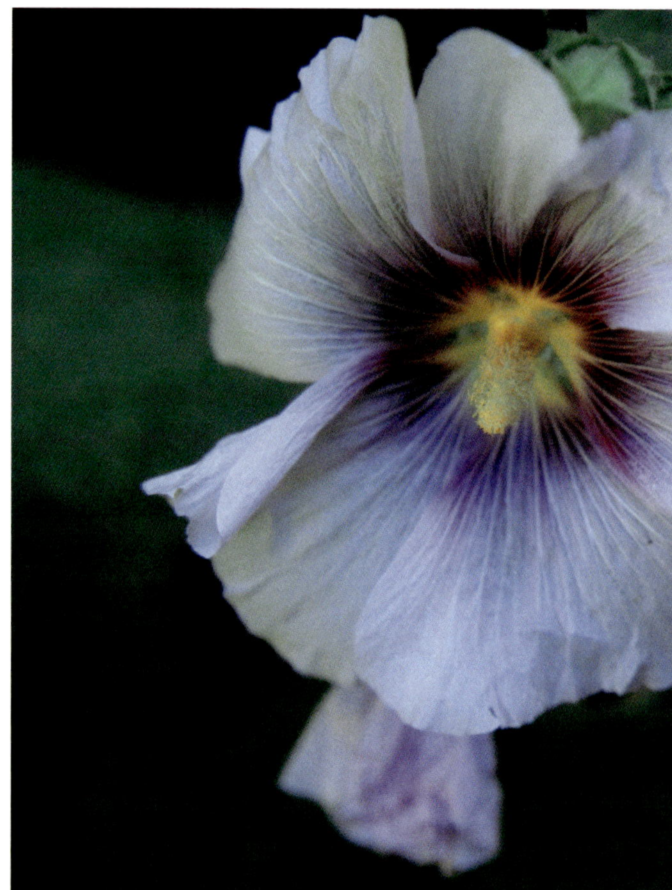

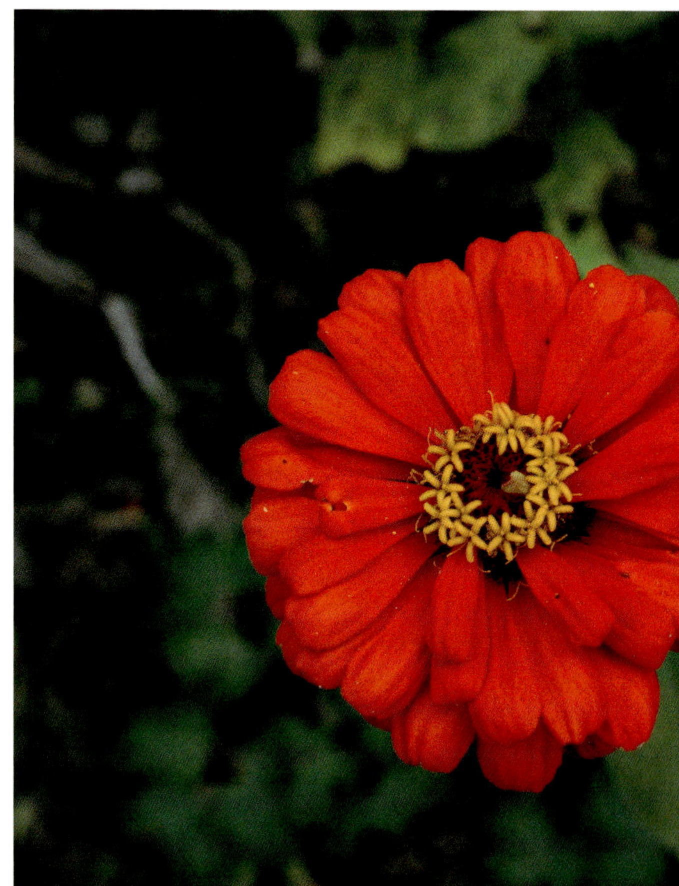

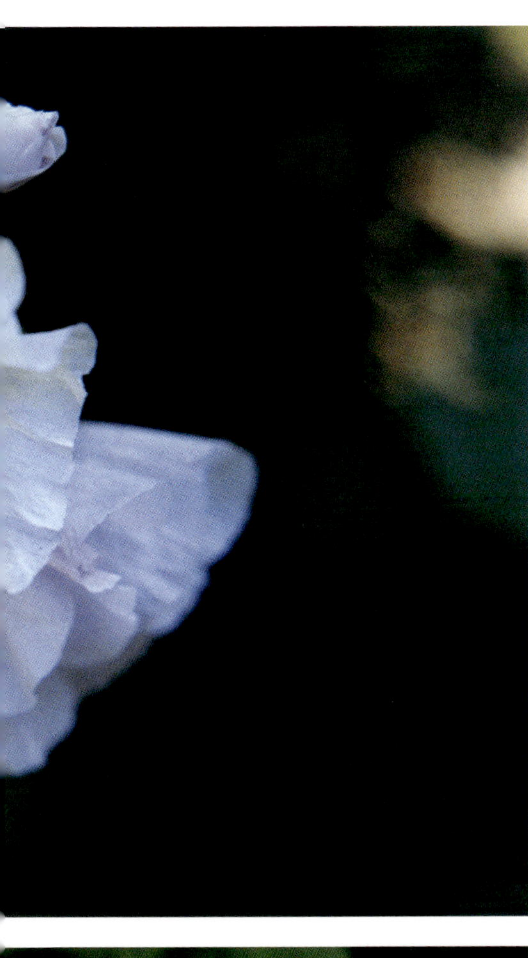

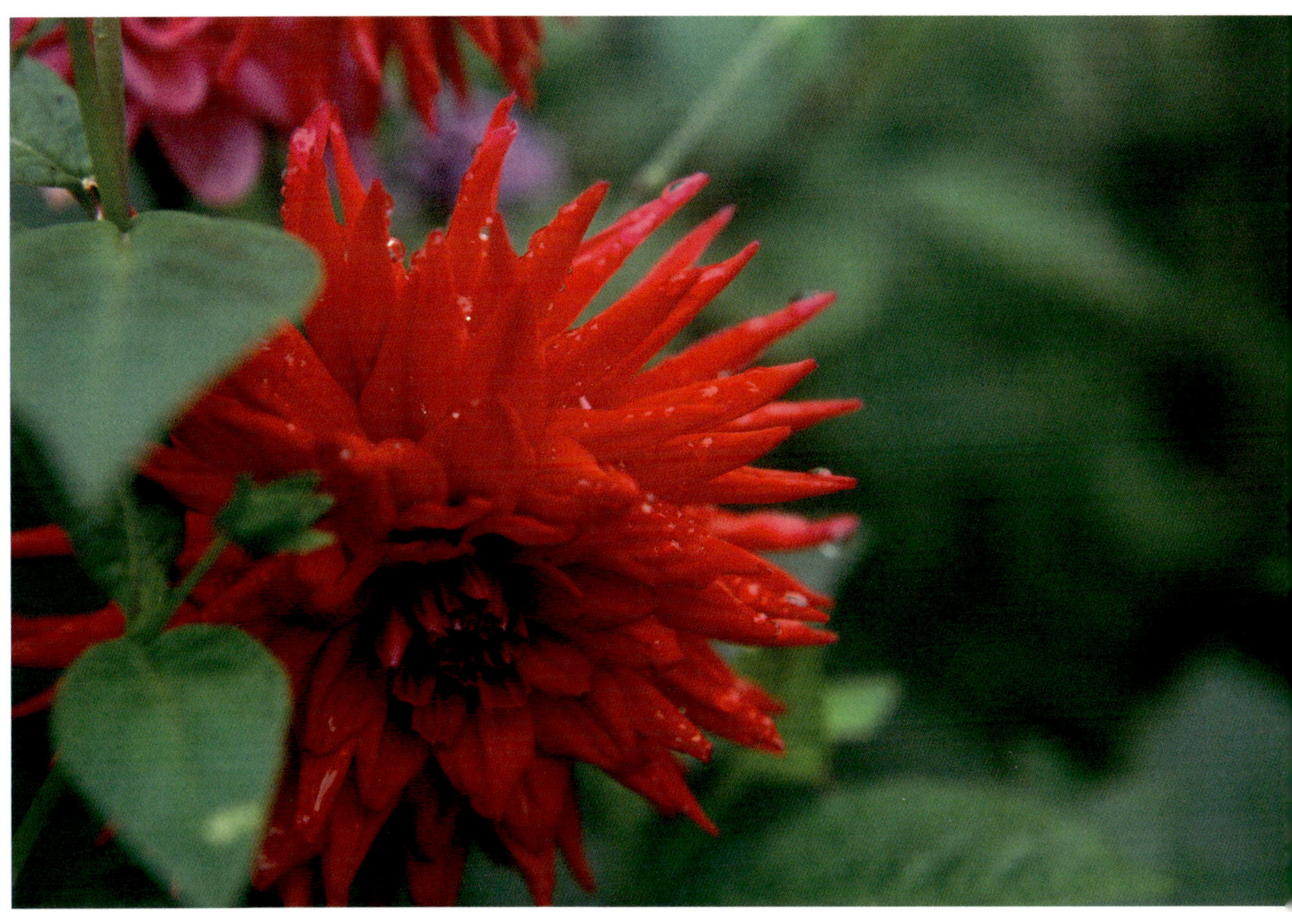

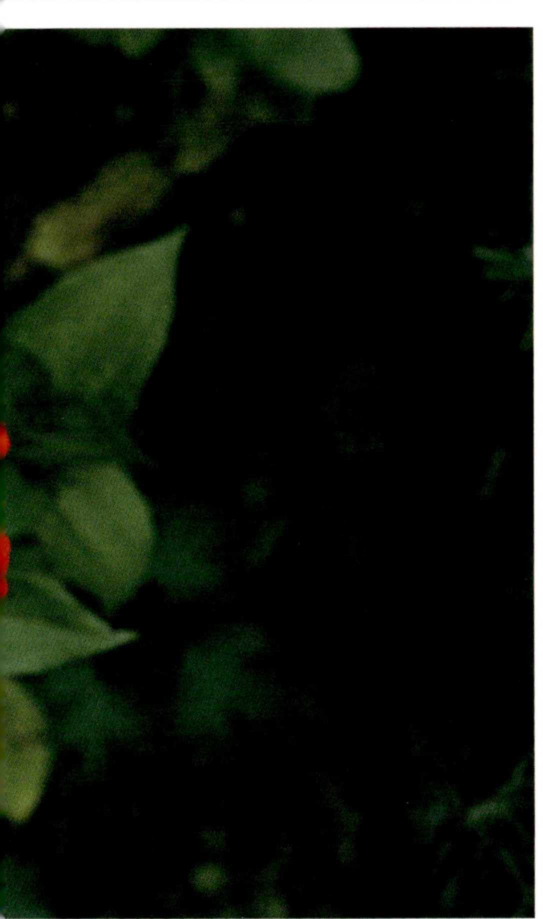

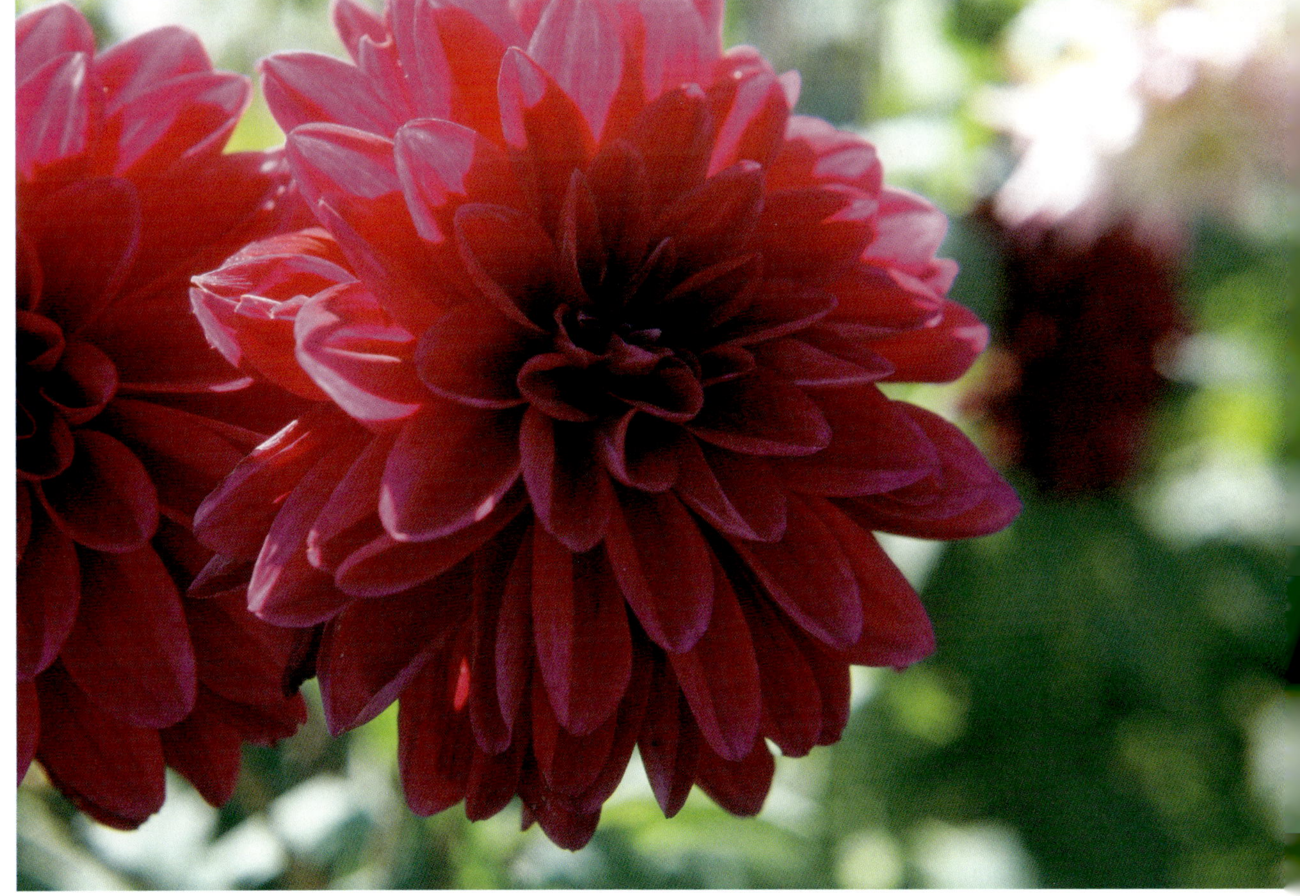

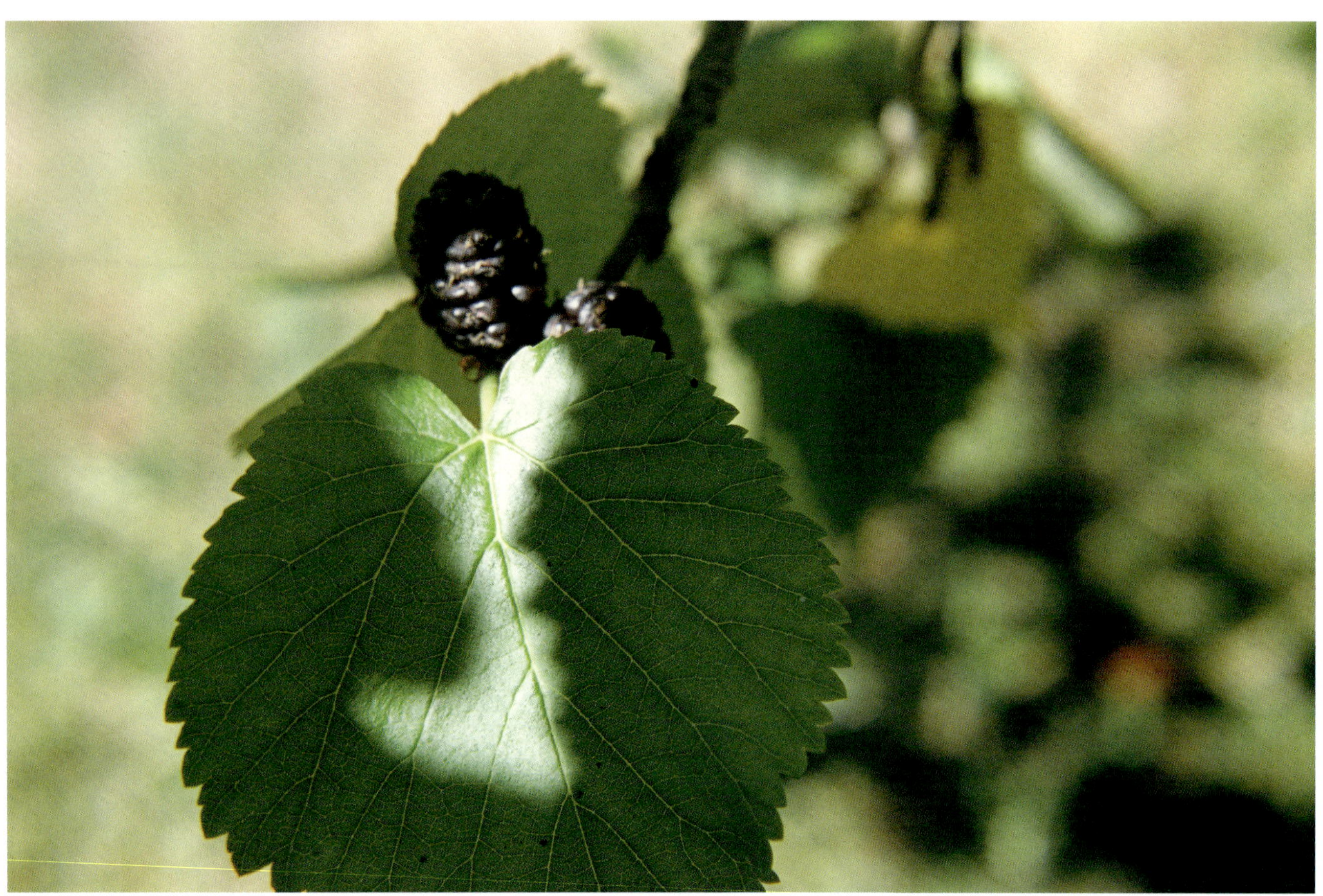
Black mulberries

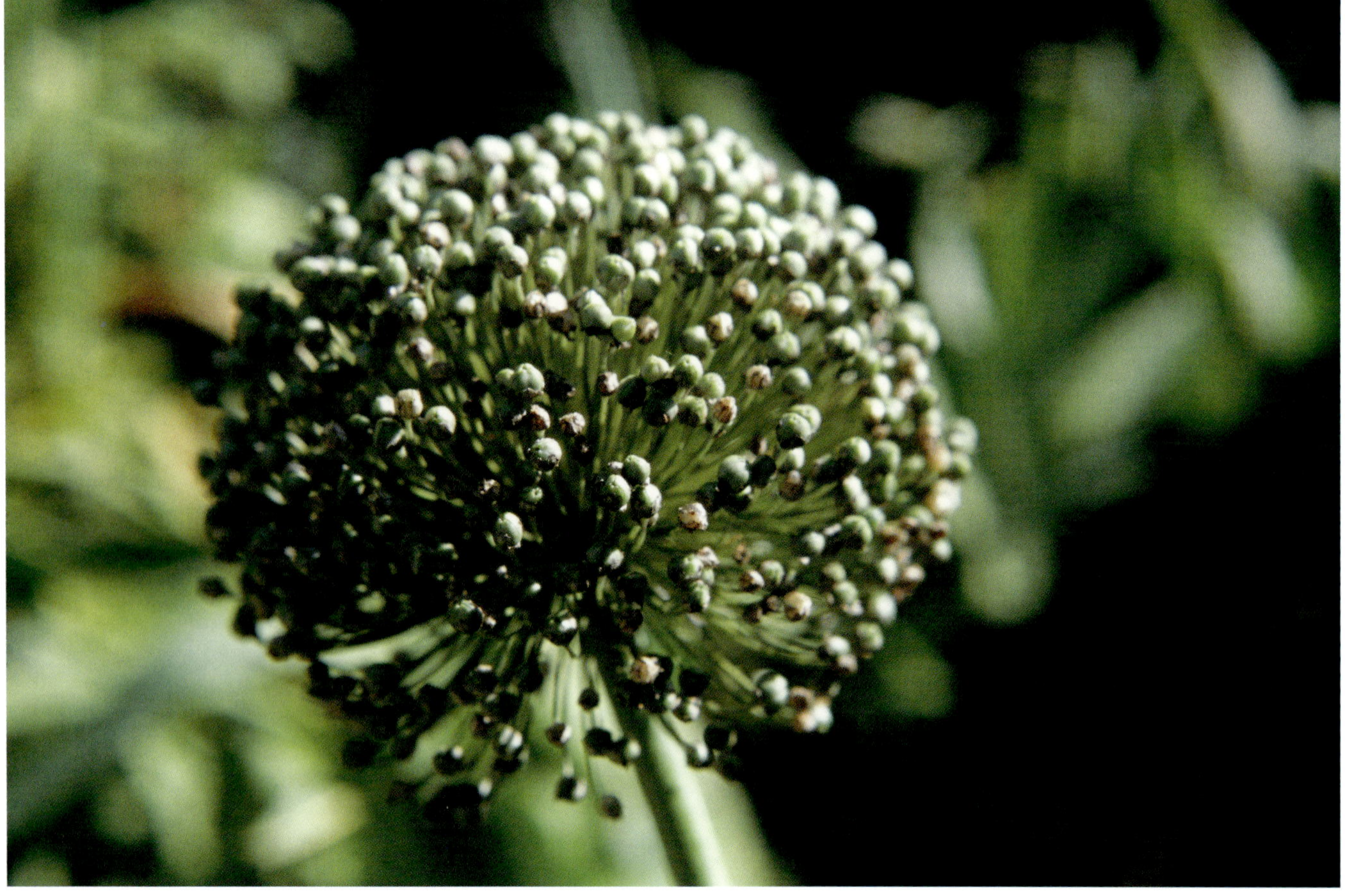
Allium seedhead

Bryony berries

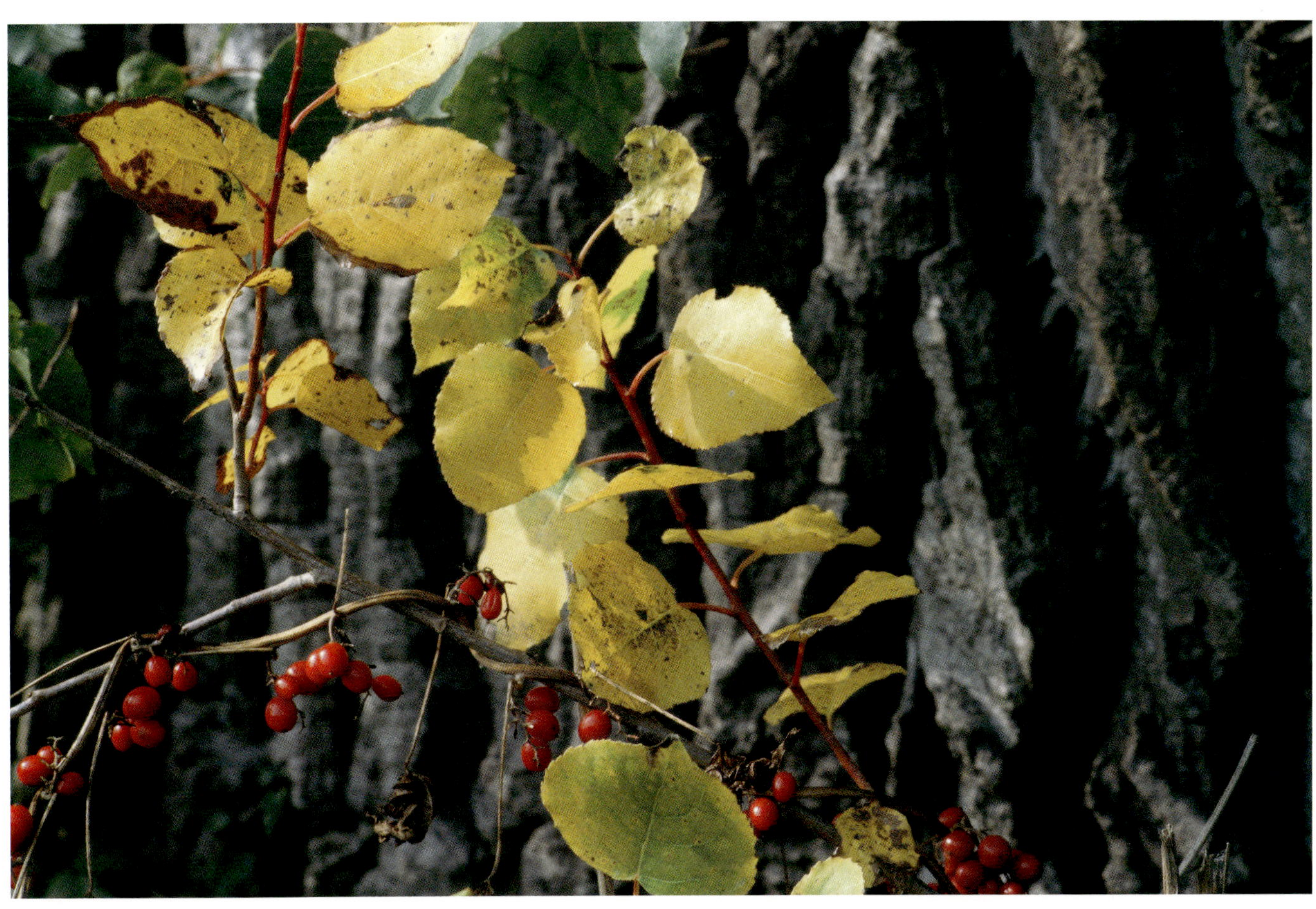

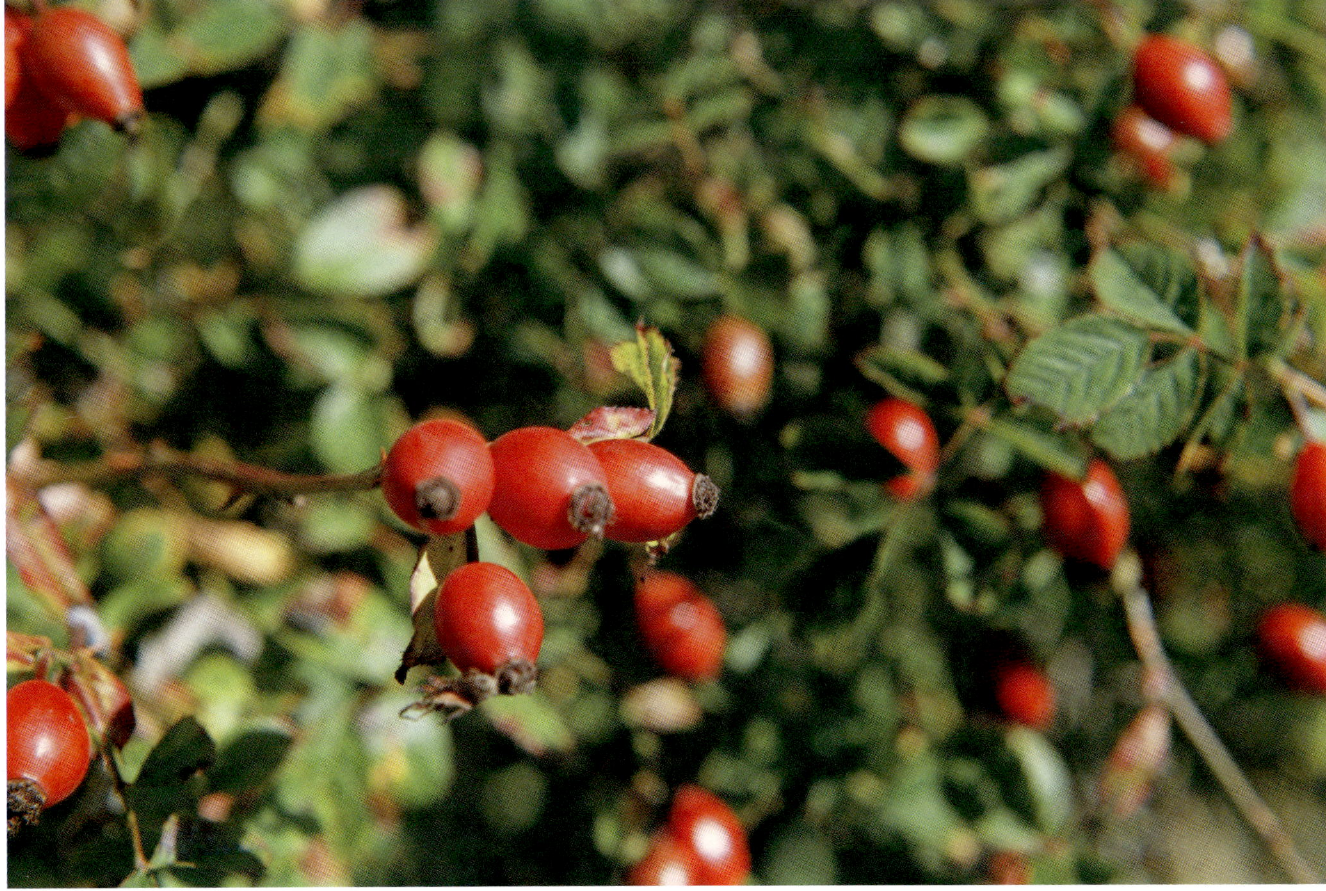

Wild rosehips

Swirling birds (above) and fig (below)

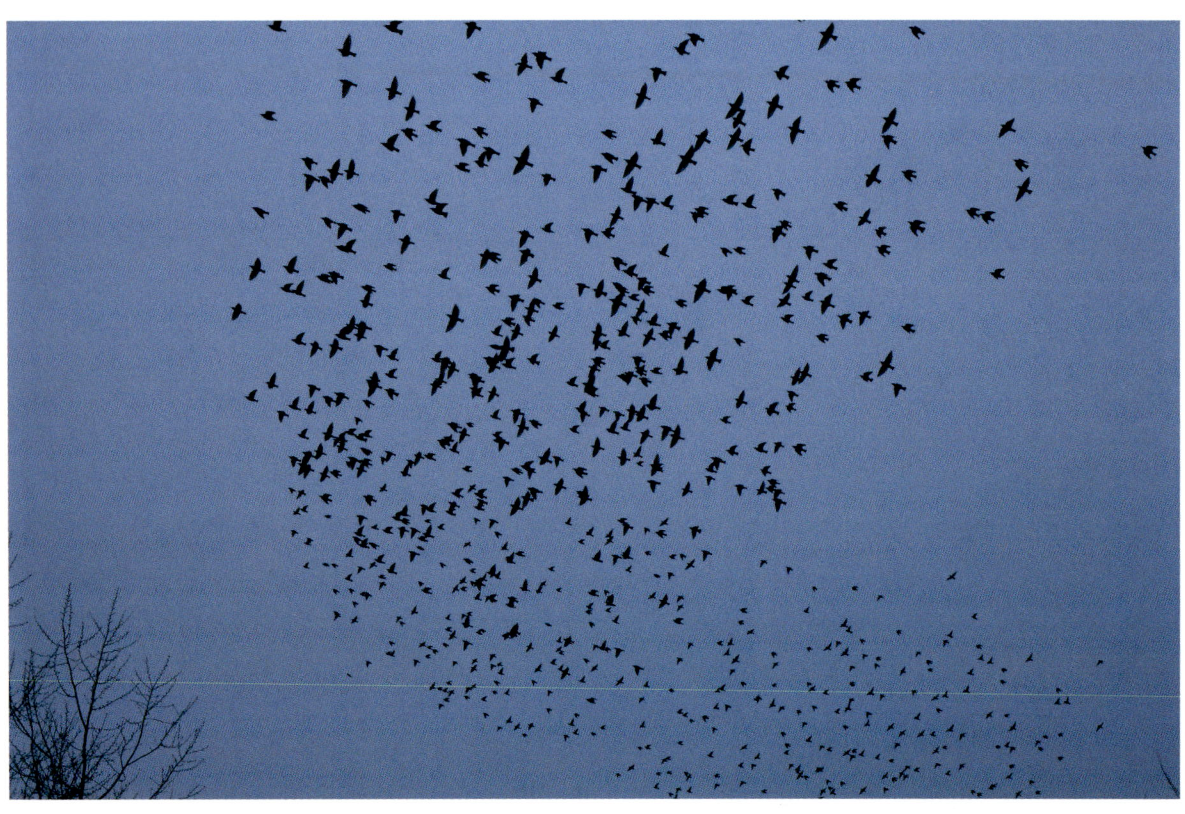

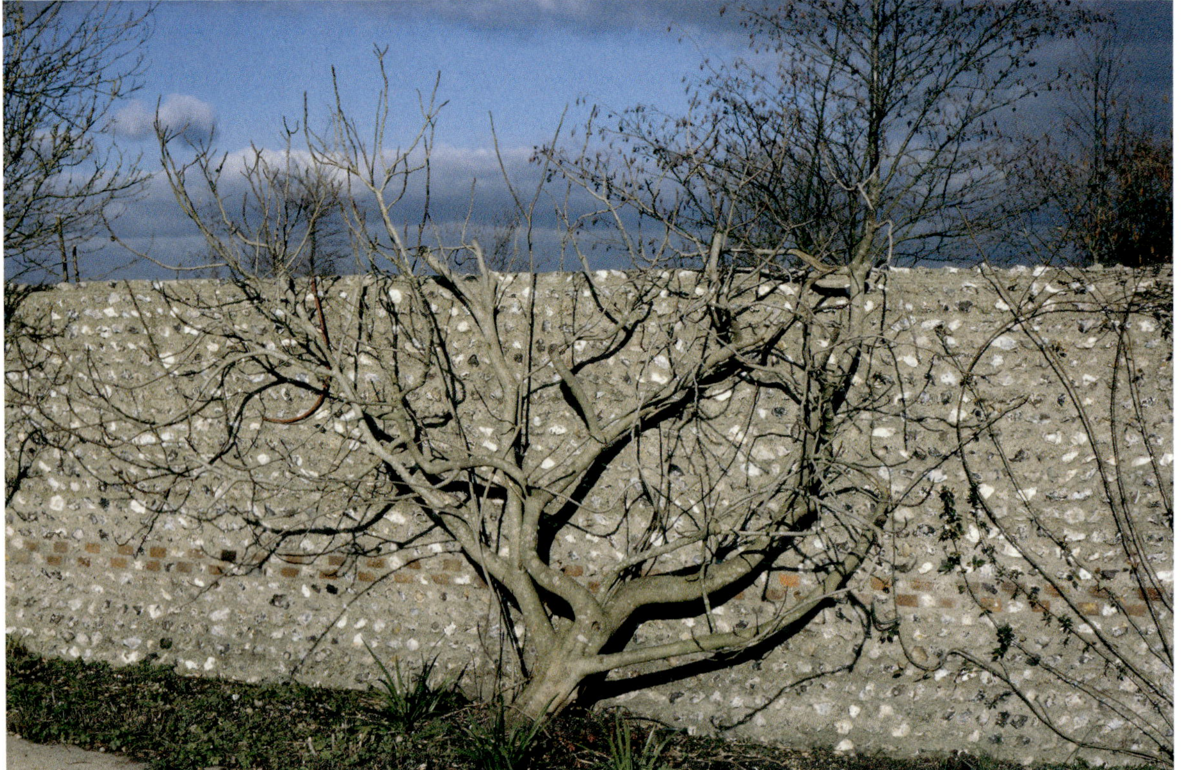

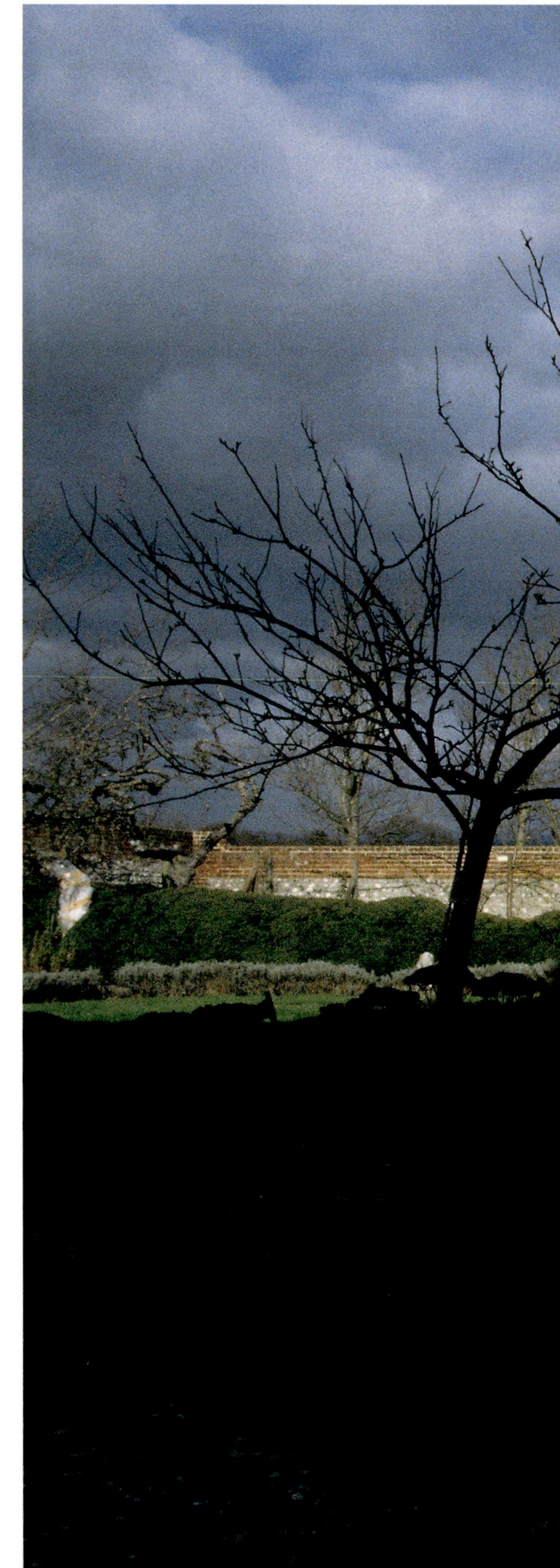

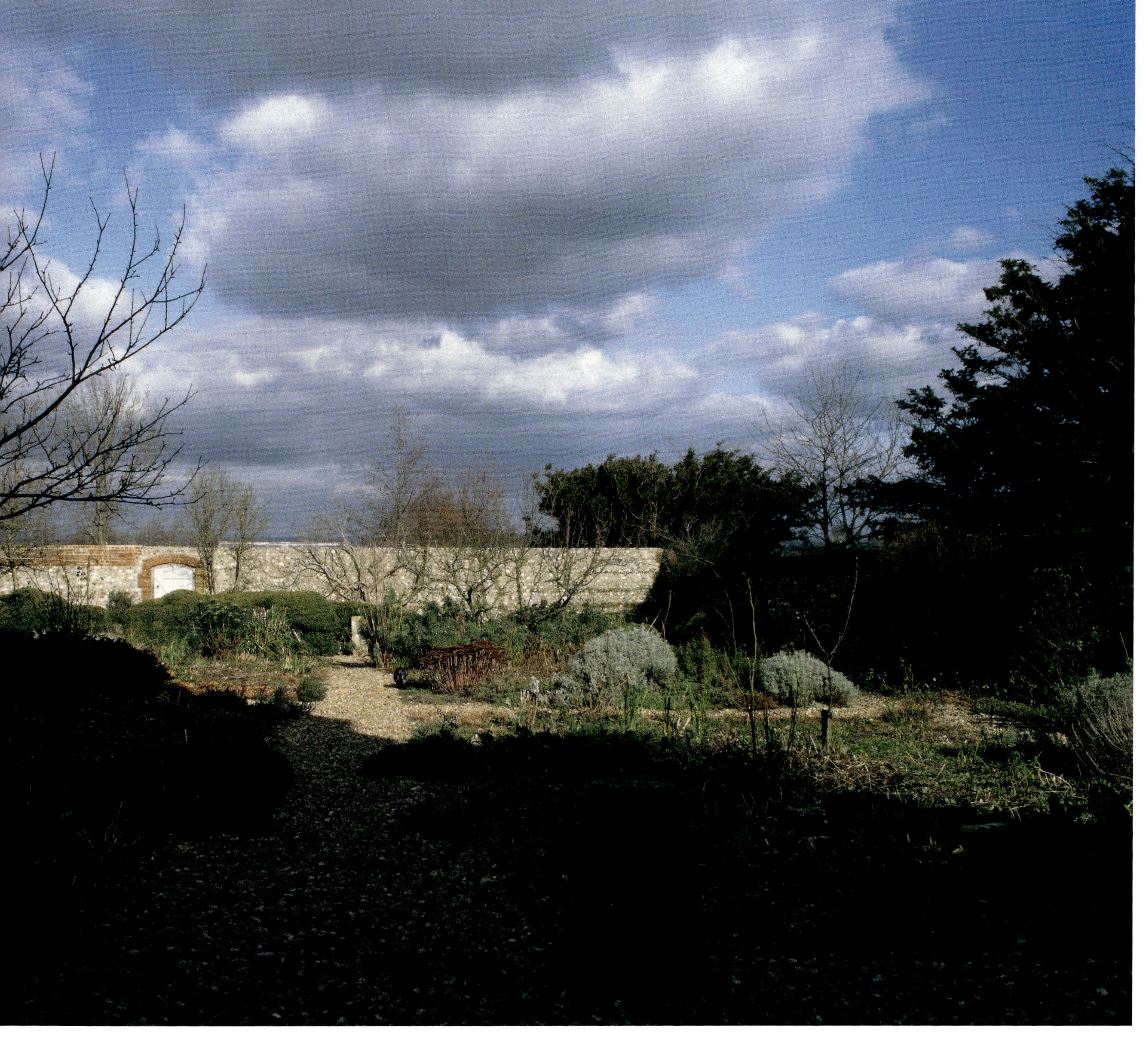

View of the farm

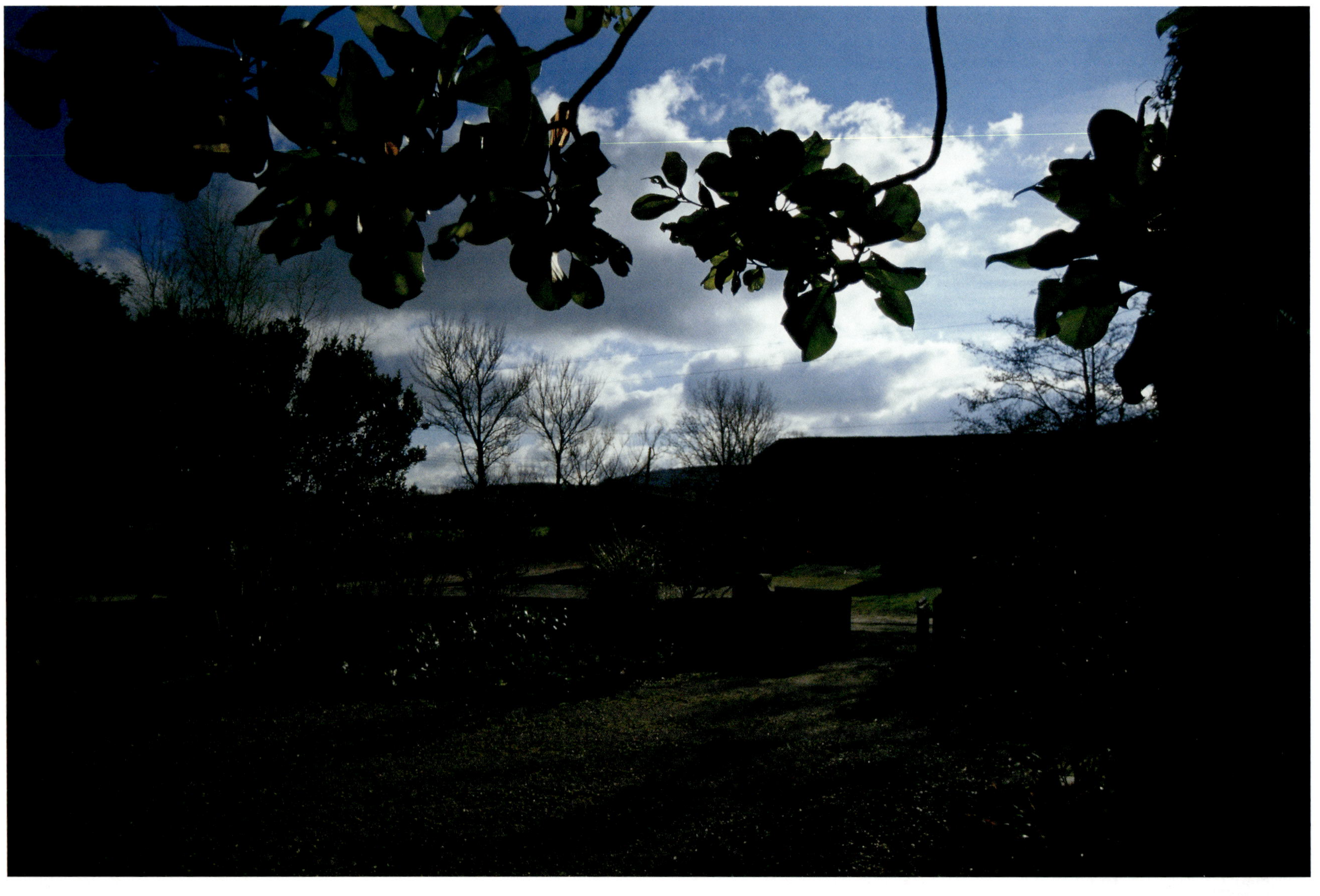

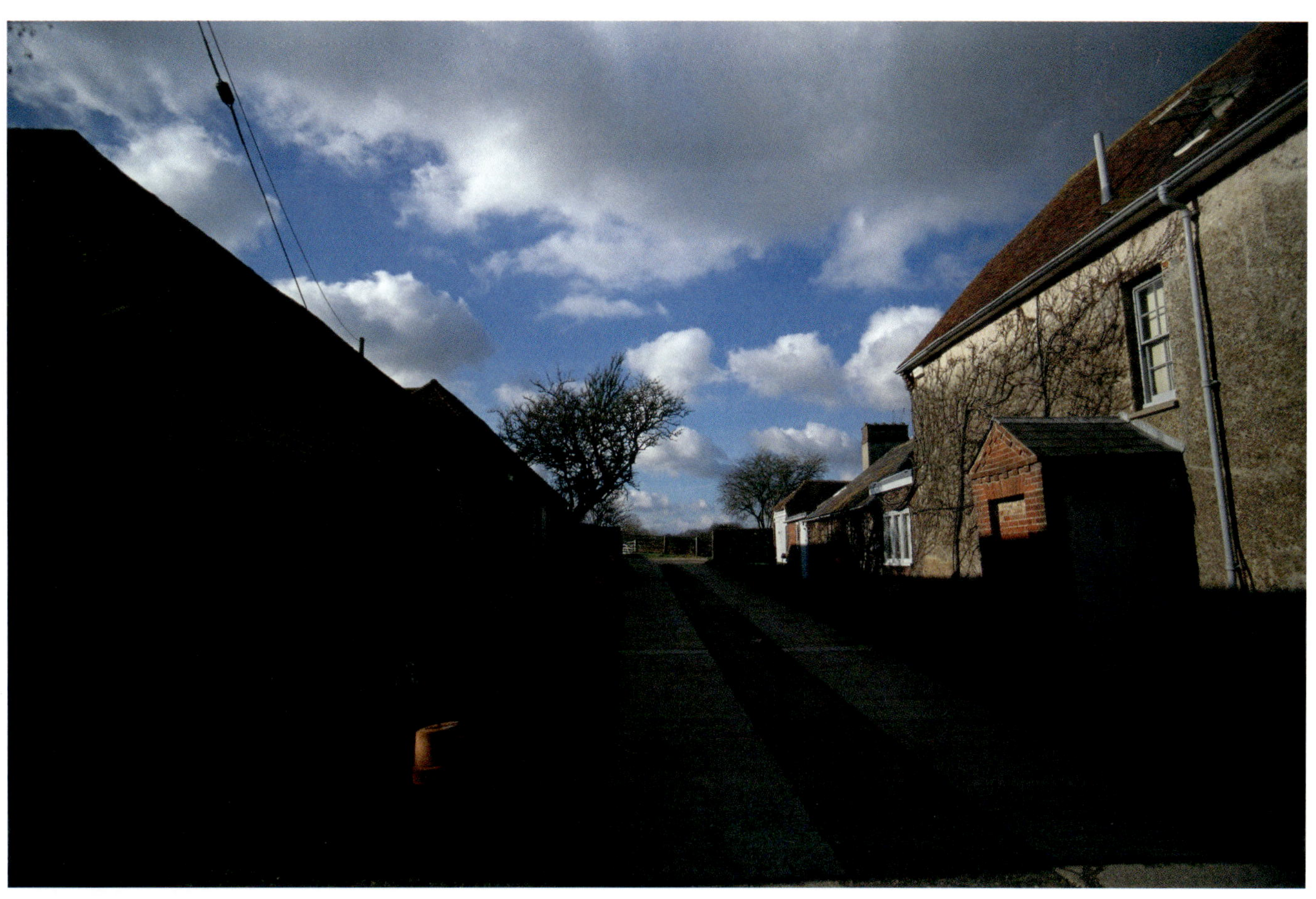
The Firle footpath

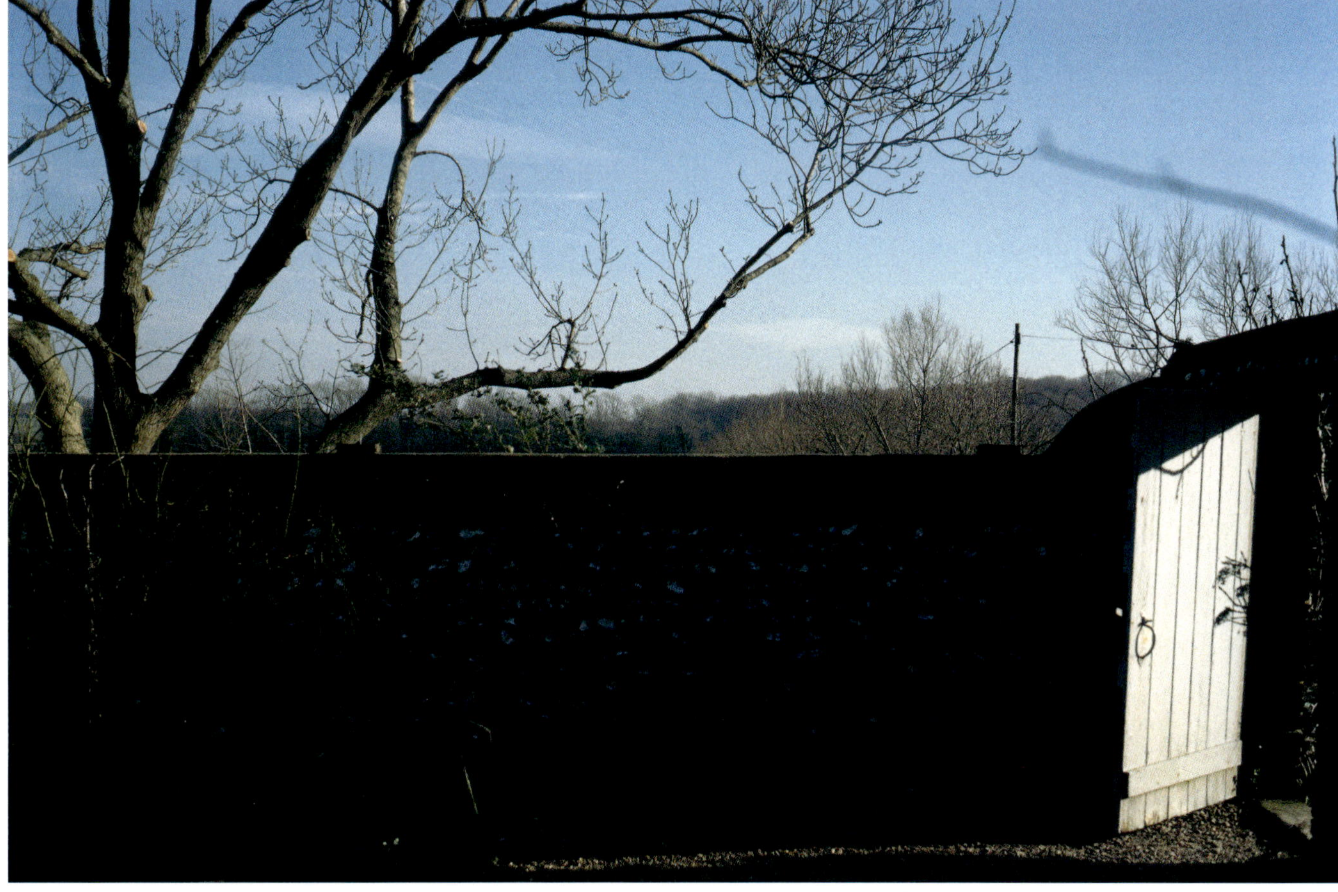
Door of the walled garden

winter

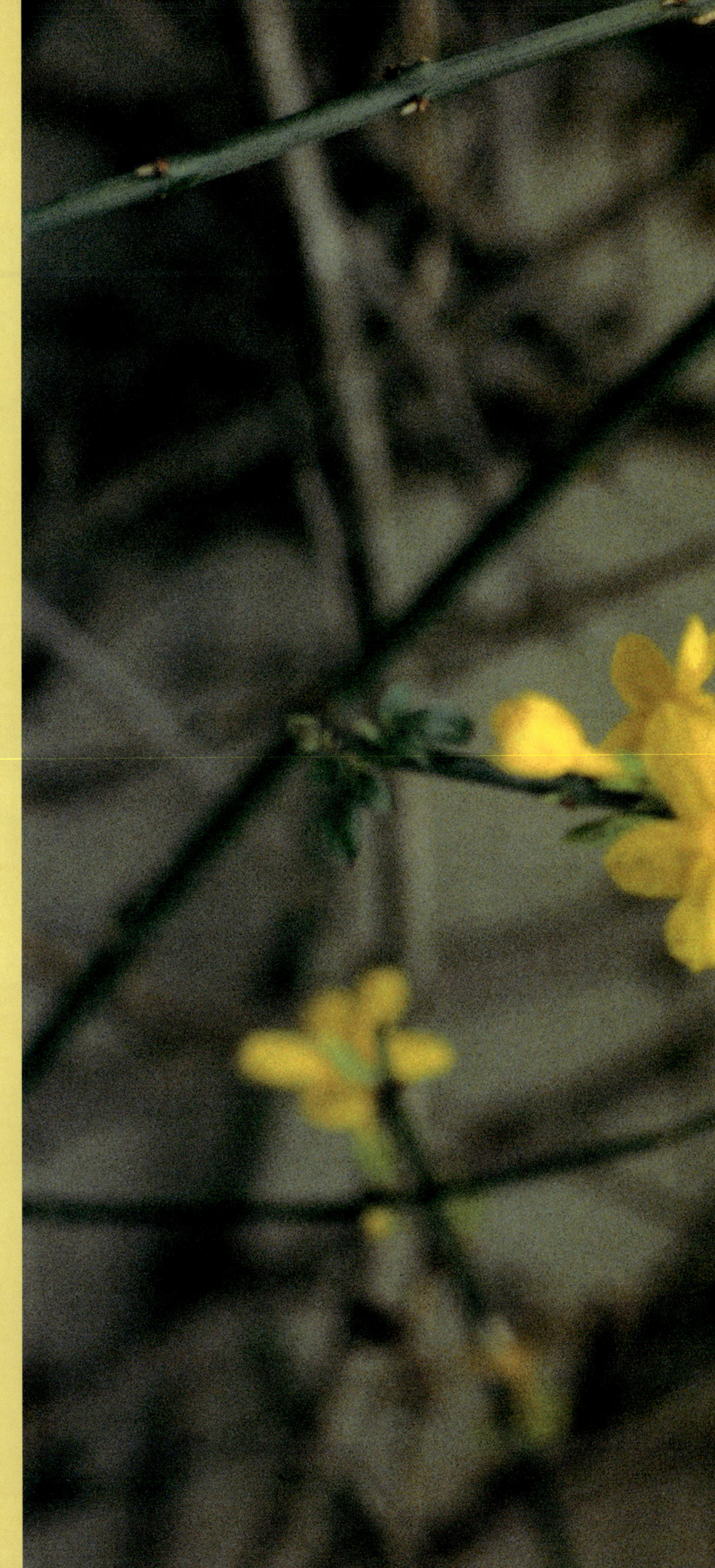

Winter jasmine

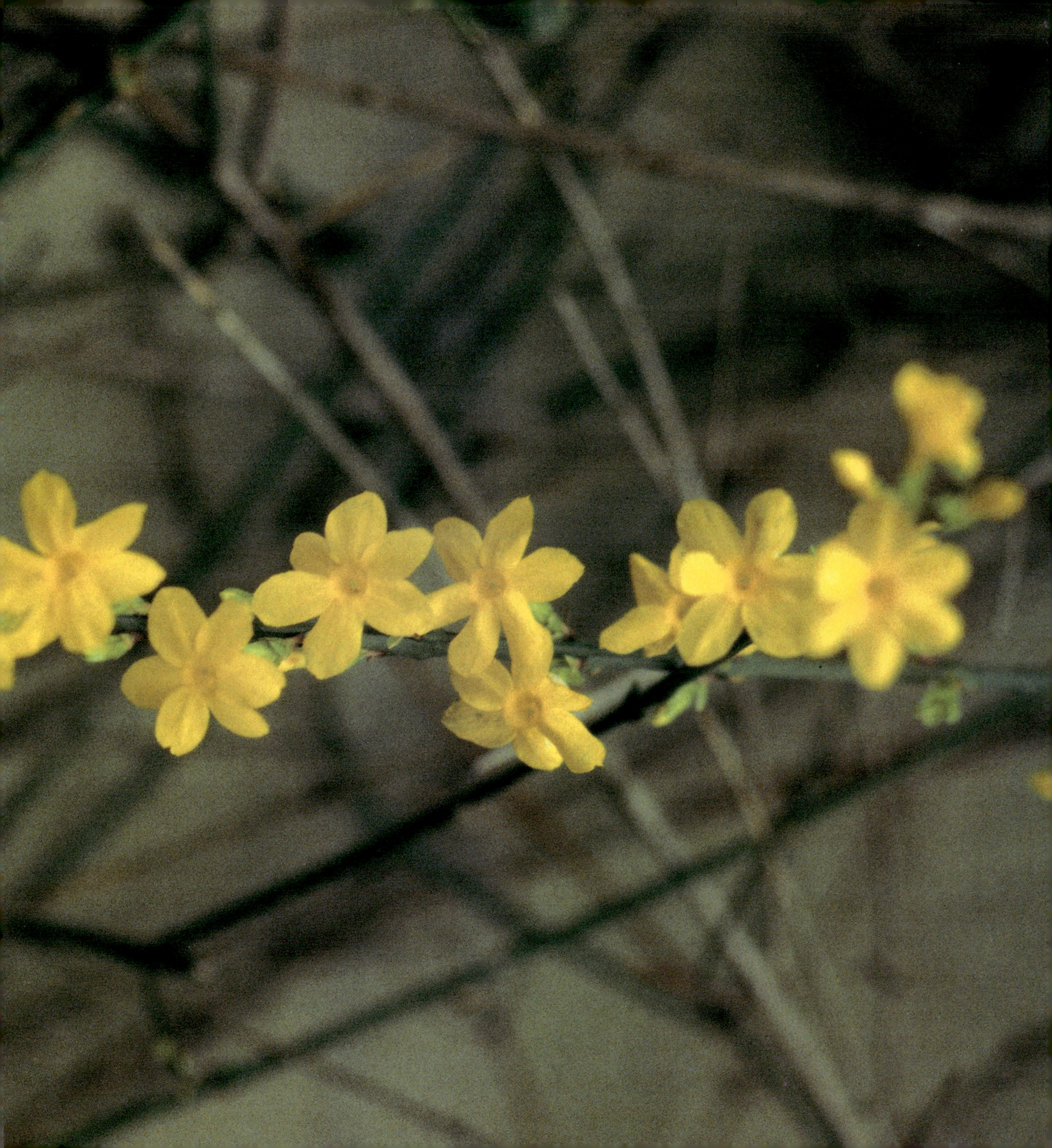

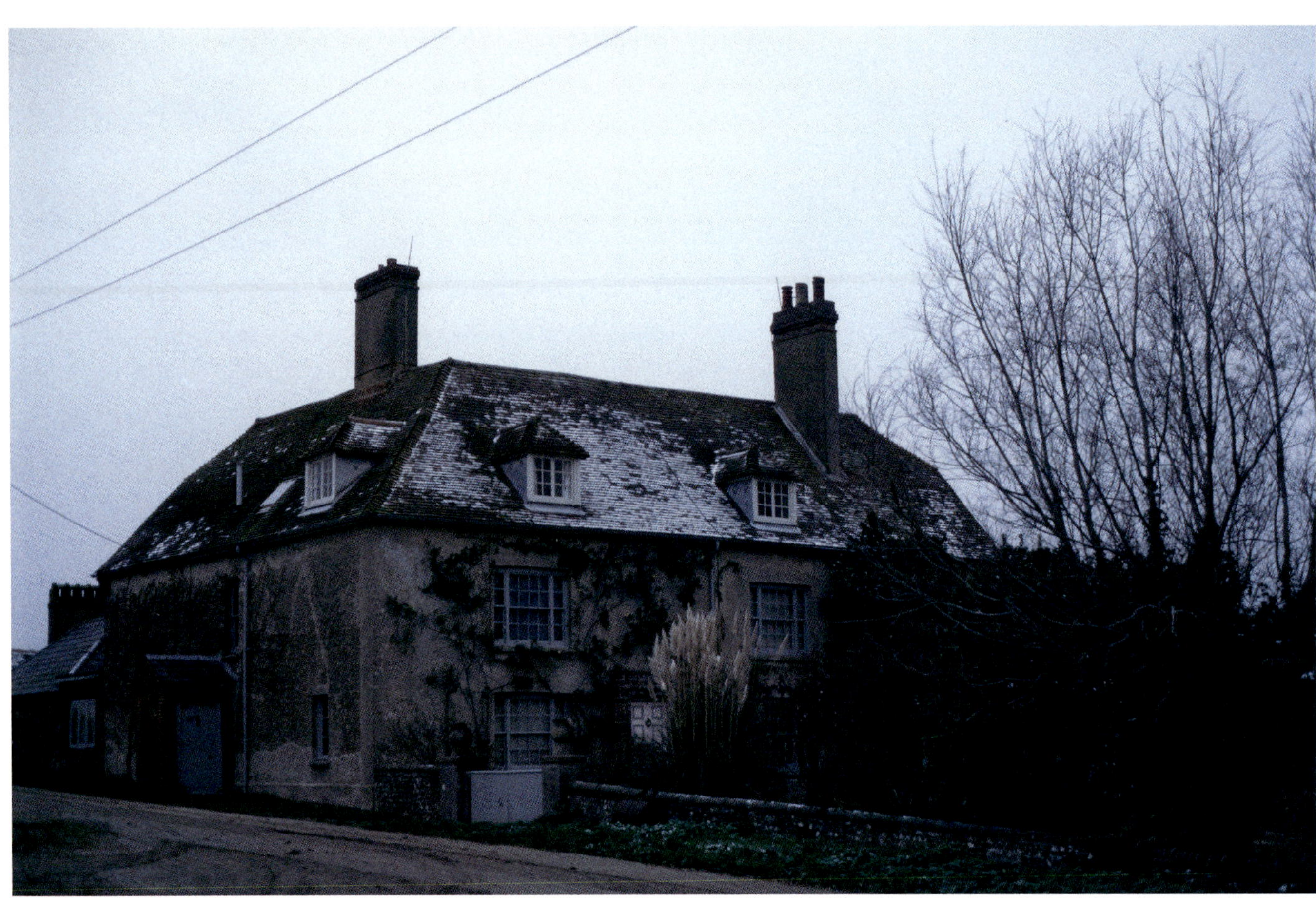

First snow

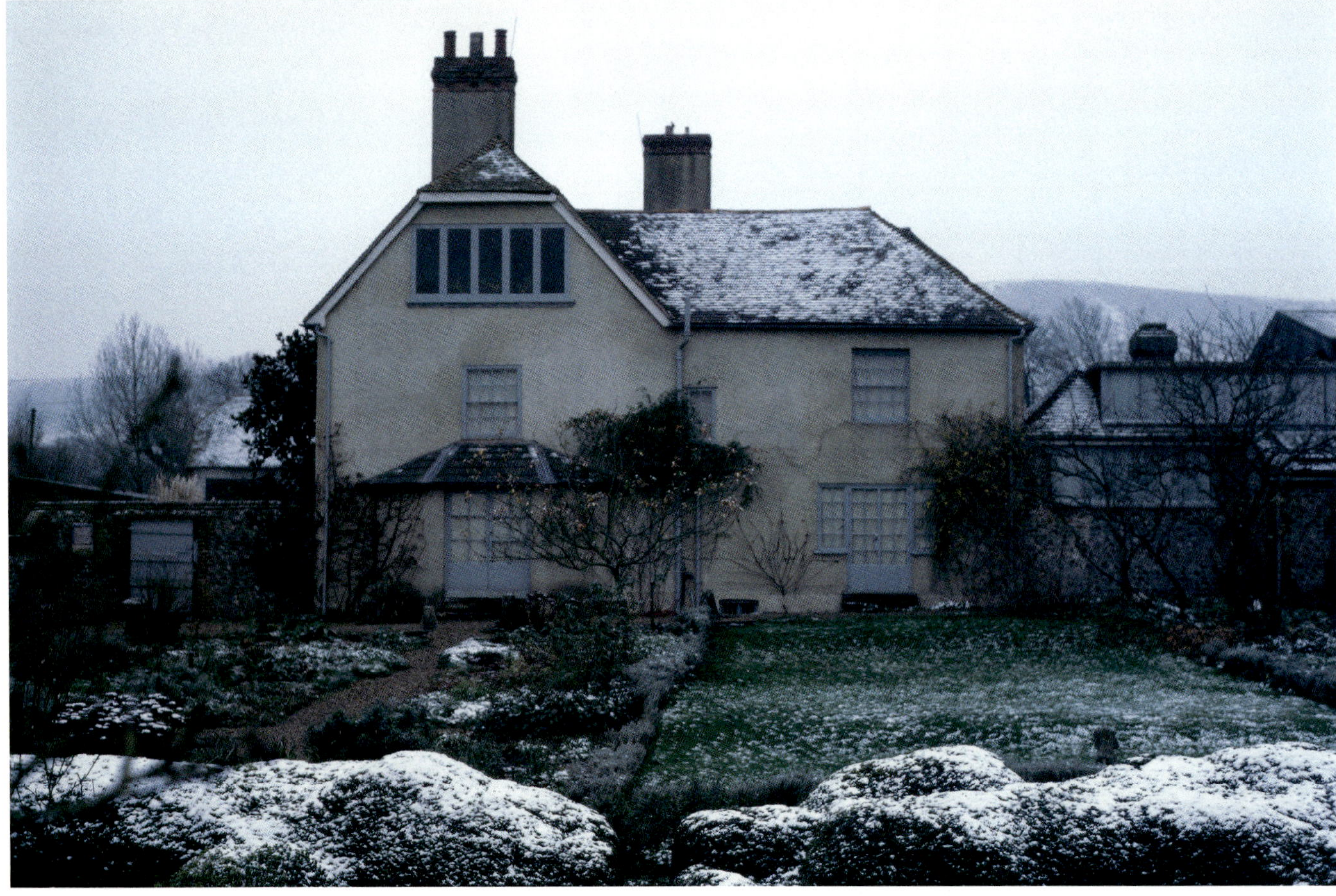

Bare trees

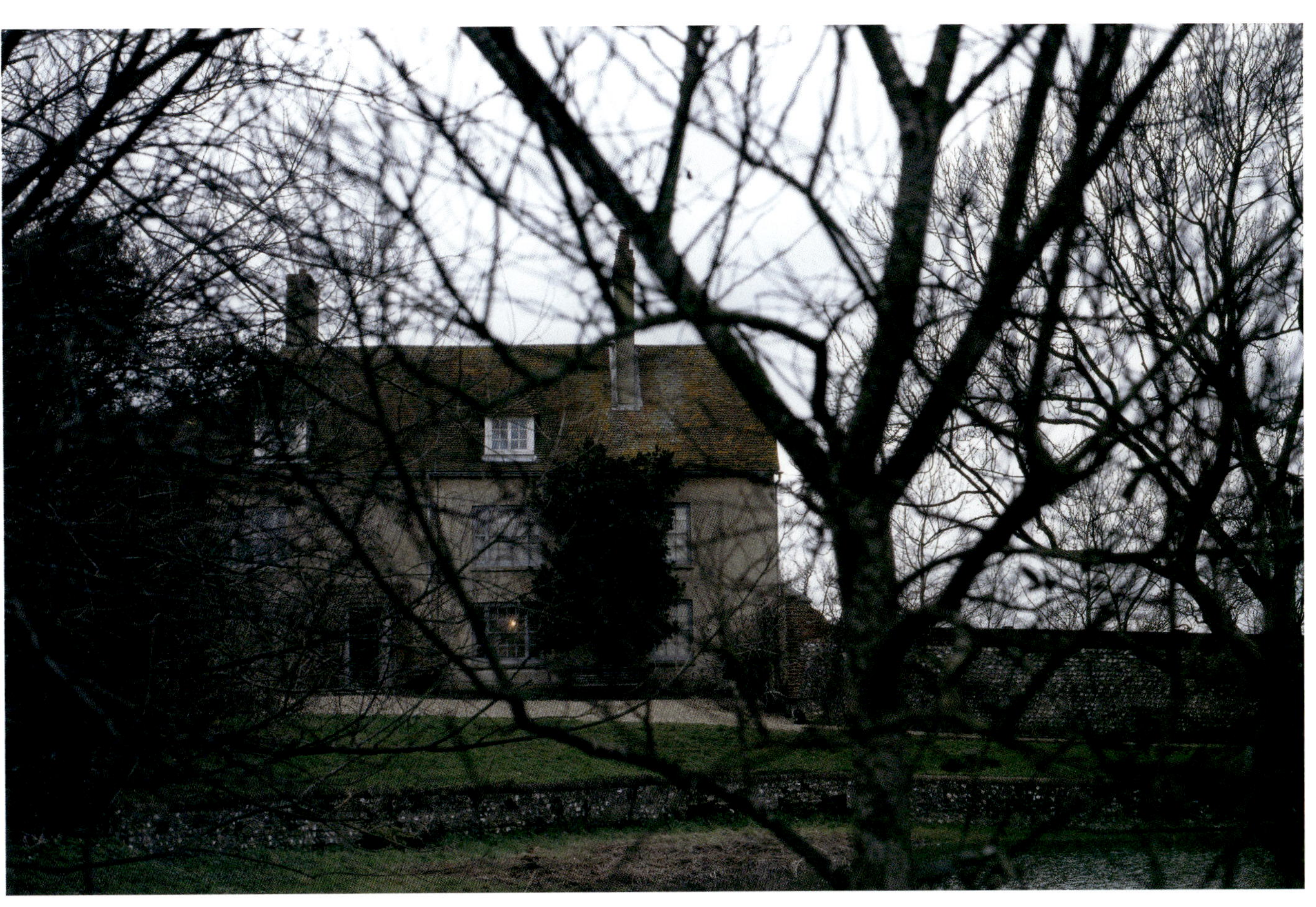

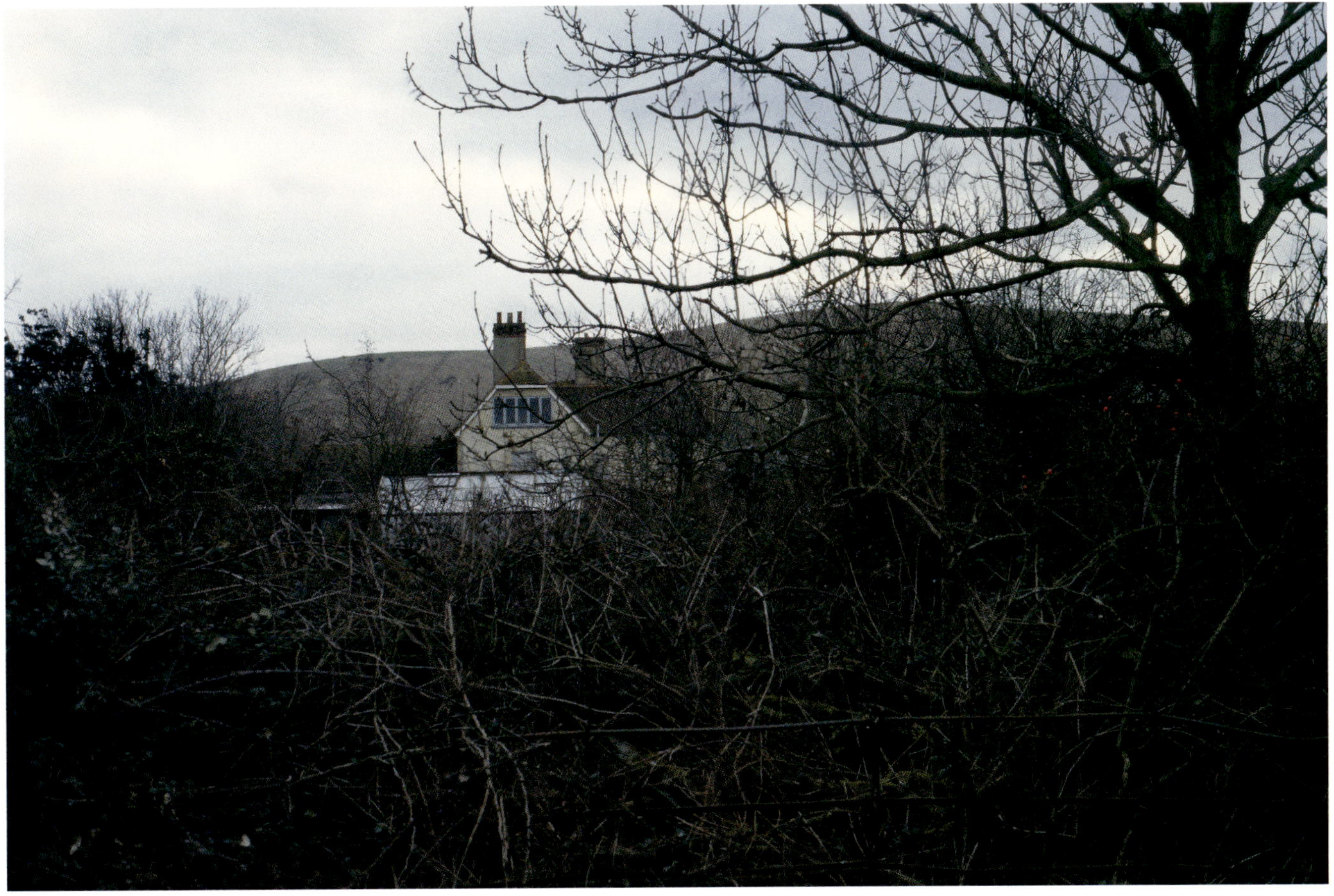

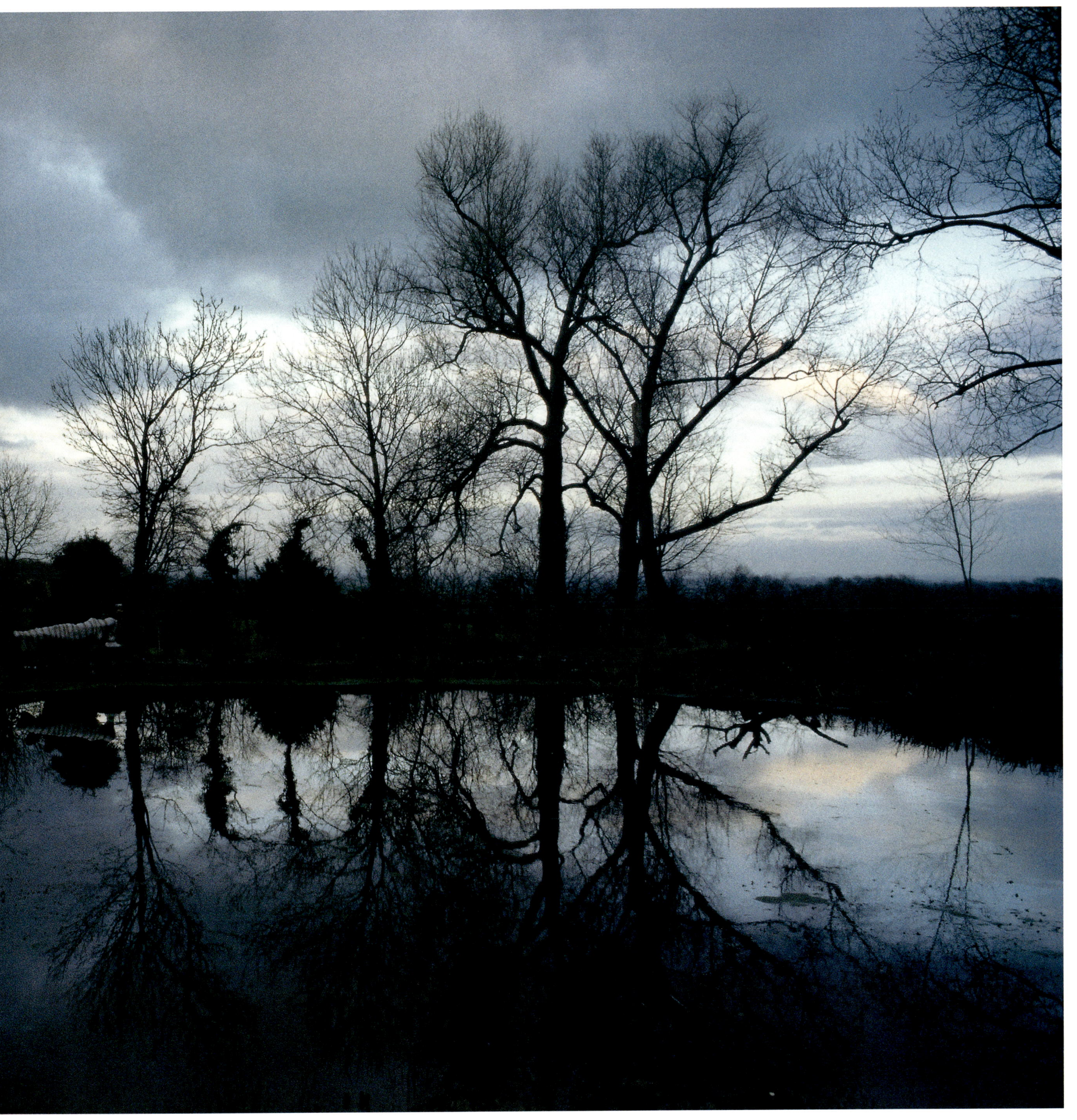

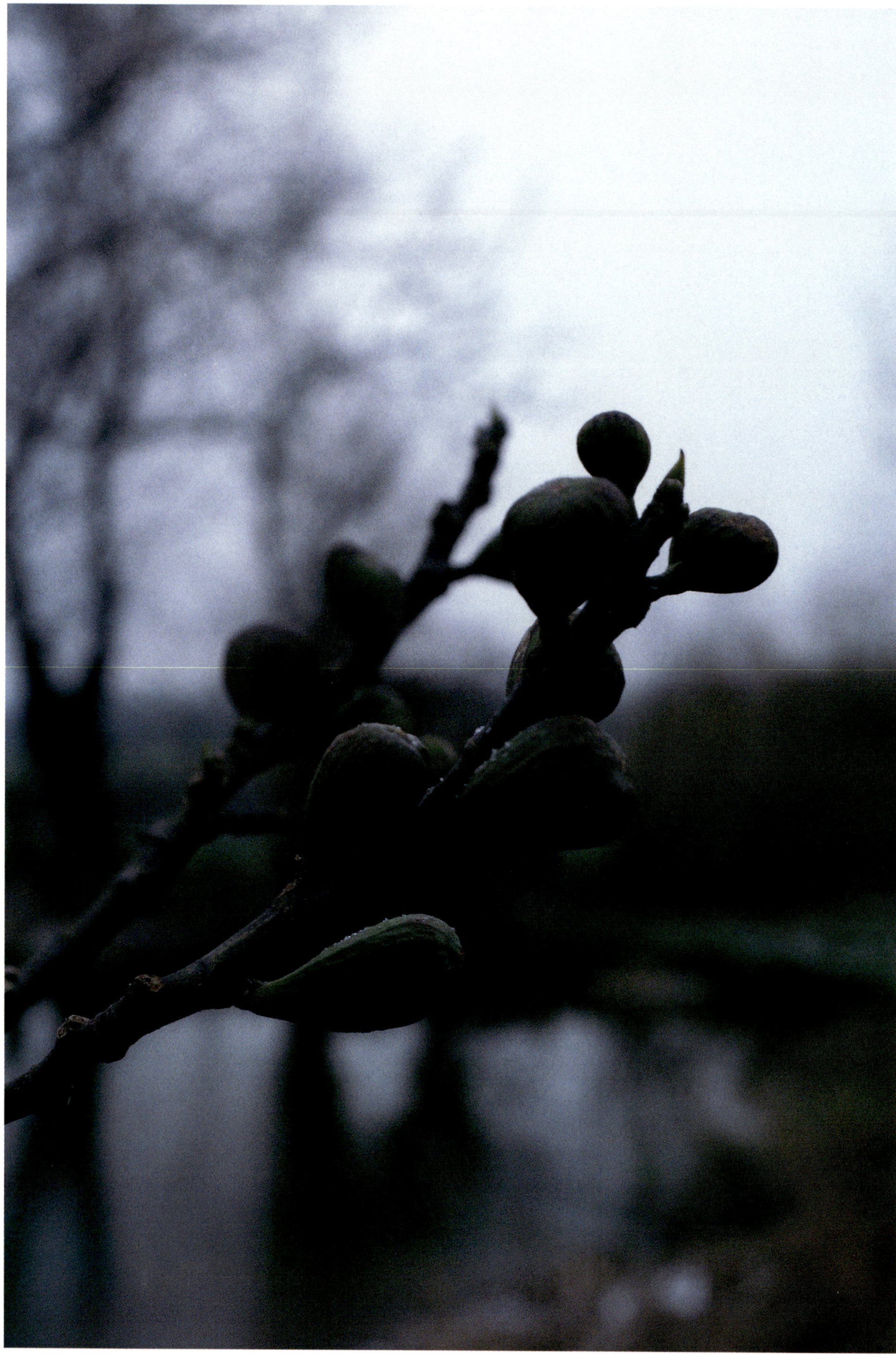

Figs

Single snowdrop

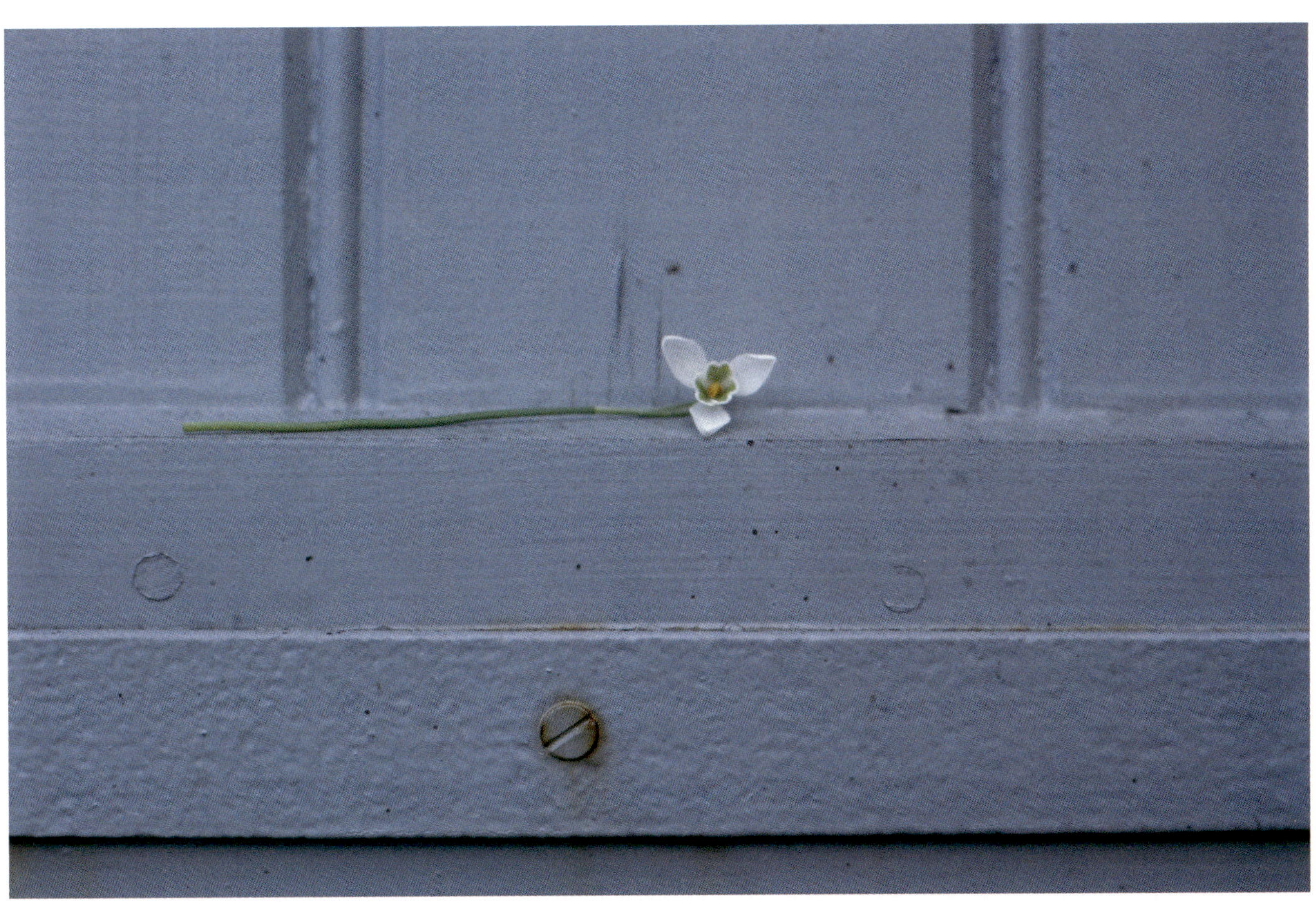

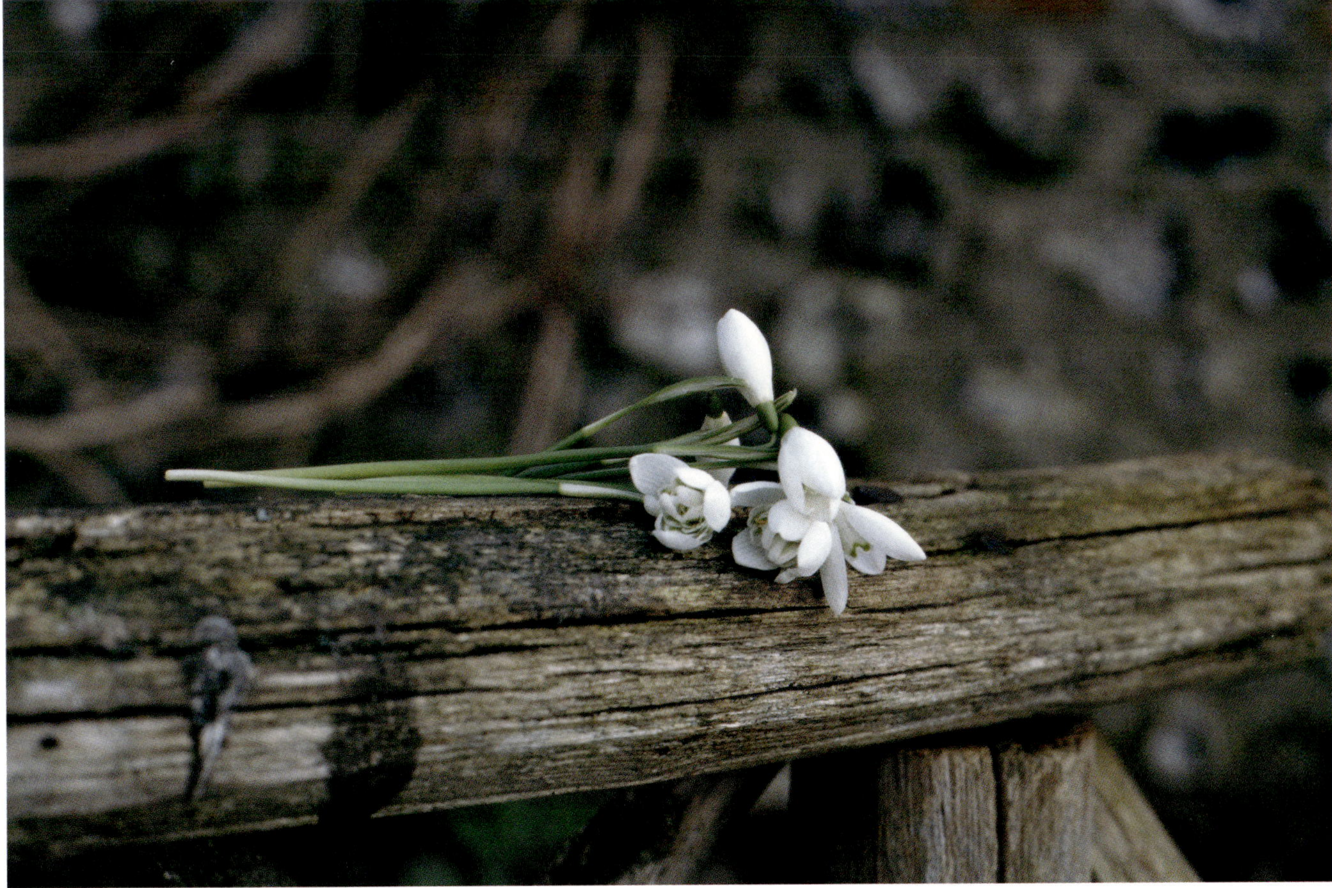

Double snowdrops

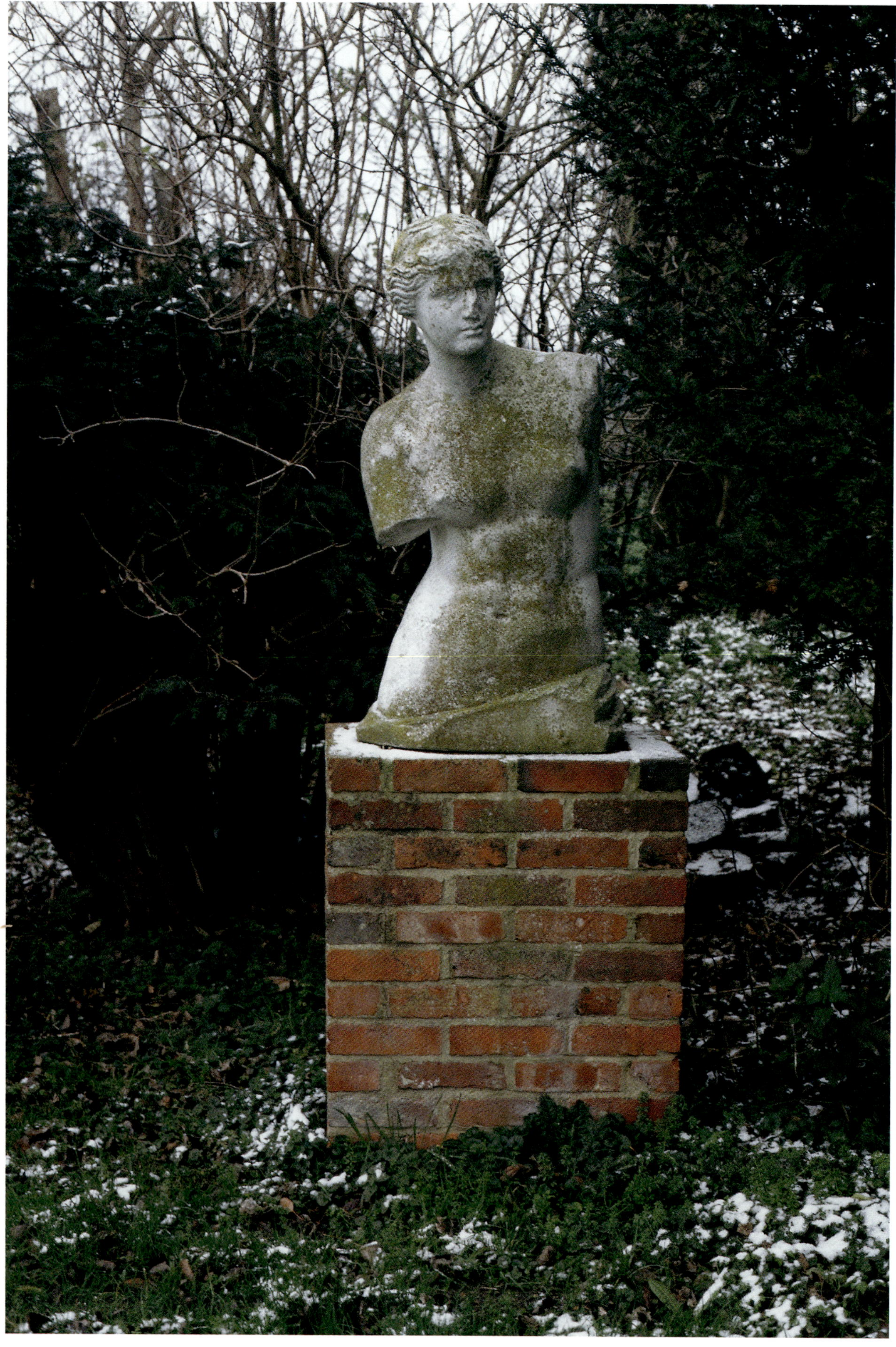

Cast after a Venus by
Giovanni da Bologna

RIGHT CLOCKWISE FROM TOP LEFT
Figurine (believed to be by Quentin Bell);
peacock butterfly;
snowdrops in the orchard

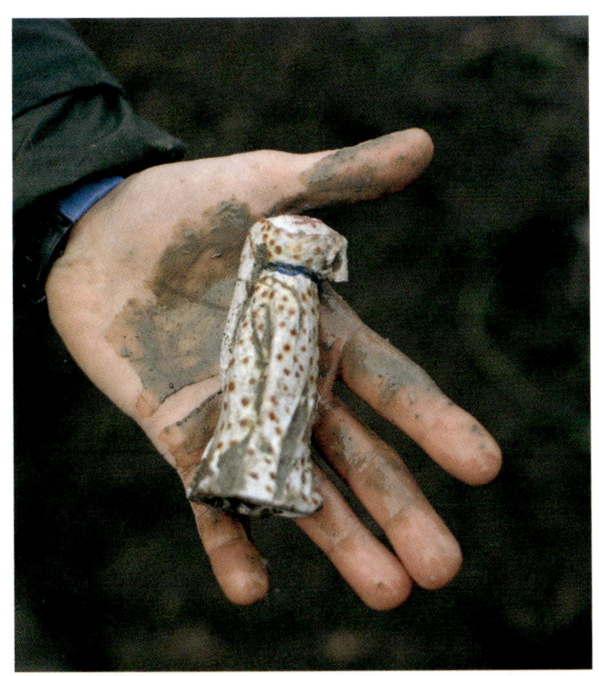

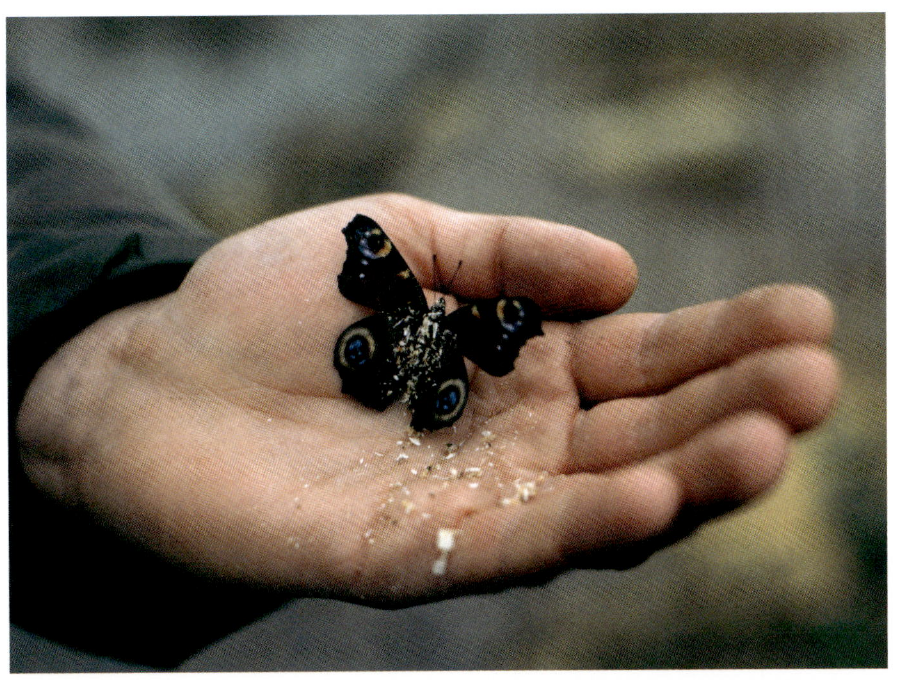

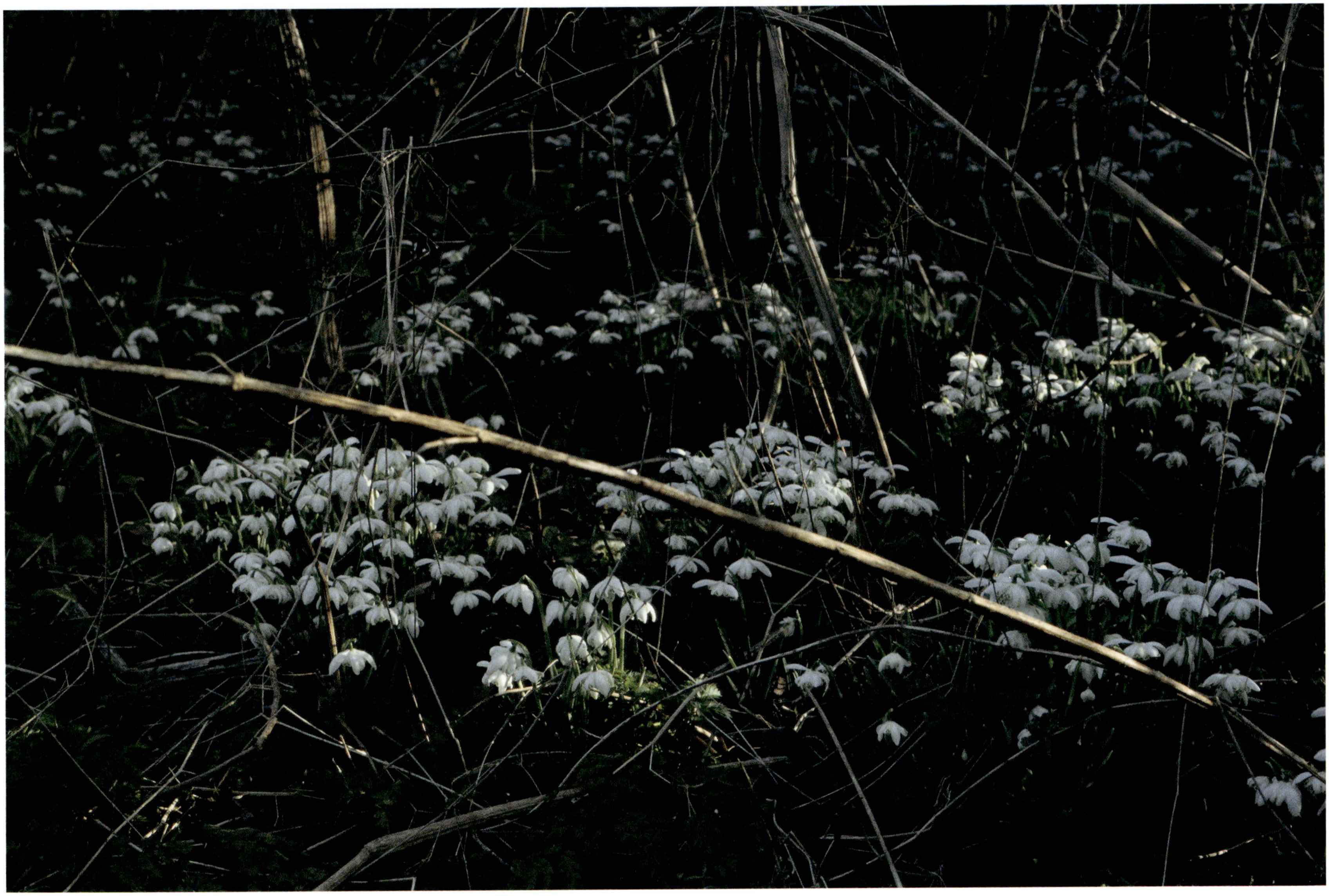

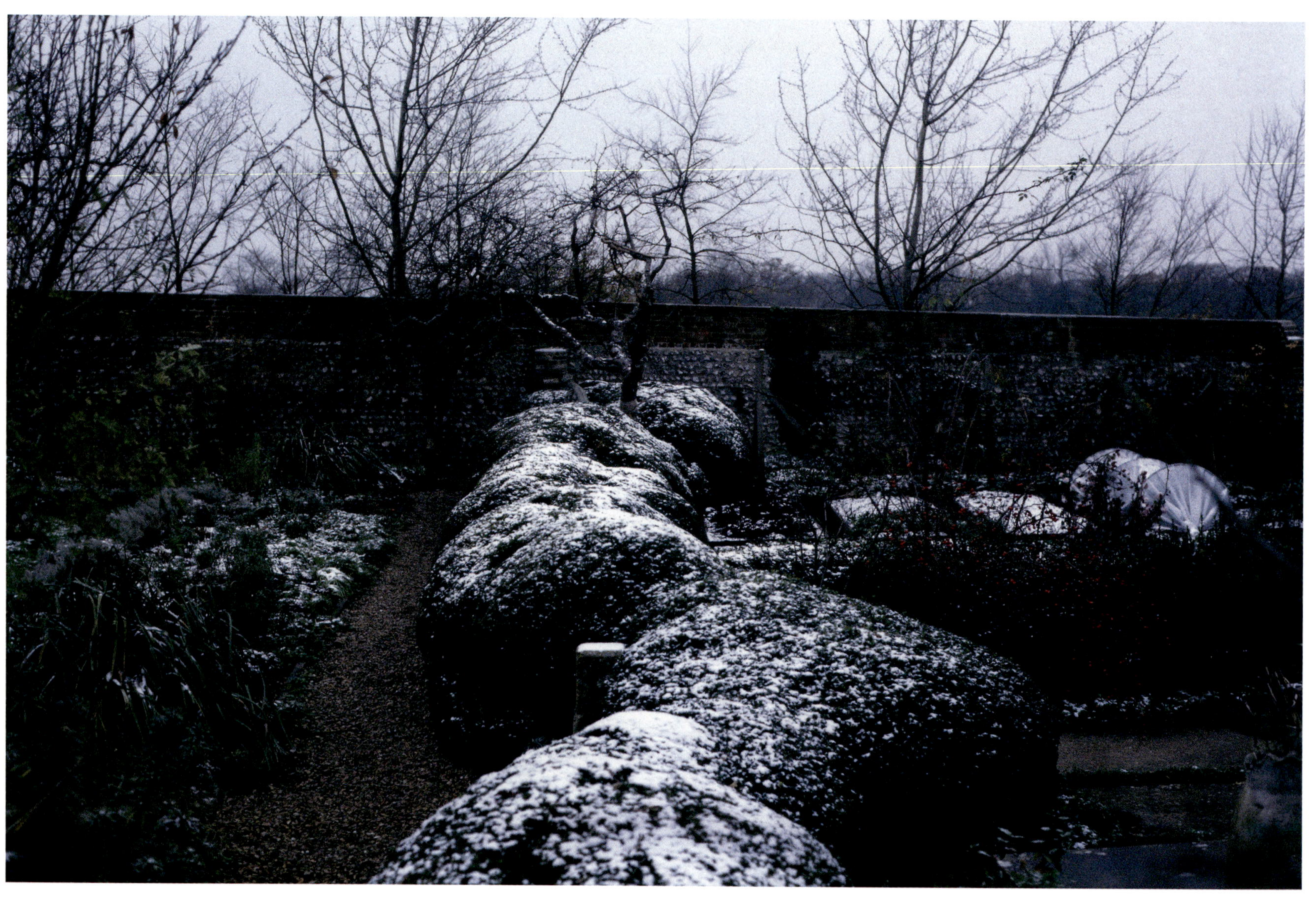

Cotoneaster berries

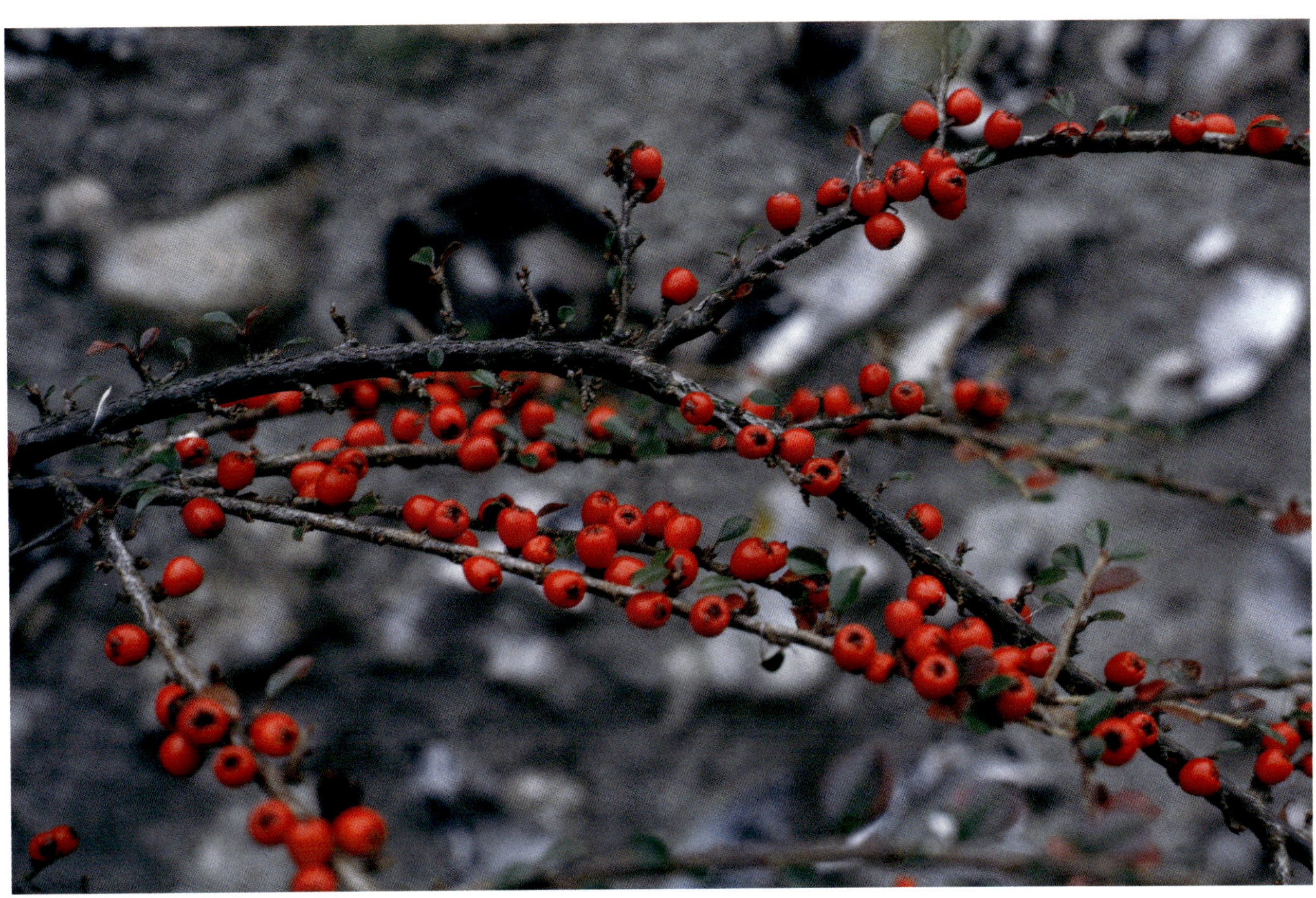

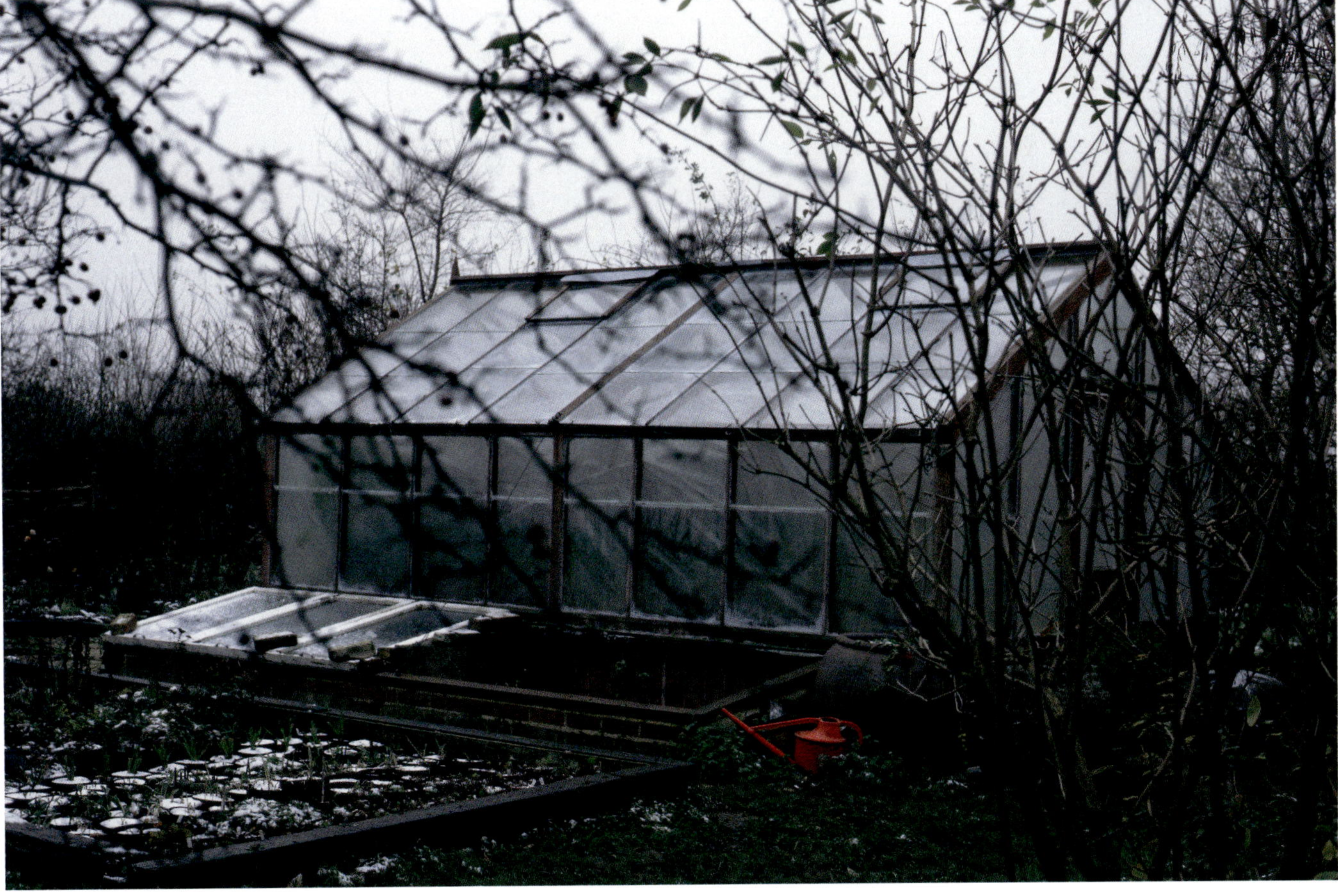

Greenhouse

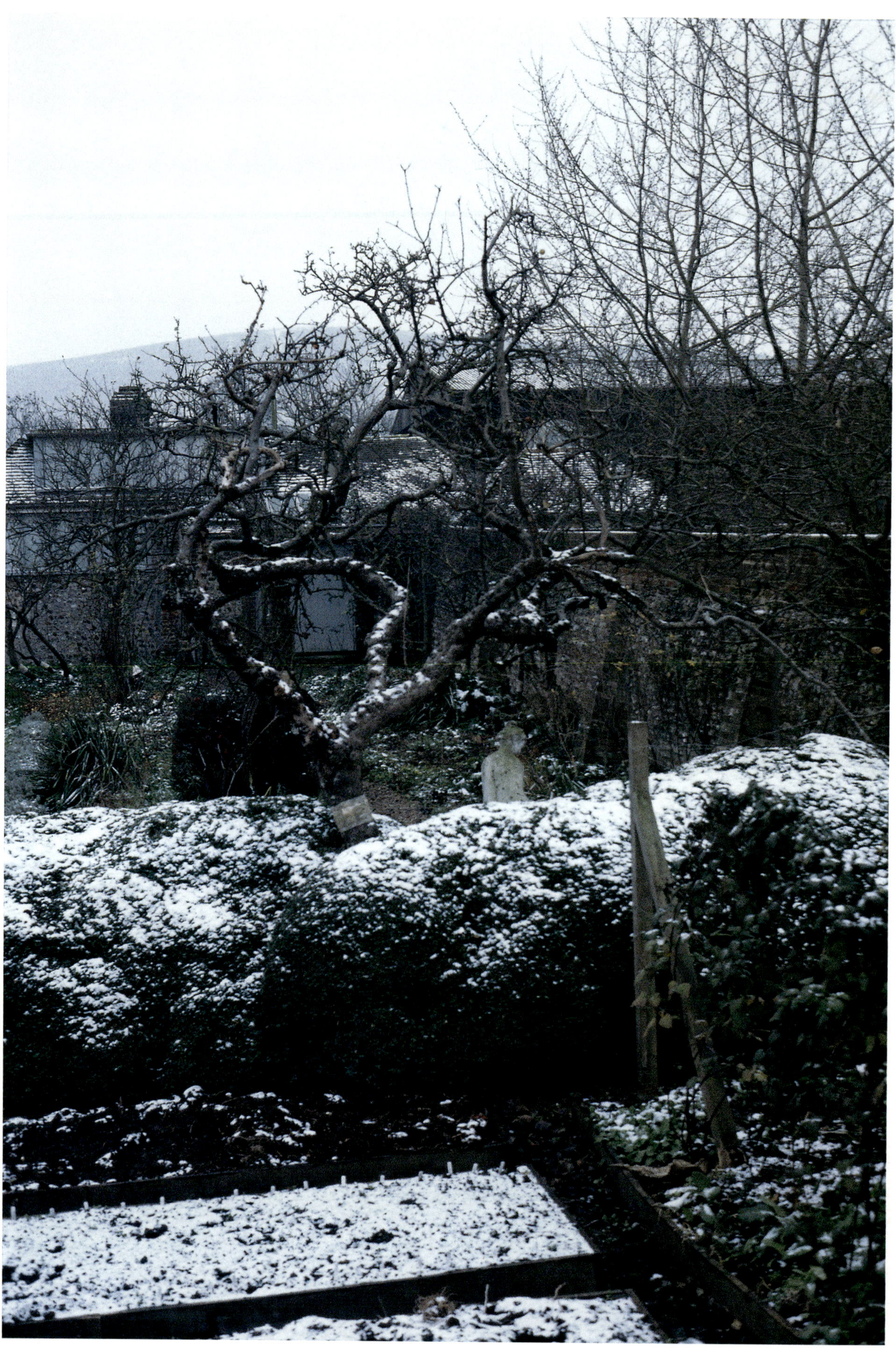

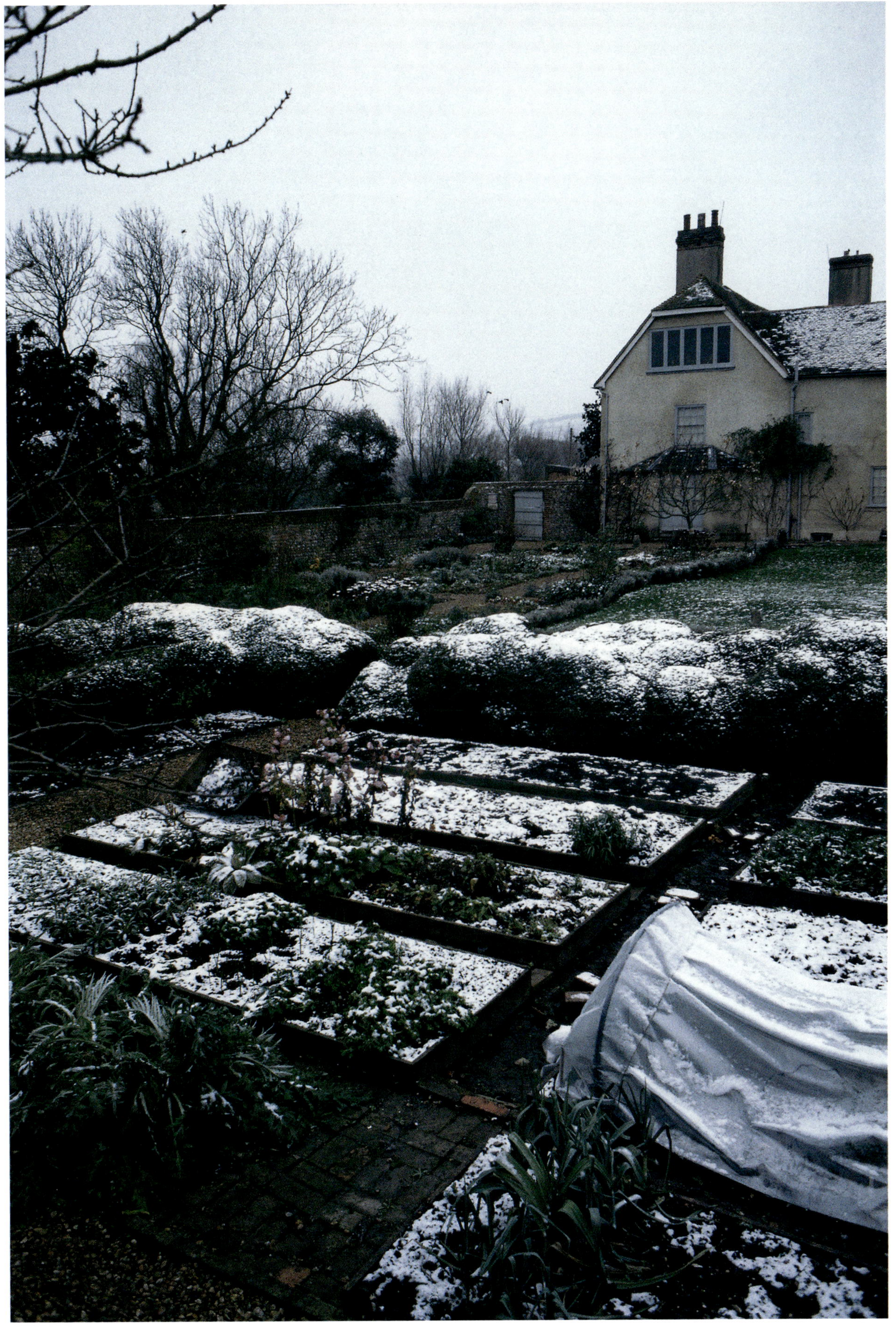

The kitchen garden

List of decorative features and sculpture
(with numbers of pages on which they appear in **bold** type)

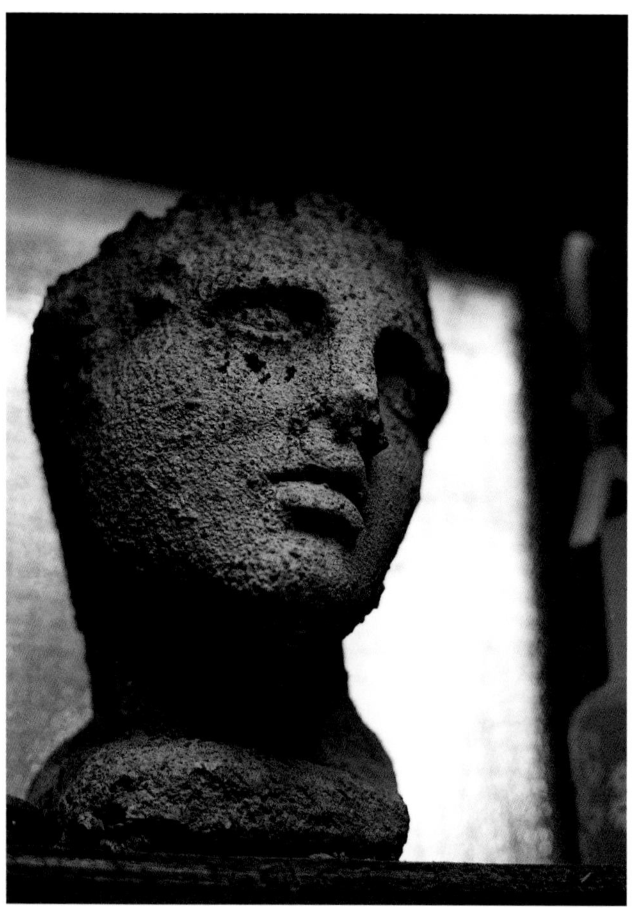

Acknowledgments

Thank you so very much to Angelica Garnett, Olivier Bell and their families, together with the Charleston Trust with its brilliant staff and volunteers, both past and present; and a special thank you to all those personally involved with my work, including Frances Partridge, Peter Miall, Shaun Romain, Myra Harud, Eleanor Gleadow, Alistair Upton, Andrew Caverly, Mark Divall, Wendy Hitchmough, Colin McKenzie and Georgia Barrington.

Thank you to the National Portrait Gallery for permission to use the Virginia Woolf postcard. Thank you also to the publisher John Nicoll at Frances Lincoln, with exceptional thanks to the art director Becky Clarke, the editor Anne Askwith and the publicist Fran Higgins; and to Nikon, Fujifilm, Danny Pope, Adrian Ensor and Metro Imaging.

And thank you to Jess Walton, Carrie McCardle, Tiffany Daneff, Erica Hunningher, Christine Fox, Tory Lawrence, Maggi Hambling, Prunella Clough, Jane Knowles, Rafaella Barruzo, Sara Scoedeller, Chantal Coady at Rococo Chocolates, Dorothee Steffens, Andrew Staffell, Gemma Hakins, Nita Amy, Adam Turnbull, Linda Peryer, Valerie Finnis, Pamela Morton and Peter Davies.

LEFT Cast head wintering in the potting shed